ENCYCLOPEDIA OF ISLAMIC DOCTRINE

VOLUME 1
BELIEFS
(*AQIDA*)

SHAYKH MUHAMMAD HISHAM KABBANI

FOREWORD BY

SEYYED HOSSEIN NASR

AS-SUNNA FOUNDATION OF AMERICA

Edited by Gabriel F. Haddad, Ph.D. (Columbia), Alexandra Bain, Ph.D. (Victoria), Karim K. Tourk, Jennifer McLennan

**Cover Design of the 8 Volume Series by
Tjahjono Abdi/Mindglow Designs, Indonesia
This publication was made possible through a grant from
Dome Publications, South Africa**

Library of Congress Cataloging in Publication Data

Kabbani, Shaykh Muhammad Hisham.
Encyclopedia of Islamic Doctrine Vol. 1. Beliefs (AQIDA)
[Arabic title: *al-Musuat al-islami aqida ahl al-sunnah wa al-jamaat*]
p.   cm.
    Indices.
Islam-doctrines. 2. Heretics, Muslim. 3. Wahhabiyah.
I. Kabbani, Shaykh Muhammad Hisham. II. Title.

ISBN: 1-871031-48-6

Published by
As-Sunna Foundation of America Publications
607A W. Dana St.
Mountain View, CA 94041
e-mail: staff@sunnah.org
www: http://sunnah.org

Distributed by
KAZI Publications
3023 W. Belmont Avenue
Chicago, IL 60618
Tel: 773-267-7001; Fax: 773-267-7002
e-mail: kazibooks@kazi.org
www: http://www.kazi.org

This work is dedicated to our Grandshaykh,
may Allah bless him,
Shaykh Abd Allah al-Daghistani,
and to his khalifa,
our Shaykh Mawlana Muhammad
Nazim Adil al-Haqqani,
who guided us to the Way of the Prophet (ﷺ)
and to his daughter, my wife,
Nazihe Muhammad Nazim Adil,
and to all Muslims around the world,
as well as to scholars of Islam—
both the living and those who passed away
in recognition of their lives' work—
who lit our road helping us to understand
the Way of the Prophet
and exemplified the fight against falsehood
and the defense of truth.

CONTENTS

ACKNOWLEDGEMENTS

The author wishes to thank Dr. G. F. Haddad for his unswerving devotion as well as all those who have contributed to the editing of this work including Dr. Laleh Bakhtiar and my special gratitude to Dr. Mateen Siddiqui for his untiring help.

FOREWORD

Normative Islam has over the centuries included schools of law, both Sunni and Shi'ite, schools of thought, both theological and philosophical, and Sufism in its multifarious manifestations. All of these schools and their teachings have together constituted Islamic orthodoxy and tradition understood in the universal sense of these terms. There have been differences of interpretation in nearly every domain from the legal to the theological and philosophical, to the esoteric. And there have been even cases of confrontation as between Ash^{c}arite and Mu^{cc}tazilite *kalām*, or *kalām* and *falsafah* or the view of certain doctors of the law and Sufism. Nevertheless all of these schools are bound to the teachings of the Noble Qur$^{\jmath}$an and the *Sunnah* and *Ḥadīth* of the Blessed Prophet (ﷺ) and the traditions followed by the generations that followed the Companions of God's last Prophet. Islam demonstrated remarkable latitude during most of its history towards differences in the interpretation of ^{c}*aqa$^{\jmath}$id*. Where there was social and political conflict of an apparently religious nature, it came usually as a result of social and political forces using different religious interpretations as ways of legitimizing or strengthening their power. In comparison with the West, during the periods when religion was strong in that world, very few people have lost their lives in the Islamic world because of differences of interpretation of the tenets of the religion, although a number have fled or gone into exile from time to time. That is not to say that there were no tragic episodes, as the cases of al-Ḥallāj and Suhrawardī demonstrate, or religious wars such as between the Ottomans and Safavids where different interpretations within the general orthodoxy of Islam were used as emblems of identity. But the universal orthodoxy of traditional Islam, embracing all the levels mentioned above, always prevailed and both sides of such conflicts usually lived and functioned within the framework of traditional Islam.

It remained for modern times for this universal orthodoxy to be attacked not only from without by the forces of modernism emanating from a secularized West but also from within by so called reform movements which in the name of purifying Islam set out to destroy that universal orthodoxy on the basis of their own narrow interpretation of Islam and as a pretext to return to the purity of the *salaf* or ancestors. Meanwhile, such movements started an aggressive opposition to Sufism, to *kalām* and philosophy or the whole of the Islamic intellectual tradition, to Shiᶜism, to nearly all the Islamic arts and sciences and even to whatever in the Sunni tradition did not agree with their views, much of which was a veritable innovation (*bidᶜah*) in the Islamic sense of the term. This opposition from within did much to weaken the Islamic world both religiously and intellectually, making it a great deal easier for the forces of modernism to dominate much of the Islamic world through the process of divide and conquer.

During the past half century the tide has begun to turn against this kind of divisive thinking among the most notable Islamic scholars both Sunni and Shiᶜite. Nearly fifty years ago the Shaykh al-Azhar Maḥmūd Shaltūt issued a religious edict (*fatwā*) about the orthodox nature of the Jaᶜfari or Twelve-Imam school of law which began to be taught at al-Azhar from that time onward and at the same time Iranian universities began to teach Sunni law especially of the Shāfiᶜi and Ḥanbalī schools. Furthermore, many younger educated Muslims, including the majority of the most intelligent and devout, have begun to realize that, far from having been an innovation and deviation, authentic Sufism is the heart of the Islamic message, its *ḥaqīqah*, and the inner force that had preserved Islam in the face of the onslaught of various alien ideas upon the Muslim mind and the soul to this day.

But the effect of the divisive forces of so-called reform has not abated. On the contrary, armed with newly gained wealth and worldly power, these forces have tried to gain domination and achieve now what they were not able to do so as long as the Ottomans ruled over much of the Islamic world. Many young Muslims, not to speak of non-Muslims who wish to learn about Islam, are thereby misled by books produced by these movements all over the globe, books which denigrate the whole of Islamic history and its achievements, charge this or that group of Muslims with infidelity and dismiss or belittle the greatest traditional *ʿulamāʾ*, thinkers and saints of Islam, creating as a result a vacuum which is then filled with the crassest forms of secularism and scientism. We therefore witness today a number of people who are pious a few hours a week and the rest of the week think in a world divorced from the sacred intellectual and artistic universe created by Islam. Consequently, while being opposed to modernism on a certain level, those affected by this so-called reformist outlook join modern secularists in their attitude towards science, the arts and even daily piety not to speak of the inner life and spirituality.

The present work by Shaykh Hisham Kabbani has the great virtue of re-stating traditional and orthodox Islamic teachings without any compromise with either modernism or so-called reformism. Rooted in the traditional interpretations of the *Sharīʿah* and schools of Islamic theology as well as the Naqshbandiyyah Order which has carried the barrier of a strictly orthodox interpretation of Sufism over the centuries, these volumes reflect the views of the greatest authorities in Islamic doctrine during Islamic history. The author brings vast scholarship, which can only be mastered in the traditional ambience, to bear upon every discussion that he carries out from the nature of God to various conditions for the daily prayers. Each volume is devoted to a particular set of beliefs starting naturally with the *ʿaqāʾid* or doctrines concerning the meaning of *tawhīd* and God's Attributes. The later volumes include elements of Islam's *praxis* that are well known and also those which have been nearly forgotten today. The work also deals with important Islamic beliefs such as "intercession" (*tawassul*) attacked by many of the so-called reformers. In each discussion Shaykh Kabbani juxtaposes the traditional Islamic views as expounded by such figures as Imam Shāfiʿi, Imam Abū Ḥanīfah, Imam al-Ghazzālī and Imam Abu 'l-Ḥasan al-Ashʿarī to the innovations in the understanding of these basic teachings some of which go back to Ibn Taymiyyah. The work is quite correctly called an encyclopedia because it is a veritable reference work in which one can find a clear and scholarly treatment of various Islamic beliefs to which one can turn with the assurance that it is the traditional and orthodox interpretation.

Shaykh Kabbani has created a major work that will do much to clear the air of the many errors that parade as Islam today and has taken a notable step in strengthening the unity between various schools of Islamic legal, theological, philosophical and Sufi thought which together have constituted traditional Islam over the centuries. All those interested in the traditional understanding of Islam must be grateful to the author and also to KAZI Publications for making this major *opus* available to the English speaking world. May God grant the author spiritual and intellectual strength to continue his efforts in this direction and reward him richly for what he has achieved in this encyclopedia which succeeds in presenting important facets of traditional Islam to both the younger generation of Muslims cut off from its own tradition and those outside the world of Islam who wish to gain genuine understanding of God's last plenar revelation to our world.

Jazāhu'Llah

Seyyed Hossein Nasr
Washington, DC
24 Safar, 1419 (A.H.)
19 June, 1998 (A.D.)

INTRODUCTION

And say, Truth has come and falsehood has vanished away. Lo! falsehood is ever bound to vanish. (17:81).

Praise be to Allah,[1] who perfected His religion and completed His favor on us. As the Quran says, *"This day have I perfected your religion for you, completed My favor upon you, and have chosen for you Islam as your religion"* (5:3). Praise be to Allah Who has made soundness of doctrine a precondition for soundness of belief and has decreed that our belief consist of knowing that He, the Exalted, is Alive, All-Knowing, and All-Powerful. He is All-Hearing without the need for ears, All-Seeing without the need for eyes, and All-Saying without need for lips or tongue. He oversees all that is, down to the finest detail. Whatever He wants is, and whatever He does not want, is not. He is free from being above anything that would raise Him, and He is free from being below anything that would abase him. He cannot be carried by a throne, contained within the heavens, shaded by a cloud, confined in a place, or moved in a direction. May Allah send abundant blessings and peace upon the Seal of Prophets and the best of mankind, our Prophet Muhammad (ﷺ), who said, "Allah existed eternally when there was nothing else."[2] May He bless his Family and Companions, particularly Abu Bakr al-Siddiq, who said, "He has not provided a way for His creation to know Him except through the need to know Him."[3] May He also bless Umar,

---

1 The following introduction isolates and addresses specific arguments that have arisen between mainstream Islam and the "Salafis." For a more comprehensive overview of this conflict, please see Appendix 1.

2 Related by Bukhari.

3 Related by al-Sufuri on the authority of al-Junayd in *Nuzhat al-majalis* (Damascus and Beirut: Dar al-iman, n.d.) p. 6.

Uthman, and Ali, who said, "Allah exists eternally without a place, and He is now as He ever was."[4] May Allah be well pleased with them and with all those who followed their path in seeking a means to Him.

Mainstream Islam consists of all of the schools of Islamic Law which follow the Straight Path (surat al-mustaqim). This means following the Quran and sunna and being, therefore, respectful of the Prophet (ﷺ), his Family and Companions and includes the Hanafi school founded by Imam Abu Hanifa an-Numani, the Hanbali school founded by Imam Ahmad Hanbal, the Maliki school founded by Imam Abu Abd Allah Malik ibn Anas, the Shafii school founded by Imam Muhammad Ibn Idris ash-Shafii and the Jafari founded by Imam Jafar Sadiq. For details on this topic, see the fatwa, summer 1959 of Mahmud Shaltut, the Rector of al-Azhar.

The unity of Muslims was fashioned under the watchful eye and guidance of scholars whose ink is dearer than the blood of martyrs. These scholars gave up the pleasures of life for the sake of spreading knowledge to Muslims from the time of the Companions and the Successors (known as the Salaf), to the present day. Among these scholars are the Imams of the the mainstream schools of Islamic law and their followers. Today, unfortunately, a sect who falsely refer to themselves as followers of the Salaf, are trying to poison the minds of Muslims for the future. Having been rejected, refuted, and condemned in prior times, these so-called "Salafi" heresies and deviations have a voice today due to the support of pseudo-scholars. Because of the immense funding these 'scholars' receive, "Salafi" literature has spread over the Muslim world along with the illusion of authority they have generated, both in their own minds and in the minds of their readers. In this way, they have fostered the growth of a new doctrine and led many Muslims, often unknowingly, to leave behind the beliefs (aqida) of the Four Caliphs, of the 2nd and 3rd centuries, of the Four Imams, and of all the scholars mentioned in this book (including Imam al-Tahawi, al-Ashari, al-Maturidi, and others). The "Salafis" consider that anyone who follows the way of these noble predecessors and the Ashari Khalaf is on the fringe of Islam.

4 Related by al-Baghdadi in al-Farq bayn al-firaq (Beirut: Dar al-kutub al-ilmiyya, n.d.) p. 256.

In fifteen centuries of Islam, there have been differences in points of view, but such differences have never put anyone outside Islam. The unprecedented trend of declaring other Muslims *kafir* was begun by the "Salafi" movement decades ago and has spread like cancer through their heavily-financed campaigns. If one examines the underlying tone of the "Salafi" message, it can clearly be seen why the Muslim community has been divided, why we are now plagued by internal conflict, and why we are engaged in armed confrontations. Sincerity has been turned into hatred, brotherhood has been made enmity, and love has been replaced with anger and rage. Of a surety, to Allah we belong and certainly to Him we will return.

In this book the reader will find comprehensive evidence against these "Salafis," and in favor of mainstream Islam based upon the exact words (*nusus*) of the scholars, the rulings of jurists (which are themselves based on Quranic verses) and many of the Prophet's hadiths. May Allah give benefit to every Muslim through this work. May every English-speaking Muslim, scholar or student, read and learn from it with Allah's permission. Through a thorough examination of mainstream Islamic scholarship, this treatise clears away the confusion caused by those who misuse certain verses of the Quran. For example, the "Salafis" frequently apply verses concerning disbelievers to believers. These innovators reject the belief (*aqida*) of the majority of Muslims, change the methodology (*usul*) of the major Imams and their schools of law, and generally deny what Sunnis accept.

Ibn Majah narrated that the Prophet (ﷺ) said:

> At the time when the last of this *umma* (Community) will curse the first of this *umma*, whoever conceals knowledge from the people will be concealing what Allah has revealed to me.

Written with these words of the Prophet (ﷺ) in mind, and with an awareness of our shortcomings in the matter of Islamic scholarship, these volumes outline the beliefs and doctrine of the majority of Muslim scholars and Muslims in general.

Before proceeding any further, it must be understood that

the name "*salaf al-salih*," or Pious Predecessors, is reserved for the time of the Prophet (ﷺ), of the blessed Companions, and of the Pious Followers of the Companions. Therefore this name cannot be rightly used to define any group or persons today.

There are established lexical and technical definitions for the word *salaf*. Lexically, *al-salaf* means: one's ancestors or older relatives, particularly the pious; one's past good deeds; an advance deposit on a sale; and a loan, like *qard*.

In the terminology of Islamic Law, the word *salaf* has the following meanings: it refers to the early *mujtahid* Imams among the schools of law who are accepted and imitated;[5] it refers to the first community of Muslims before Muhammad ibn al-Hasan al-Shaybani.[6] In the Shafii school, it refers to 'Those who came first in the history of this Community,' (*awail hadhihi al-umma*); it refers to the Companions, the Successors, and the immediate followers of the Successors, who are included in the Prophet's hadith, "The best of centuries is my century, then the one that follows it, then the one that follows that."

Muhammad Said Ramadan al-Buti offers the following definition of *salaf*:

> The established technical definition of the term *salaf* is: the first three centuries in the age of this Muslim Community, the Community of our Master Muhammad (ﷺ). This is derived from his saying according to the narration of the Two Shaykhs [Bukhari and Muslim] from Abd Allah ibn Masud: "The best of people are my century, then those that follow them, then those that follow the latter. After that there will come people who will be eager to commit perjury when bearing witness."[7]

Nuh Keller wrote:

> The word *salafi* or 'early Muslim' in traditional Islamic scholarship means someone who died within the first four hundred years after the Prophet (ﷺ), including scholars such as Abu Hanifa, Malik, Shafii, and Ahmad ibn Hanbal. Anyone

5 According to the definition of Ibn Abidin, this refers to people like Abu Hanifa and his companions, Abu Yusuf and Muhammad al-Shaybani, the Companions of the Prophet, and the Followers (*tabiin*).

6 This is Abd al-Al's definition.

7 Muhammad Said Ramadan al-Buti, *al-Salafiyya marhalatun zamaniyyatun mubarakatun la madhdhabun islami*. The Salafiyya is a blessed period of history, not an Islamic school of law. (Damascus: Dar al-fikr, 1408/1988).

who died after this is one of the *khalaf* or 'latter-day Muslims.'

The term *'salafi'* was revived as a slogan and movement, among latter-day Muslims, by the followers of Muhammad Abduh (the student of Jamal al-Din al-Afghani) some thirteen centuries after the Prophet (ﷺ), approximately a hundred years ago. Like similar movements that have historically appeared in Islam, its basic claim was that the religion had not been properly understood by anyone since the Prophet (ﷺ) and the early Muslims and themselves.[8]

According to "Salafi" ideology, a "Salafi" is one who has a special understanding or ability, above most Muslims, to follow the beliefs of the Salaf. They also acknowledge a very limited number of scholars from later times. Of course, this definition is challenged by mainstream Muslims. Even the term, "Salafi," as understood by the "Salafi" movement, is rejected on the grounds that it is the result of an innovation and a term that the mainstream Muslims have never used.

Where mainstream Muslims further differ from the "Salafis" is in the "Salafi" promotion of a handful of dubious scholars as representing all Islamic scholarship since the time of the true Salaf. They praise and promote these individuals over and above the established, unquestioned mainstream scholars. Those supported by the "Salafis" include:

• Ibn Taymiyya and his student Ibn al-Qayyim,
• Ibn Abd al-Wahhab and his Najdi epigones, and
• Modern day "scholars" such as Bin Baz, Uthaymin, Albani, and their propagandists.[9]

Mainstream Muslims disagree with "Salafi" claims because these scholars neither belong to the time of the Salaf, nor do they represent the belief and practice of the Salaf, and for these reasons they are not recognized as authorities by mainstream Islam. In fact, the condemnation of Ibn Taymiyya, Ibn al-

---

8 Nuh Keller's essay is entitled, *Who or What is a Salafi? Is Their approach valid?* Available at the website: http://ds.dial.pipex.com/masud/ Islam/Nuh/salafi.htm.

9 Examples of "Salafi" claims can be found in a booklet entitled, "*A Brief Introduction to the Salafi Dawah*" (Ipswich, UK: Jamiat ihya minhaj al-sunnah, 1993) p. 2. The "Salafis" add Imam al-Dhahabi alongside Ibn Taymiyya and his student.

Qayyim, and Ibn Abd al-Wahhab by many scholars is widely-known. Furthermore, it is interesting to note that al-Dhahabi, whom the "Salafis" recognize alongside Ibn Taymiyya, himself characterized Ibn Taymiyya as an innovator. His precise words were:

> He [Ibn Taymiyya] was a virtuous and outstanding scholar, very accurate and meticulous in his intellectual examinations, but guilty of introducing innovations in the religion (*mubtadi*).[10]

The most definitive proof that the modern day "Salafis" have no right to claim any connection with the pious Salaf of the past lies in five fundamental characteristics of their ideology.

• "Salafis" attribute anthropomorphic traits to Allah; assigning a place, direction, and corporal identity to Allah Almighty, Who is exalted far above each of these.
• Through their disparaging of meritorious activities such as the commemoration of the birth of the Messenger (*mawlid al-nabi*), the Nocturnal Journey and Ascent *(isra wal mira*j), and the repetition of blessings upon the Messenger (*salawat*), the "Salafis" disrespect the Prophet (ﷺ) his Family(*Ahl al-Bayt*), and his relatives (*itra*).
• "Salafis" have adopted a "modern" approach to the Quran and hadith that disregards the traditional need for scholars, the mastery of Arabic, traditional accreditation (*ijaza*), and the Islamic sciences.
• "Salafis" are quick to disparage adherence to the four Sunni schools of law (*madhahib*), the two schools of doctrine (Asharis and Maturidis), and all the schools of self-purification (*tasawwuf*).
• Finally, the most disturbing practice of the "Salafis" is the practice of declaring other Muslims disbelievers (*takfir*).

Recently, it has been suggested that the "Salafis" are essentially Westernized modernists striving to distance themselves

---

10 These words were reported by the hadith master of al-Sakhawi in his book *al-Ilan wa al-tawbikh*. Dhahabi's own disclaimer of the errors of Ibn Taymiyya is stated explicitly in his stern *al-Nasiha al-dhahabiyya*, which was published in Damascus in 1347 together with his *Bayan zaghal al-ilm* (Damascus: Qudsi, 1347, 1928-1929). Ibn Hajar mentioned Dhahabi's *Nasiha* in *al-Durar al-kamina* (1:166), and so did al-Sakhawi in *al-Ilan wa al-tawbikh* (p. 504). Two extant manuscripts of the *Nasiha* are kept, one in Cairo and one at Damascus at the Zahiriyya library (#1347).

from their own "messy" past. Instead, they favor a more "tidy" history which they associate, in youthful revisionist fashion, with that of the pious Salaf. Muhammad al-Abbasi writes:

> With the neatness of mind which they had learnt from the West, and driven by a giddy enthusiasm which blinded them to the finer aspects of the classical heritage, many of the fundamentalists announced that they found the Islam of the people horribly untidy. Why not sweep away all the medieval cobwebs, and create a bright new Islam, streamlined and ready to take its place as an ideology alongside Marxism, capitalism, and secular nationalism? To achieve this aim, it was thought that the four schools of law of Islamic jurisprudence (*fiqh*) had to go. Ditto for the Ashari and Maturidi theological traditions. The Sufi orders were often spectacularly exotic and untidy; they of course had to be expunged as well. In fact, at least ninety percent of the traditional Islamic texts could happily be consigned to the shredding machine: while what was left, it was hoped, would be the Islam of the Prophet (ﷺ), stripped of unsightly barnacles, and presiding over a reunified Muslim world, striding towards a new and shining destiny.[11]

Unfortunately, the principal activity of these "unbarnacled," revisionist "Salafis" has been, like their Wahhabi forerunners,[12] to denounce other Muslims as disbelievers (*kafir*) for not thinking in the same terms as they do.

These so-called "Salafis" claim to follow the Quran and *sunna*, but they fail to do so according to the obligations of the Salaf. These obligations dictate that religious knowledge be learned and taught only from the mouth of an established, knowledgeable shaykh or scholar of Islam. The institution of the 'chain of transmission,' or *isnad*, and the certification of knowledge, or *ijaza*, are the basic building-blocks of the transmission of knowledge in Islam.

The importance of the chain of transmission is indicated by the fact that the narrators of hadith always used terms that

---

11 Muhammad al-Abbasi, in his essay entitled *Protestant Islam*, which is available at http://ds.dial.pipex.com/masud/Islam/MISC/pislam.htm.

12 See Appendix 1 for a thorough discussion of the forerunners of the "Salafi" movement.

denote oral transmission. This is not because they did not use books, which they all did, but because unless they said, "I heard X say to me: Y told me: Z said to us . . . etc.," one could never verify that the transmission of someone's report of X's report from Y was authentic, unless that someone had actually heard X say he had actually heard Y say it. This is why one also had, and still has, to evaluate the power of memorization, legal and linguistic ability, and moral character of each narrator involved, as well as when and where they lived, who they studied under, and who studied under them.

This is a clear illustration of the mainstream Islamic principle that Islam is taken not from books, or from un-Islamic sources, but from the pious and knowledgeable teachers of Islam. This is enunciated by Umar ibn al-Khattab in his saying, "This religion is not taken except from the mouths of reliable people (al-rijal),[13] therefore let each investigate from whom he is taking it."

Consequently, one of the sciences particular to Islam is that of "narrator criticism" (ilm al-rijal). This science became a veritable gauntlet in the preservation of Prophetic narrations. Thanks to this and other related sciences, we know that the Prophet (ﷺ) said such-and-such a hadith, not merely because it is in print under Bukhari or Muslim's name, but because we can find A among us who has verifiably and authentically heard B tell him face-to-face that C told him that D told him, etc., that the Prophet (ﷺ) told them the hadith. Each transmitter bequeathed to his successor the hadith based on his faith in the competence and integrity of the junior transmitter. This system is called the chain of transmission (isnad). The isnad is part and parcel of the religion of Islam, and the mainstream Islamic scholars have been granted leadership in the pursuit of this science. In addition, the certification of knowledge (ijaza), is granted to the student by the teacher, who was himself granted ijaza by his teacher. The ijaza is the central form of accreditation in Islamic knowledge. In recent years, the ijaza has unfortunately been neglected in favor of more Western forms of recognition, such as the university degree. Those who grant such degrees to Muslims are, in many cases, non-Muslims.

---

13 Al-rijal literally means "men." However, many major hadith scholars were women. See M. Z. Siddiqui, Hadith Literature and Its Early Development (ITS), appendix entitled "Women Scholar of Hadith."

Chains of transmission exist for every single science in Islam, including exegesis (*tafsir*), grammar (*nahw*), purification of the self (*tasawwuf*), recitation of the Quran (*tajwid*), and even for the recitation of the call to prescribed prayer (*adhan*). The chains of the science of purification of the self (*tasawwuf*) and grammar almost all pass through Ali ibn Abi Talib, those of the call to prescribed prayer (*adhan*) through Bilal, and all chains go back to the Prophet (ﷺ).

Below is an example of an *ijaza* in jurisprudence that belongs to a late great scholar of the Hanafi school, the *faqih* and *muhaddith* Imam Muhammad Zahid al-Kawthari. He was the last renewer of the Community (*mujaddid*), and the deputy of the last Shaykh al-Islam (highest religious authority) of the Ottoman Islamic State. He died in Cairo, in exile from his native land, Turkey.

Imam Kawthari (d. 1371H.) received certification (*ijaza*) from his father, and also from Hafiz Ibrahim Haqqi (d. 1345), and from Shaykh Zayn al-Abidin al-Alsuni (d. 1336).

Kawthari's father received certification from Ahmad Dia al-Din al-Kamushkhanawi (d. 1311), who received certification from Sayyid Ahmad al-Arwadi (d. 1275), who received certification from *hafiz* Muhammad Amin, Ibn Abidin (d. 1252), whose chain is given elsewhere.

Both Haqqi and Alsuni received certification from the *hafiz* Ahmad Shakir (d. 1315), who received certification from *hafiz* Muhammad Ghalib (d. 1286), who received certification from Sulayman ibn al-Hasan al-Kraydi (d. 1268), who received certification from Ibrahim al-Akhiskhawi (d. 1232), who received certification from Muhammad Munib al-Aynatabi (d. 1238), who received certification from Ismail ibn Muhammad al-Qunawi (d. 1195), who received certification from Abd al-Karim al-Qunawi al-Amidi (d. 1150), who received certification from Muhammad al-Yamani al-Azhari (d. 1135), who received certification from Abd al-Hayy al-Shurunbali who received certification from Abu al-Ikhlas al-Hasan al-Shurunbali (d. 1069), who received certification from Abd Allah ibn Muhammad al-Nuhrayri; and from Shams al-Din Muhammad al-Muhibbi al-Qahiri (d. 1041), who received certification in jurisprudence both from Ali al-Maqdisi (d. 1004), who received certification from Ahmad ibn Yunus al-Shalabi (d. 948), who received certification from Abd al-Barr ibn al-Shahna (d. 921), who received certification from Imam ibn al-Hammam (d. 861), who received certification from Siraj al-Din Umar ibn Ali Qari al-Hidaya (d. 829).

Siraj al-Din Umar ibn Ali Qari al-Hidaya received certification: 1) from Ala's al-Din al-Sirami (d. 790), who received certification from Jalal al-Din al-Karlani who received certification from Abd al-Aziz al-Bukhari (d. 730),[14] who received certification from Hafiz al-Din Abd Allah ibn Ahmad al-Nasafi (d. 701), who received certification from the Sun of Imams Muhammad ibn Abd al-Sattar al-Kardari and 2) from Akmal al-Din Muhammad al-Babarti (d. 796), who received certification from Qawwam al-Din Muhammad al-Kaki (d. 749), who received certification from al-Husayn al-Saghnaqi (d. 711), who received certification from Hafiz al-Din al-Kabir Muhammad ibn Muhammad ibn Nasr al-Bukhari (d. 693), who also received certification from Muhammad ibn Abd al-Sattar al-Kardari (d. 642).

Al-Kardari received certification from the author of *al-Hidaya*, Ali ibn Abi Bakr al-Marghinani (d. 593) who received certification from al-Najm Abu Hafs Umar al-Nasafi (d. 537) who received certification from the two Bazdawi brothers: Fakhr al-Islam (d. 482) and Sadr al-Islam (d. 493), the first of whom received certification from the Sun of Imams al-Sarkhasi (d. 483), the author of *al-Mabsut*, who received certification from the Sun of Imams al-Halwai (d. 448) who received certification from al-Husayn ibn Khidr al-Nasafi (d. 423), who received certification from Muhammad ibn al-Fadl al-Bukhari (d. 381), who received certification from Abd Allah ibn Muhammad al-Harithi (d. 340), who received certification from Muhammad ibn Ahmad ibn Hafs (d. 264), who received certification from his father Abu Hafs al-Kabir (d. 217), who received certification from the Imam Muhammad ibn al-Hasan al-Shaybani (d. 189), the companion of Abu Hanifa.

Sadr al-Islam received certification from Ismail ibn Abd al-Sadiq who received certification from Abd al-Karim al-Bazdawi

---

14 Abd al-Aziz al-Bukhari is the author of *Kashf al-asrar*, a manual of *Usul al-fiqh* recently edited by Muhammad al-Baghdadi at *Dar al-kitab al-arabi*.

(d. 390) who received certification from the Imam of Guidance Abu Mansur al-Maturidi (d. 333) who received certification from Abu Bakr al-Jawjazani who received certification from Abu Sulayman Musa ibn Sulayman al-Jawjazani who also received certification from the Imam Muhammad ibn al-Hasan al-Shaybani.

Al-Shaybani received certification from the founder of the Hanafi school of law (*madhhab*), Abu Hanifa al-Numan (d. 150), who received certification from Hammad ibn Abi Sulayman (d. 120) who received certification from Ibrahim ibn Yazid al-Nakhi (d. 95) who received certification from:

1. Alqama ibn Qays (d. 62),
2. Al-Aswad ibn Yazid (d. 75), and
3. Abu Abd al-Rahman Abd Allah ibn Hubayyib al-Sulami (d. 74 or 73)

Alqama and al-Aswad received certification from Abd Allah ibn Masud (d. 32), may Allah be well pleased with him, while al-Sulami received certification from Sayyidina Ali, upon him be peace, who was martyred in Kufa in the month of Ramadan of the year 40, and both Ibn Masud and Sayyidina Ali took from the Seal of Prophets and Leader of the Radiant-faced ones, the Master of the First and the Last among angels, *jinn*, and human beings including prophets and messengers, who was taken to the Highest Company in the late morning of the second day of the week, the 13th of the month of Rabi al-Awwal in the year 11, blessings and peace of Allah upon him, honor, generosity, and mercy, and upon his excellent and chaste Family as well as his pure and Godfearing Companions. And the last of our case is, Praise belongs to Allah, Lord of the worlds.[15]

The author wishes to stress that the intention of this *Encyclopedia of Islamic Doctrine* is to clarify for Muslims around the world the beliefs (*aqida*) of mainstream Muslims, or the People of the Way of the Prophet (ﷺ) and the Congregation of Muslims, and that of our predecessors whom we may truly call *al-salaf al-salih*, the Pious Predecessors. We ask Allah to guide all Muslims in their belief and to bring all who have strayed back to the truth, far from likening Allah to creation (*tashbih*) and attributing a body to Allah (*tajsim*) and back to

15 *Maqalat al-kawthari* (Riyadh: Dar al-ahnaf, 1414/1993) p. 29-31.

the guidance of the righteous predecessors.

This work is only a modest foundation for the correct representation of the doctrine of mainstream Islam in schools and mosques around the English-speaking world. It is a preliminary step in returning to the traditional Islamic understanding regarding the doctrine of Oneness (*aqida al-tawhid*), and the words of the Prophet Muhammad, blessings and peace be upon him, as the Messenger of Allah.

The "Salafis" have deviated far from the original teachings of Islam, and have stifled the more genuine voices in their pursuit to claim authority in the Muslim world. The podium of scholarly discourse has been hijacked, through politics and pressure, by a sect who deny a voice to anyone but themselves. The free pulpit of mainstream Muslims no longer exists in the way that it did as recently as fifty years ago. Huge amounts of money and political resources have facilitated the publicization of beliefs (*aqida*) that had hitherto been kept in check.

In all other times in history, false doctrine, or *tashbih*, was condemned without recourse by scholars who fought fiercely to preserve the faith of Muslims. For example, Ibn Taymiyya was incarcerated for his arrogance and deviation when he went so far as to state that Ali ibn Abi Talib was wrong on seventeen matters and Umar ibn Khattab in more than that (thus challenging the Prophet's advice to, "Follow my *sunna* and the *sunna* of my rightly guided companions after me,"[16] and then made an attempt to replace the mainstream doctrine with views that suggested anthropomorphism in the Divine Essence and Attributes.

When Ibn Taymiyya tried to promote his false doctrines, he and his student were condemned. This occurred despite the fact that he was a scholar of jurisprudence and language, whose learning was generally commended. The reverse is true in recent days, as political and financial support is helping to promulgate false doctrines, moving them from the outskirts of Islam to the center, and suppressing the way of mainstream Muslims.

The Prophet (ﷺ) ordered us to follow the Congregation of

---

16 As related by Ibn Hajar from al-Tufi al-Hanbali in *al-Durar al-kamina* (8:154-155).

Muslims when he said, "You have to follow the congregation for verily Allah will not make the largest group of Muhammad's community agree on error" (*alaykum bi al-jamaa fa inna Allaha la yajmau ummata Muhammadin ala dalala*).[17] Today, the best witnesses to the knowledge of the Congregation are the scholars and imams who are quoted extensively in the following volumes.

Without the guidance of the imams of traditional Islam, it would be left to each and every individual Muslim to seek out and learn the truth concerning sound doctrine, jurisprudence (*fiqh*), and the ways of self-purification (*tazkiyat al-nafs*). Fortunately, Muslims are inextricably attached to their scholars, from the Salaf and Khalaf, and they will not be fooled by a mere label flaunted by a vocal minority. The rope of unity is the rope of the Salaf and the Khalaf, who form not two, but one saved group.

This work is intended to bring Muslims together according to Sunni teachings. This is done in strict accordance with the following hadiths of the Prophet (ﷺ):

> My Community shall never agree upon misguidance; therefore, if you see divergences, you must follow the greater mass or larger group (*inna ummati la tajtamiu ala dalalatin fa idha raaytum al-ikhtilaf fa alaykum bi al-sawad al-azam*).[18]

> Allah's hand is over the group, follow the largest mass, for verily whoever dissents from them departs to hell (*yadu Allah ala al-jamaa, ittabiu al-sawad al-azam fa innahu man shadhdha shadhdha ila al-nar*).[19]

Also, Haythami relates:

---

17 Ibn Abi Shayba relates it from Abu Umama with a sound (*sahih*) chain. Ibn Majah (2:1303 #3950) also narrates it from Anas with a weak chain, but Imam Ahmad narrates it *mawquf* through three sound chains to Abu Umama al-Bahili and Ibn Abi Awfa. Furthermore, it is *marfu* to the Prophet from Abu Umama as narrated by Ibn Jarir al-Tabari and al-Tabar and al-Tabarani with a sound chain, whose narrations, like Ibn Abi Shayba's, state that Abu Umama heard this from the Prophet up to seven times. Bayhaqi in *al-Madkhal* narrates something similar from Ibn Abbas.

18 Already cited.

19 Narrated by al-Hakim and al-Tabari from Ibn Abbas, and al-Lalikai in *al-Sunna* and al-Hakim also narrated it from Ibn Umar.

Abu Ghalib said that during the crisis with the Khawarij in Damascus he saw Abu Umama one day and he was crying. He asked him what made him cry and he replied, 'They followed our religion.' Then he mentioned what was going to happen to them the next day. Abu Ghalib asked, 'Are you saying this according to your opinion or from something you heard the Prophet (ﷺ) say?' Abu Umama said, 'What I just told you I did not hear from the Prophet (ﷺ) only once, or twice, or three times, but more than seven times. Did you not read this verse in Al-Imran: *The day faces will be white and faces will be dark . . .?'* (3:106). Then he said, 'I heard the Prophet (ﷺ) say, "The Jews separated into 71 sects, 70 of which are in the fire; the Christians into 72 sects, 71 of which are in the fire; and this Community will separate into 73 sects, all of them are in the fire except one which will enter paradise." We said, 'Describe it for us.' He said, 'The *sawad al-azam*.'[20]

The s*awad al-azam* means "a massive gathering of human beings," which is established by the following sound hadith in Tirmidhi (*hasan sahih*):

Ibn Abbas narrated, "When the Prophet (ﷺ) was taken up to heaven, he passed by prophets followed by their nations and he passed by prophets followed by their groups and he passed by prophets followed by no one until he saw a tremendous throng of people (*sawad azim*) so he asked, 'Who are these?' and the answer was, 'These are Moses and his nation, but raise your head and look up,' whereupon the Prophet (ﷺ) said, '(I raised my head and saw) a tremendous throng (*sawad azim*) that had blocked the entire firmament from this side and that!' And it was said, 'This is your Community . . .'"

The *sawad al-azam* is therefore as Ibn Masud said in his authentic narration: That which the Muslims deem good, Allah deems good.[21]

---

20 Haythami said in *Majma al-zawaid*: Tabarani narrated it in *al-Mumam al-kabir* and *al-Awsat* and its narrators are trustworthy (*thiqa*).

21 Ahmad in the Musnad (#3599) relates it from the words of Ibn Masud (*mawquf*) with a sound chain.

The above is also Imam al-Shafii's understanding of the Congregation of Muslims, as he said, "We know that the people at large cannot agree on an error and on what may contradict the *sunna* of the Prophet (ﷺ)." This statement is found in his *Risala*, which is the foremost exposition of the *Principles of the Law* which the Salaf bequeathed to us. This is also the consensus of Muslims, the rope to which all mainstream Muslims cling, and our firm conviction, by Allah's grace and His favor.

The Prophet (ﷺ) warned against those who would rend the unity of Muslims using newfangled ideas. As Muslim narrated in his *Muqaddima*, the Prophet (ﷺ) said:

> There will be towards the end of time Dajjals and arch-liars who will say to you what neither you nor your forebearers ever heard before. Beware of them lest they misguide you and bring you confusion.

An example of what the Muslims and their forebears never heard before the advent of "Salafi" ideology is the categorization of *tawhid* (the Oneness of Allah) into two and three areas, such as *tawhid al-uluhiyya* (unity of Godship) *tawhid al-rububiyya* (unity of Lordship) and *tawhid al-asma wa al-sifat* (unity of Names and Attributes).

Bedouins used to come into the presence of Prophet (ﷺ) Muhammad (ﷺ) and bear witness, "There is no god but Allah and Muhammad is the Messenger of Allah (*la ilaha illa Allah, Muhammadun rasulullah*)," and he accepted that from them. He never said to them, "Accept also unity of Godship and unity of Lordship." It is established throughout the Islamic sciences that there is no difference between the Lord and God (*al ilahu wa al-rabbu wahid*)." The Prophet (ﷺ) said, as narrated by Muslim, "Whoever accepts Allah as his Lord (*rabb*), Islam as his religion, and Muhammad as his Prophet (ﷺ) will taste faith (*dhaqa tama al-imani man radia billahi rabban wa bi al-islami dinan wa bi Muhammadin rasulan*)."

The Prophet (ﷺ) did not differentiate between the meaning of "Allah" and the meaning of "*rabb*." If they were different, he would have said, "Whoever accepts Allah as *ilah* and Allah as *rabb*. . ." The sayings, *ashadu an la ilaha illa-Allah wa ashadu an la rabba illallah* and *wa ashadu anna Muhammadan Rasulullah wa ashhadu anna Muhammadan rasul al-rabb* have never been among the requirements of Islam. Rather, the Prophet (ﷺ) said, *ashadu an la ilaha illa-Allah then wa ashadu anna Muhammadan rasulullah.*

The *shahada* is complete and unchangeable. Muslim and Bukhari narrated in their *Sahih*s that the Prophet (ﷺ) said, "I have been ordered to fight people until they say *la ilaha illa Allah Muhammadun rasulullah.* If they say it, then their blood is protected, their possessions are safe and their judgement is with Allah." He did not say, I have been ordered to fight people until they say *la ilaha illa-Allah wa la rabba illallah*" and "*Muhammadun rasulullah wa Muhammadan rasul al-rabb.*"

The Prophet (ﷺ) decreed that whoever says the *shahada* is a Muslim unitarian. However, "Salafi" doctrine considers those who say the *shahada*, but differ from them in anything, to be polytheists (*mushrik*). They put them outside the range of Islam by labeling what they do as polytheism (*shirk*), disbelief (*kufr*), innovation (*bida*) and forbidden (*haram*). Yet, the Prophet (ﷺ) was far more lenient with the servant-girl who worked as a shepherdess, when he asked her, "Where is Allah?" She replied, "In heaven," and he asked her, "Who am I?" to which she replied, "You are the Messenger of Allah." On this alone he confirmed her faith and her Islam, and said, "She is a believer (*hiya mumina*)."[22]

"Salafis" curse many worshippers—especially those who are pious, who remember Allah often (practice *dhikr* Allah), and believe in intercession—by claiming they are out of the fold of Islam. They forget that the Prophet (ﷺ) explicitly enjoined kindness and gentleness upon those who would convey the Message of Islam, even to non-Muslims. Abd Allah ibn Abi Bakr said that he was told that when the Prophet (ﷺ) sent Muadh ibn Jabal to the people of Yemen he gave him instructions and then said:

> Deal gently and not harshly; announce good news and do not repel people. You are going to one of the people with Scripture who will ask you about the key to Heaven. Say to them it is the witness that there is no god except Allah, Who has no partner.[23]

---

22 This is narrated by Muslim, Ahmad, and others.
23 Ibn Hisham narrates it in his *Sira* and it is authentic. English version p. 644.

As the Prophet (ﷺ) ordered Muadh to be lenient with the People of the Book, it is all the more our responsibility to be lenient with one another. Still, our "Salafi" brethren continuously condemn other Muslims. Allah said, *"Behold, ye received it on your tongues, and said out of your mouths things of which ye had no knowledge. Ye thought it to be a light matter, while it was most serious in the sight of Allah"* (24:15); and, *"It is a grievous saying that issues from their mouths; what they say is nothing but falsehood!"* (18:5)

The Prophet (ﷺ) said, as narrated in *Sahih Muslim*:

> Do not envy one another, do not argue with another, do not have hatred for one another and do not show your backs to one another. Do not intervene in your brother's transactions but be servants of Allah, brothers. A Muslim is the brother of a Muslim. He never oppresses him, never puts him down and never humiliates him. Sincerity is here, said the Prophet (ﷺ), pointing to his heart. Anyone is evil if he will humiliate his Muslim brother. Everything between Muslims is sacrosanct; his blood, his money and his honor.

To further the controversy, the "Salafis" assume that the seventy-two sects other than the saved sect are condemned to hellfire forever like disbelievers (*kufar*). This is not the correct position. Even Ibn Taymiyya says in his book *al-Iman*:

> Whoever says the seventy-two divisions of the Islamic nation are disbelievers (*kufar*), he has opposed the Holy Quran and the *sunna*, the consensus of the Companions, the consensus of the four Imams and the rest of the scholars. None of the above have accused any from the seventy-two divisions of being disbelievers except the Mutazila and those who are associated with them.[24]

Imam al-Ghazali said, in his explanation of the same hadith, that when the Prophet (ﷺ) said that all of these groups are in the fire except one, he meant that although they have

---

24 Ibn Taymiyya, *al-Iman*, ed. Muhammad Nasir al-Din al-Albani (Cairo: Maktabat Anas ibn Malik, 1400/1980).

done things that are considered a sin, they died in the Oneness of Allah (*tawhid*). Therefore, to say they are in the fire, actually means they will go to the fire to be punished and later enter paradise with the intercession of the Prophet (ﷺ). They will enter paradise with the Prophet's intercession, but it is not known whether this will occur after punishment or before they enter hell, as it is known that his intercession takes place on the Day of Judgment.

However, the Prophet (ﷺ) warned very sternly against the sects that will enter the fire. He said:

> There will be people in my Community whose mark is that they shave (their heads) [*simahum al-tahliq*]. They will recite Quran, but it will not go past their throats. They will pass through religion the way an arrow passes through its quarry. They are the worst of human beings and the worst of all creation.[25]
>
> He also said: "O Allah, bless our Sham and our Yaman!" They said: "O Messenger, and our Najd!" He did not reply. He blessed Sham [the North] and Yaman [the South] twice more. They asked him to bless Najd twice more but he did not reply. The third time he said: "There [in Najd] are earthquakes and dissensions, and through it will dawn the epoch [or horn] of satan."[26]

The Prophet (ﷺ) also said: Belief is Yemenite while afflictions appear from there (the East) from where the side of the head of satan will appear.[27]

Bukhari and Muslim also narrated from Ibn Masud that

---

25 Note: This is the penultimate hadith in the entire book of *Sahih al-Bukhari*, #7007. The Prophet's prediction of the *tahliq* of the People of *fitna* was fulfilled by the early followers of Muhammad ibn Abd al-Wahhab, who used to require that anyone who joined him shave his head as a sign of loyalty. See the relevant sections of Abd Allah ibn Alawi al-Haddad's *Misbah al-anam* and Ahmad Zayni Dahlan's *Khulasat al-kalam fi umara al-balad al-haram*.

26 Nawari in *Tahrir al-tanbih* (Dar al-fikr 1990 ed. p. 157, s.v. "najd") said: "Najd is the area that lies between Jurash (in Yemen) all the way to the rural outskirts of Kufa (in Iraq), and its Western border is the Hijaz. The author of *al-Matali* said: Najd is all a province of al-Yamama." Al Fayruzabadi said in *al-Qamus al-muhit*: "al-Najd": Its geographical summit is Tihama and Yemen. Its bottom is Iraq and Sham. It begins at Dhat Irqin from the side of the Hijaz.

27 English *Bukhari*, Volume 5, Book 59, Number 672.

the Prophet (ﷺ) pointed to al-Yaman and said:

> Verily, belief is there; but hardness and coarse-
> ness of heart is with the desert-people (al-faddadin),
> the people of many camels, where the two sides of the
> head of satan shall appear: among (the tribes of)
> Rabia and Madar.

A Muslim might ask, "How did the Prophet (ﷺ) predict, in his hadith, that from the area of Najd will come satan, dissension, and *fitna*, when we know that it is an Islamic area?" The response is in another hadith in Muslim: "Whoever calls a believer an unbeliever, it is true of one of them." Therefore, if one condemns two Muslims as disbelievers, he makes himself doubly an unbeliever. If he condemns three Muslims as disbelievers, he triples his unbelief, and so on. Thus, his attitude directly reflects his unbelief. Since a small group, the Wahhabi inhabitants of Najd, declared as disbelievers everyone opposed to the ideology of Muhammad ibn Abd al-Wahhab, it compounded their own unbelief to make it global and all-encompassing.

Furthermore, the Wahhabi inhabitants of Najd believe that all the inhabitants of the world, aside from themselves, are disbelievers. According to their thinking, there is no place in heaven but for them, as the only way to enter paradise is to accept their ideology and dismiss 1400 years of mainstream Islamic beliefs.

They went even further by naming Najd "the land or home of the believers," (*dirat al-muminin* and *dar al-muminin*), whereas mainstream Muslims know that these sacred titles apply to Madina (Tayba) and Makka al-Mukarrama as the places of *iman*. The "Salafis," who are the modern perpetuators of the Wahhabi creed, use the name *dar al-iman* to refer to Najd exclusively, and so devalue the Two Holy Cities.

According to mainstream Islam, the prohibition of something that lacks scholarly consensus is forbidden. Yet, the "Salafis" persist in their prohibition of the celebration of the birth of the Messenger (*mawlid*) and *tawassul* (among other issues). Imam Nawawi and Ibn Taymiyya together say:

Scholars only protest against that which is (governed by) unanimous consensus; as for that which is not (governed by) unanimous consensus, then there is no permission to protest.[28]

In the Quran Allah said:

Jesus the son of Mary said, "O Allah, our Lord! send down to us food from heaven which should be to us an ever-recurring happiness, to the first of us and to the last of us, and a sign from Thee, and grant us means of subsistence, and Thou art the best of the Providers" (5:114).[29]

Prophet Jesus (🕊) asked Allah to send him a feast so they could celebrate. Explanations of the Quran have shown that the feast consisted of a table of seven loaves of bread and seven fish. If that table was a festival (*id*) for them, what is Allah's gift of the Perfect Man, who holds the authority for intercession from Allah, whose followers go to paradise before those of all other Prophets, and who is the most noble in Allah's Eyes? Which "ever-recurring happiness" is more worthy of commemoration, the gift of food or the birth of the Seal of Prophets, whose Message lives until the end of time?

It is therefore justified if Muslims meet at a table to thank Allah for bringing the Prophet Muhammad (🕊) to this world on the 12th of Rabi al-Awwal. They may also remember Allah that day, through calling on Him through His Holy Names and Attributes, reciting the Quran, reading the story of the Prophet's life, reminding people of the duties of Islam, and distributing food, presents, and sweets. Even though it is not called a festival (*id*), this feast is better than the *id* of bread and fish of Prophet Jesus (🕊). The appearance of the Prophet Muhammad was a mercy for all humanity that believers have been ordered to celebrate. Allah said, *"We did not send you except as a Mercy to the worlds"* (21:107) and *"Say, in the bounty of Allah and in His mercy, therein let them rejoice. It is better than what they hoard"* (10:58).

To continue to dispute issues about which scholars have dis-

---

28 Imam Nawawi said this in his commentary on *Sahih Muslim*, Chapter entitled *al-Amr bi al-maruf wa al-nahi an al-munkar* (Enjoining Good and Prohibiting Evil), and identically, Ibn Taymiyya in his *Fatawa al-kubra* (2:33).

29 M. Shakir translation.

agreed opposes the authentic hadith narrated by Tirmidhi, Ibn Majah, Ahmad, and Malik: "Of the excellence of someone's Islam is that the Muslim leaves alone what does not concern him" (*min husni islam al-mari tarkuhu ma la yanih*). Similarly, Darimi narrated in his *Sunan*:

> When the Caliph Sulayman ibn Abd al-Malik passed by Madina he asked to see who was still alive among the Companions of the Prophet (ﷺ) and he was referred to Abu Hazim. Among many other questions he asked him, "Who among the believers is the biggest loser?" Abu Hazim replied, "He who goes to extreme against the idle desire of his brother and thereby commits injustice, so he sells out his hereafter (*akhira*) due to someone else's *dunya* (lower world)."

Also, al-Junayd said, "Among the marks of Allah's wrath against a servant is that He makes him very busy with that which is of no concern to him."[30]

It is no accident that the most violent verbal outrages committed by "Salafis" are against the Sufis. The Sufis are, on the whole, the most staunch adherents of traditional Islamic beliefs and practices. They have been successful in spreading Islam through jihad, learning, and spirituality as no other group has. As a result, they have roused the envy of the "Salafis," who have neither enjoyed such success, nor achieved their reputation. The "Salafis" see in the Sufis the reflection of their own shortcomings.

In an explanation of the hadith, "The believer is the mirror of the believer," al-Munawi wrote:

> In a mirror, man sees nothing but his own face and person. And if he exerts himself to the utmost in order to see the body of the mirror, he does not see it because his own image veils him. Al-Tibi said, "Concerning the unveiling of his brother's defects, the (examined) believer is like a polished mirror which displays all images reflected in it, no matter how minute . . ." Therefore whoever has gathered the features of Iman, accomplished the manners of Islam,

---

30 As related by Ibn al-Jawzi in his *Sifat al-safwa*.

and excelled internally against the blameworthy fea-
tures of his ego (*nafs*), then his heart raises to the
peak of *ihsan* (excellence), so pure that it becomes like
a mirror; if the believers look at him, they see the
darkness of their own condition reflected within the
purity of his, and they see the ill state of their own
manners reflected within the excellence of his."[31]

A state of confusion has currently emerged due to the
migration of many Muslims of today's generation into certain
so-called "Islamic countries." There, they have found that
"Salafi" ideology has spread unchecked while traditional
Islamic knowledge has been cast aside. Their lack of understanding has made these immigrants easy prey for the influence of "Salafi" dogmas. Unaware of the mainstream Islamic
approach to many issues, and disarmed by their love of the
Arabic language, the immigrants quickly embraced "Salafi"
teachings and, believing them to be true, they began to propa-
gate these teachings in their own countries. This is precisely
how the "Salafis" have managed to turn a marginal heresy into
a significant threat. As Ibn Abbas said, "Misguidance contains
sweetness in the hearts of those who spread it." Allah said in
the Quran:

> *Is he then, to whom the evil of his conduct is made*
> *alluring, so that he looks upon it as good (equal to one*
> *who is rightly-guided)? For Allah leaves to stray whom*
> *He wills, and guides whom He wills* (35:8).

The innovators use any and every of the considerable
means at their disposal to spread their innovations, i.e.
through the free distribution of books, pamphlets and other
publications, through the granting of scholarships, through
widely-broadcast television programs, through financing
imamships, or through conducting large-scale fundraising.
Allah said in the Holy Quran:

> *Their intention is to extinguish Allah's Light (by*
> *blowing) with their mouths. But Allah will complete*

31 Al-Munawi, *Fayd al-qadir* (6:251-252 #9141-9142). A fair (*hasan*) narration,
cited by Tabarani from Anas and by Bukhari in his *Adab al-mufrad* and Abu Dawud
from Abu Hurayra.

His Light, even though the disbelievers may detest (it)
(61:8).

Until today, the pious Salaf and all Muslims have sought
shafaa (intercession), *istighatha* (aid), *tabarruk* (blessing), and
tawassul (means), have celebrated *mawlid*, and have sat for
the blessed *dhikr*. According to the "Salafis," all such Muslims
are polytheists (*mushrik*).

The "Salafi" hypothesis is therefore that previous generations are for the most part *mushrik*, and hence *murtadd* (apostate). Their assertion is that the majority of Muslims today are
either apostates or the children of apostates. As such, their
death is obligatory, their money is forfeited, they cannot inher-
it, cannot be inherited from, and cannot be prayed for in death.

Allah ordered Muslims to pray for their parents who have
died. *"My Lord, bestow on them Thy Mercy even as they cher-
ished me in childhood"* (17:24). *"And those who came after them
say, 'Our Lord! Forgive us, and our brethren who came before
us into the faith, and leave not in our hearts rancor (for sense of
injury) against those who have believed. Our Lord! Thou art
indeed full of kindness, most Merciful"* (59:10).

As the Prophet (ﷺ) said, "There is nothing better than
these two matters: having good assumption (*husn al-zann*)
about Allah and having good assumption about the servants of
Allah." There is no doubt that whoever accuses a Muslim of disbelief (*kufr*) becomes a *fasiq* (transgressor) and that whoever
accuses a Muslim of adultery will be cursed in this life and in
the next. What about accusing the Muslims of *shirk, irtidad*,
and *kufr*? Allah said in the Quran:

> *And those who followed would say, 'If only we had
> one more chance! We would clear ourselves of them, as
> they have cleared themselves of us.' Thus will Allah
> show them (the fruits of) their deeds as (nothing but)
> regrets, nor will there be a way for them out of the fire"*
> (2:166).

> *If you desire their guidance, yet surely Allah does
> not guide him who leads astray, nor shall they have
> any helpers"* (16:37).

> *Of no profit will be my counsel to you. Much as I desire to give you (good) counsel. If it be that Allah willeth to lead you astray, He is your Lord! And to Him will ye return!* (11:34).

Al-Bayhaqi and Ibn Abi al-Dunya narrated from Fatima that the Prophet (ﷺ) said, "The most evil are those who have been enriched with wealth, those who eat all different kinds of food, wear all different kinds of clothes and rant and rave in their speech."

In the same respect, the Prophet (ﷺ) said, "I do not fear for you only the anti-Christ." They asked, "Then who else are you afraid from?" He said, "The misguided scholars."[32] The Prophet (ﷺ) also said, "What I fear most for my nation is a hypocrite who has a scholarly tongue."

Allah calls upon Muslims to come together without prejudice, and act as one hand; *"And hold fast to the Rope of Allah, all together, and do not separate"* (3:103). Ninety-five percent of all Muslim scholars follow the belief (*aqida*) of mainstream Islam. These scholars occupy positions of authority as ministers, deputy ministers, muftis, university presidents, deans of faculties, professors, writers, lecturers, and imams throughout the Muslim world. Unfortunately, whenever one of them wants to speak about *aqida* nowadays, he faces violent opposition from the very vocal minority of "Salafi" scholars.

The freedom of speech and action afforded by mainstream Islamic scholars of Islamic law must be preserved. Of the "Salafis" it is demanded that they leave everyone to decide freely what he wants to say and do. Mainstream Islam follows a sound doctrine, revealed and clarified by the Prophet (ﷺ) and implemented and transmitted by the Pious Predecessors (*salaf al-salih*). May Allah help our brothers and sisters to be steadfast in this path, and forgive us our sins, *wa al-salamu alaykum wa rahmatullah.*

O Allah, bear witness that I have delivered my message. I hope and pray that my Lord will turn this work, which was three years in the making, into a deed that is accepted and

---

32 Ahmad narrated it in his *Musnad* with a good chain.

blessed in His presence, and in the court of His Beloved Muhammad (ﷺ). May Allah grant that this book be solely for His Glorious Countenance and grant its author the intercession of the blessed Prophet (ﷺ) on the Day of Resurrection. We have presented the kind reader with many radiant proofs and trenchant swords from the statements of mainstream scholars beginning with the Companions of the Prophet (ﷺ), and continuing to our time. We finished writing this book on *yawm al-khamis* the twelfth day of Rabi al-Awwal, 1418, which corresponds to Thursday the 17th of July, 1997, in San Francisco, California. The imams Tirmidhi, Ahmad, Ibn Majah, and al-Hakim narrated from Ibn Umar:

> The Prophet (ﷺ) took hold of my shirt and said: "Abd Allah! Live in the world a stranger, a wayfarer, and consider yourself one of the dwellers of the graves."

It is understood from this hadith that one must be in the world like the traveling merchant who came from the world of souls to the lower world, and whose wares include knowledge of Allah, friendship with Allah, and the means to achieve nearness to Allah. He does not care to look at the adornments of the world, so that the sun of spirituality will never set for him, nor will he ever be cut off from the paths of rightful guidance. The last of our speech is: Glory and praise belongs to Allah, Lord of the worlds.

The Servant of the Noble Way of the Prophet (ﷺ)
Muhammad Hisham Kabbani

1. THE UNITY OF DOCTRINE AND ITS ENEMIES

What are the beliefs and doctrine of mainstream Muslims as opposed to those who call themselves "Salafis" with regard to the Names and Attributes of Almighty Allah?

1.1. MAINSTREAM ISLAM

Scholars have observed that the the Community's (*umma*) greatest achievement over the past millennium has undoubtedly been its internal intellectual cohesion. They point out how from the beginning of the Islamic era to almost the present day, Muslims have maintained an astounding sense of unity despite the clash of the numerous dynasties under which they lived. No major religious hostilities have divided Muslims. At least, this was true until the physical and intellectual assault on Islamic unity initiated by Muhammad ibn Abd al-Wahhab (1703-1792 CE), his immediate successors, and by the self-named "Salafi" sect of the present day (see Appendix 1).

Before the advent of Abd al-Wahhab, as today, a genuine Muslim is one who strives to achieve salvation. A hadith of the Prophet (ﷺ) relates:

> "My Community will split into seventy-three sects. All of them will be in the fire except one group. "They asked, "Who are they, O Messenger of Allah?" He said, "Those that follow my way (*sunnati*) and that of my companions."[1]

---

1 A sound (*sahih*) hadith related by Tirmidhi, Abu Dawud, and al-Darimi.

Scholars unanimously define this group as mainstream Muslims (the People of the Way of the Prophet (ﷺ) and of the Congregation of Muslims) among whom are those who follow the path of the *sunna* embodied in the Sharia as set forth by the four Imams: Abu Hanifa (80-150 AH), Malik (93-179 AH), Shafii (150-204 AH), and Ahmad Ibn Hanbal (164-241 AH). The doctrine of the followers of these four Imams adheres strictly to the way of the Prophet (ﷺ) and the practice of the Companions. This doctrine received a classic formulation at the hands of Abu al-Hasan al-Ashari (d. 324). A descendant of the Companion Abu Musa, al-Ashari was born in Basra, Iraq, as was his contemporary Abu Mansur al-Maturidi (d. 333 AH).[2] Both were motivated by the incredible confusion and strife caused by various groups who espoused erroneous beliefs about Allah, His Attributes, the nature of the afterlife, the Decree, and other essentials of Muslim doctrine.

1.1.1. IMAM AL-ASHARI AND THE ASHARI SCHOOL

The Ashari school has been the standard-bearer for the faith of mainstream Muslims for most of its history. During the infamous period of the Inquisition (*mihna*) under the Caliphs al-Mamun and al-Mutasim, mainstream Muslims were the only scholars who stood against the Mutazila or rationalist heresy. A prominent opponent of the Mutazila school was Ahmad Ibn Hanbal, who was jailed and beaten for upholding the true doctrine. Most unfailing against the Mutazila was Imam Abu al-Hasan al-Ashari.

What made Ashari such a formidable foe against heresy was that he only began his mission of clarifying and formulating the correct beliefs of Muslims after having himself followed the Mutazila school. He left them after seeing a dream three times during Ramadan in which the Prophet (ﷺ) asked him to support the truth that had been transmitted from him. Ashari thus realized the invalidity of the Mutazila school and began his work in establishing a true creed according to the teachings of the Prophet (ﷺ). He authored many works, including:

---

2 The substantive differences between the two Imams amount to about six questions.

- *Al-Ibana an usul al-diyana*[3]
- *Istihsan al-khawd fi ilm al-kalam*[4]
- *Kitab al-luma fi al-radd ala ahl al-zaygh wa-al-bida*[5]
- *Maqalat al-islamiyyin wa ikhtilaf al-musallin*[6]
- *Usul ahl al-sunna wa al-jamaa* (*Risalat ahl al-thughar*).[7]

The Mutazila position on Allah's attributes was extreme. They claimed that the Quran's mention of His Seeing and Hearing, as well as the believers' seeing their Lord in the afterlife, was purely metaphorical. Their most famous error was their view that the Quran is a creation. In addition to this, they asserted that the Night-Ascension of the Prophet (ﷺ) (*miraj*), was in spirit only, against the consensus of scholars. They held that the punishment of the grave, the Scale, the Bridge (*sirat*) and other matters pertaining to the afterlife are all figurative. While it is true that they acknowledged bodily resurrection, the physical reality of paradise, its physical enjoyments, and the torments of hell, they differed with the Sunnis in their beliefs about destiny and freewill, and in their position regarding the Companions of the Prophet (ﷺ).

Faced with this onslaught of dissent, Imam al-Ashari maintained that Allah, the Creator, the Sustainer, the Nourisher, Lord, the Single Unique Divine Being, Exalted and Glorious, is above all conception of His creation. He is exalted above any description or likeness. As He has revealed about Himself: *"There is nothing whatsoever like Him."* (42:11).

3 Ashari, *al-Ibana an usul al-diyana*, Hyderabad: Dairat al-maarif, 1321/1903; Cairo: Idarat al-matbaa al-muniriyya, 1348/1930; ed. Fawqiyya Husayn Mahmud, 2 vol. (Cairo: Dar al-ansar, 1977); ed. Abbas Sabbagh (Beirut: Dar al-nafais, 1994); also translated as Abu al-Hasan Ali ibn Ismail al-Ashari's *al-Ibana an usul al-diyana* (The elucidation of Islam's foundation): a translation with introduction and notes by Walter C. Klein (New York: Kraus Reprint Corp., 1967; Reprint. Originally published: New Haven, Conn.: American Oriental Society, 1940).

4 Ashari, *Istihsan al-khawd fi ilm al-kalam*, Hyderabad: Dairat al-maarif, 1344/1925. Reprinted in Richard J. McCarthy, *The Theology of al-Ashari* (Beirut: Imprimerie Catholique, 1953). Its attribution to al-Ashari is greatly open to doubt.

5 Ashari, *Kitab al-luma fi al-radd ala ahl al-zaygh wa-al-bida*, Ed. Abd al-Aziz Izz al-Din Sayrawan (Beirut: Dar lubnan li al-tibaa wa al-nashr, 1987), together with Imam al-Haramayn al-Juwayni's *Luma al-adilla fi qawaid aqaid ahl al-Sunna*; ed. Hammuda Ghuraba (Cairo: al-Maktaba al-azhariyya li al-turath, 1993). Ed. and trans. in McCarthy. op. cit.

6 Ashari, *Maqalat al-islamiyyin wa ikhtilaf al-musallin*, Ed. H. Ritter, 2 vol. (Istanbul: Government Press, 1929-1930); (Damascus and Beirut: al-Hikma, 1994).

7 Ashari, *Usul ahl al-sunna wa al-jamaa*, Ed. Muhammad al-Sayyid al-Julaynad (Cairo: Matbaat al-taqaddum, 1987).

This belief is the cornerstone of all beliefs concerning Allah. It is the fabric from which Muslim unity and consensus was woven and its defense against the danger of image worship that is inherent in the anthropomorphic interpretation of the Divine Attributes.

At the same time, Imam Ashari refuted the Mutazila's denial of the positive significance of the divine attributes and their explaining away the reality of the afterlife. For the most part, he did not offer figurative explanations for problematic expressions of divine Attributes (such as Allah's "Hand" etc.), but urged that they be accepted as they have come without asking how they are meant. All the while, Ashari maintained Allah's absolute transcendence above created things in accordance with the verse above. Yet, as Nuh Keller explains, "Later members of his school did give such interpretations in rebuttal of anthropomorphists, preserving the faith of Islam from their innovations in the same spirit and with the same dedication that the Imam had preserved it before them by his rebuttal of the Mutazila."[8]

1.1.2. IMAM AL-MATURIDI

Abu Mansur Muhammad ibn Muhammad al-Maturidi (d. 333) learned and transmitted the doctrine and jurisprudence (fiqh) of Abu Hanifa from his teacher, al-Nasr ibn Yahya al-Balkhi, who was a student of Abu Hanifa. He was born in Maturid, near Samarqand, and became famous in Basra for his eloquence and clarity in stating the Sunni doctrine. He gave a greater role to reason than al-Ashari in the determination of legal rulings. He authored *Kitab tawil al-quran* (Interpretation of the Quran), *al-Usul fi usul al-din* (Foundational principles of the religion), *Kitab al-tawhid* (Book of the doctrine of Oneness), and others. His commentary on Imam Abu Hanifa's *al-Fiqh al-akbar* has also been published.[9]

1.1.3. IMAM AL-TAHAWI

Imam Abu Jafar Ahmad ibn Muhammad al-Azdi, known as

8 Nuh Ha Mim Keller, editor and translator, *The Reliance of the Traveller: A Classic Manual of Islamic Sacred Law*, by Ahmad ibn Naqib al-Misri (Dubai: Modern Printing Press, 1991) p. 1030.

9 Abu Mansur Muhammad ibn Muhammad al-Maturidi, in *Majmuat rasail* (Hyderabad: Matbaat majlis dairat al-maarif al-nizamiyya, 1321/1903).

Imam Tahawi after his birthplace in Egypt, is among the most outstanding authorities of the Islamic world on hadith and jurisprudence (*fiqh*). He lived at a time when both the direct and indirect disciples of the Imams of law were teaching and practicing. This period was the greatest age of hadith and jurisprudence (*fiqh*) studies, and Imam Tahawi studied with all the living authorities of the day. Al-Badr al-Ayni said that when Ahmad died, Tahawi was 12; when Bukhari died, he was 27; when Muslim died, he was 32; when Ibn Majah died, he was 44; when Abu Dawud died, he was 46; when Tirmidhi died, he was 59; and when Nisai died, he was 74.

Kawthari also relates this, adding the consensus of scholars that Tahawi allied in himself the knowledge of both hadith and jurisprudence (*fiqh*). This consensus included, among others, al-Ayni and al-Dhahabi, with Ibn Taymiyya singling himself out in his opinion that Tahawi was not very knowledgeable in hadith. This is flatly contradicted by Ibn Kathir, who says in his notice on Tahawi in *al-Bidaya wa al-nihaya*, "He is one of the trustworthy narrators of established reliability, and one of the great memorizers of hadith." Kawthari calls Ibn Taymiyya's verdict "another one of his random speculations," and states, "No-one disregards Tahawi's knowledge of the defective hadith except someone whose own defects have no remedy, and may Allah protect us from such."[10]

Tahawi began his studies with his maternal uncle Ismail ibn Yahya al-Muzani, a leading disciple of Imam Shafii. However, Tahawi felt instinctively drawn to the corpus of Imam Abu Hanifa's works. Indeed, he had seen his uncle and teacher turning to the works of Hanafi scholars to resolve thorny issues of jurisprudence drawing heavily on the writings of Abu Hanifa's two leading companions, Muhammad Ibn al-Hasan al-Shaybani and Abu Yusuf, who had codified Hanafi jurisprudence. This led him to devote his attention to studying the Hanafi works, and to eventually join the Hanafi school. He now stands out not only as a prominent follower of that school, but, in view of his vast erudition and remarkable powers of assimilation, as one of its leading scholars. His monumental scholarly works, such as *Sharh maani al-athar* and *Mushkil*

---

10 Kawthari, *Maqalat* p. 500.

al-athar, are encyclopedic in scope and have long been regarded as indispensable for training students of jurisprudence. He was, in fact, a *mujtahid* across the board and was thoroughly familiar with the jurisprudence of all four schools, as stated by Ibn Abd al-Barr and related by Kawthari, and as shown by Tahawi's own work on comparative law entitled *Ikhtilaf al-fuqaha*.[11]

Tahawi's "Doctrine" (*al-aqida*), though small in size, is a basic text for all times, listing what a Muslim must know, believe, and inwardly comprehend. There is consensus among the Companions, the Successors and all the leading Islamic authorities, including the major Imams and their followers, on the doctrines presented in this work. Tahawi's doctrines are entirely derived from the undisputed primary sources of religion: the Holy Quran, and the confirmed Hadith. Being a text on Islamic doctrine, this work summarizes arguments set forth in these two sources in order to define sound belief and to refute the views of sects that have deviated from the *sunna*.

As Tahawi makes frequent, and often vague references to various sects, such as the Mutazila, the Jahmiyya, the Karramiyya, the Qadariyya, and the Jabriyya, it would be helpful to be familiar with Islamic history up to the time of the author. *Al-aqida* also contains allusions to other views that were considered unorthodox and outside the way of the Sunnis. There is an explicit reference in the work to the controversy on the creation of the Quran in the times of al-Mamun and others.

While the permanent relevance of the statements of belief in *al-Aqida* is clear, the historical weight of these statements can be properly appreciated only if the work is studied with the guidance of some learned person. Since the present book is intended to help elucidate Tahawi's arguments with reference to the intellectual and historical background of the sects, it is hoped that the quotation of the entire text of Tahawi's "Doctrine" will be of benefit to the reader.

Imam Abu Jafar al-Tahawi (239-321) can be said to represent the creed of both Asharis and Maturidis (especially the latter), as he also followed the Hanafi school of law. Therefore, it

---

11 Tahawi, *Ikhtilaf al-fuqaha li al-imam Abu Jafar Ahmad ibn Muhammad al-Tahawi*, ed. Muhammad Saghir Hasan al-Masumi (Islamabad: Mahad al-abhath al-islamiyya, 1971).

was decided to include the entire translated text of his Statement of Islamic Doctrine, commonly known as the *aqida Tahawiyya*. This text is one of the most representative of the mainstream view, and is the widely acclaimed source of indispensible evidence for Muslim beliefs. The text below is a complete English translation.

1.1.3.1.IMAM TAHAWI'S STATEMENT OF ISLAMIC DOCTRINE
In the Name of Allah, the Merciful, the Compassionate
Praise be to Allah, Lord of all the worlds.

The great scholar Hujjat al-lslam Abu Jafar al-Warraq al-Tahawi al-Misri, may Allah have mercy on him, said: "This is a presentation of the beliefs of Sunnis, according to the school of the jurists of this religion, Abu Hanifa al-Numan ibn Thabit al-Kufi, Abu Yusuf Yaqub ibn Ibrahim al-Ansari and Abu Abd Allah Muhammad ibn al-Hasan al-Shaybani. May Allah be pleased with them all, and with what they believe regarding the fundamentals of the religion and their faith in the Lord of the worlds."

We say about Allah's unity, believing by Allah's help that:

1 Allah is One, without any partners.

2 There is nothing like Him.

3 There is nothing that can overwhelm Him.

4 There is no god other than Him.

5 He is the Eternal without a beginning and enduring without end.

6 He will never perish nor come to an end.

7 Nothing happens except what He wills.

8 No imagination can conceive of Him and no understanding can comprehend Him.

9 He is different from any created being.

10 He is living and never dies and is eternally active and never sleeps.

11 He creates without His being in need to do so and provides for His creation without any effort.

12 He causes death with no fear and restores to life without difficulty.

13 He has always existed together with His attributes since

before creation. Bringing creation into existence did not add anything to His attributes that was not already there. As He was, together with His attributes, in pre-eternity, so He will remain throughout endless time.

14 It was not only after the act of creation that He could be described as "the Creator" nor was it only by the act of origination that He could be described as "the Originator."

15 He was always the Lord even when there was nothing to be Lord of, and always the Creator even when there was no creation.

16 In the same way that He is the "Bringer to life of the dead," after He has brought them to life a first time, and deserves this name before bringing them to life, so too He deserves the name of "Creator" before He has created them.

17 This is because He has the power to do everything, everything is dependent on Him, everything is easy for Him, and He does not need anything. *"There is nothing like Him and He is the Hearer, the Seer"* (42:11).

18 He created creation with His knowledge.

19 He appointed destinies for those He created.

20 He allotted to them fixed life spans.

21 Nothing about them was hidden from Him before He created them, and He knew everything that they would do before He created them.

22 He ordered them to obey Him and forbade them to disobey Him.

23 Everything happens according to His decree and will, and His will is accomplished. The only will that people have is what He wills for them. What He wills for them occurs and what He does not will, does not occur.

24 He gives guidance to whomever He wills, and protects them, and keeps them safe from harm, out of His generosity; and He leads astray whomever He wills, and abases them, and afflicts them, out of His justice.

25 All of them are subject to His will either through His generosity or His justice.

26 He is Exalted beyond having opposites or equals.

27 No one can ward off His decree or delay His command or overpower His affairs.

28 We believe in all of this and are certain that everything comes from Him.

29 And we are certain that Muhammad (may Allah bless him and grant him peace) is His chosen Servant and elect Prophet (ﷺ) and His Messenger with whom He is well pleased,

30 And that he is the Seal of the Prophets and the Imam of the Godfearing and the most honored of all the messengers and the Beloved of the Lord of all the worlds.

31 Every claim to prophethood after Him is falsehood and deceit.

32 He is the one who has been sent to all the *jinn* and all mankind with truth and guidance and with light and illumination.

33 The Quran is the word of Allah. It came from Him as speech; it is not possible to say how. He sent it down on His Messenger as revelation. The believers accept it as absolute truth; they are certain that it is, in truth, the word of Allah. It is not created as is the speech of human beings, and anyone who hears it and claims that it is human speech has become an unbeliever. Allah warns him and censures him and threatens him with fire when He, Exalted is He, says: "*I will burn him in the fire*" (74:26). When Allah threatens with the fire those who say, "*This is just human speech*" (74:25), we know for certain that it is the speech of the Creator of mankind and that it is totally unlike the speech of mankind.

34 Anyone who describes Allah as being in any way the same as a human being has become an unbeliever. All those who grasp this will take heed and refrain from saying things such as the disbelievers say, and they will know that He, in His attributes, is not like human beings.

35 The Seeing of Allah by the People of the Garden is true, without their vision being all-encompassing and without the manner of their vision being known. As the Book of our Lord has expressed it: "*Faces on that Day radiant, looking at their Lord*" (75:22-3). The explanation of this is as Allah knows and wills. Everything that has come down to us about this in

authentic Traditions from the Messenger, may Allah bless him and grant him peace, in authentic traditions, is as he said and means what he intended. We do not delve into that, trying to interpret it according to our own opinions or letting our imaginations have free rein. No one is safe in his religion unless he surrenders himself completely to Allah, the Exalted and Glorified, and to His Messenger (ﷺ) and leaves the knowledge of ambiguous things to the One who knows them. 36 A person's Islam is not secure unless it is based on submission and surrender. Anyone whose intellect is not content with surrender, and desires to know things which are beyond his capacity, will discover that his desire veils him from a pure understanding of Allah's true unity, clear knowledge and correct belief, and that he veers between disbelief and belief, confirmation and denial and acceptance and rejection. He will he subject to whisperings and find himself confused and full of doubt, being neither an accepting believer nor a denying rejecter.

37 Belief of a person in the seeing of Allah by the People of the Garden is not correct if he interprets or imagines what it is like according to his own understanding, since the interpretation of this seeing (or indeed, the meaning of any of the subtle phenomena which are in the realm of Lordship), is in avoiding its interpretation and strictly adhering to the submission. This is the religion of Muslims. Anyone who does not guard himself against negating the attributes of Allah, or likening Allah to something else, has gone astray and has failed to understand Allah's glory, because our Lord, the Glorified and the Exalted, can only be described in terms of oneness and absolute singularity and no creation is in any way like Him.

38 He is beyond having limits placed on Him, or being restricted, or having parts or limbs. Nor is He contained by the six directions as all created things are.

39 The Ascent through the heavens (al-miraj) is true. The Prophet (ﷺ), may Allah bless him and grant him peace, was taken by night and ascended in his bodily form, while awake, through the heavens, to whatever heights Allah willed for

him. Allah ennobled him in the way that He ennobled him and revealed to him what He revealed to him, *"And his heart was not mistaken about what it saw"* (53:11). Allah blessed him and granted him peace in this world and the next.

40 The Pool (*al-hawd*), which Allah has granted the Prophet (ﷺ), as an honor to quench the thirst of his Community on the Day of Judgment, is true.

41 The intercession (*al-shafaa*), which is stored up for Muslims, is true, as related in the hadiths.

42 The covenant which Allah made with Adam and his offspring is true.

43 Allah knew, before the existence of time, the exact number of those who would enter the garden and the exact number of those who would enter the fire. This number will neither be increased nor decreased.

44 The same applies to all actions done by people, which are done exactly as Allah has known they would be done. Everyone is eased towards what he was created for and it is the action with which a man's life is sealed which dictates his fate. Those who are fortunate are fortunate by the decree of Allah, and those who are wretched are wretched by the decree of Allah.

45 The exact nature of the decree is Allah's secret in His creation, and no angel near the Throne, nor any prophet sent with a message, has been given knowledge of it. Delving into it and reflecting too much about it only leads to destruction and loss, and results in rebelliousness. So be extremely careful about thinking and reflecting on this matter or letting doubts about it assail you, because Allah has kept knowledge of the decree away from human beings, and forbidden them to enquire about it, saying in His Book, *"He is not asked about what He does, but they are asked"* (21: 23). Therefore, anyone who asks: "Why did Allah do that?" has gone against a judgement of the Book, and anyone who goes against a judgement of the Book is an unbeliever.

46 This, in sum, is what those of Allah's Friends with enlightened hearts need to know and constitutes the level of those firmly endowed with knowledge. For there are two kinds of

knowledge: knowledge which is accessible to created beings, and knowledge which is not accessible to created beings. Denying the knowledge which is accessible is disbelief, and claiming the knowledge which is inaccessible is disbelief. Belief can only be firm when accessible knowledge is accepted and the inaccessible is not sought after.

47 We believe in the Tablet (al-lawh) and the Pen (al-qalam) and in everything written on the former. Even if all created beings were to gather together to prevent the existence of something whose existence Allah had written on the Tablet, they would fail. And if all created beings were to gather together to make something exist which Allah had not written on it, they would not be able to do so. The Pen has dried having written down all that will be in existence until the Day of Judgment.Whatever a person has missed he would have never gotten, and whatever he gets he would have never missed.

48 It is necessary for the servant to know that Allah already knows everything that is going to happen in His creation and has decreed it in a detailed and decisive way. There is nothing that He has created in either the heavens or the earth that can contradict it, or add to it, or erase it, or change it, or decrease it, or increase it in any way. This is a fundamental aspect of belief and a necessary element of all knowledge and recognition of Allah's Oneness and Lordship. As Allah says in His Book: *"He created everything and decreed it in a detailed way"* (25:2). And He also says: *"Allah's command is always a decided decree"* (33:38). So woe to anyone who argues with Allah concerning the decree and who, with a sick heart, starts delving into this matter. In his deluded attempt to investigate the Unseen, he is seeking a secret that can never be uncovered, and he ends up an evil-doer, telling nothing but lies.

49 The Throne (al-arsh) and the Chair (al-Kursi) are true.

50 He is independent of the Throne and that which is beneath the Throne.

51 He encompasses all things and that which is above it, and what He has created is incapable of encompassing Him.

52 We say with belief, acceptance, and submission that Allah

took Abraham as an intimate friend and that He spoke directly to Moses.

53 We believe in the angels, and the prophets, and the books which were revealed to the messengers, and we bear witness that they were all following the manifest Truth.

54 We call the people of our *qibla* Muslims and believers as long as they acknowledge what the Prophet, may Allah bless him and grant him peace, brought, and accept as true everything that he said and told us about.

55 We do not enter into vain talk about Allah nor do we allow any dispute about the religion of Allah.

56 We do not argue about the Quran and we bear witness that it is the speech of the Lord of all the Worlds which the Trustworthy Spirit came down with and taught the most honored of all the Messengers, Muhammad, may Allah bless him and grant him peace. It is the speech of Allah and no speech of any created being is comparable to it. We do not say that it was created and we do not go against the Congregation (*jamaa*) of the Muslims regarding it.

57 We do not consider any of the people of our *qibla* to be disbelievers because of any wrong action they have done, as long as they do not consider that action to have been lawful.

58 Nor do we say that the wrong action of a man who has belief does not have a harmful effect on him.

59 We hope that Allah will pardon the people of right action among the believers and grant them entrance into the Garden through His mercy, but we cannot be certain of this, and we cannot bear witness that it will definitely happen and that they will be in the Garden. We ask forgiveness for the people of wrong action among the believers and, although we are afraid for them, we are not in despair about them.

60 Certainty and despair both remove one from the religion, but the path of truth for the People of the *qibla* lies between the two.

61 A person does not step out of belief except by disavowing what brought him into it.

62 Belief consists of affirmation by the tongue and acceptance by the heart.

63 And the whole of what is proven from the Prophet regarding the Sharia and the explanation (of the Quran and of Islam) is true.

64 Belief is, at base, the same for everyone, but the superiority of some over others in faith is due to their fear and awareness of Allah, their opposition to their desires, and their choosing what is more pleasing to Allah.

65 All the believers are Friends of Allah and the noblest of them in the sight of Allah are those who are the most obedient and who most closely follow the Quran.

66 Belief consists of belief in Allah, His angels, His books, His messengers, the Last Day, and belief that the Decree—both the good of it and the evil of it, the sweet of it and the bitter of it—is all from Allah.

67 We believe in all these things. We do not make any distinction between any of the messengers, we accept as true what all of them brought.

68 Those of the Community of Muhammad, may Allah bless him and grant him peace, who have committed grave sins will be in the fire, but not eternally, provided they die and meet Allah as believers affirming His unity even if they have not repented. They are subject to His will and judgement.

69 If He wants, He will forgive them and pardon them out of His generosity, as is mentioned in the Quran when He says: *"And He forgives anything less than that (shirk) to whomever He wills"* (4: 116). If He wants, He will punish them in the fire out of His justice, and then bring them out of the fire and send them to the garden through His mercy, and by the intercession of those who were obedient to Him. This is because Allah is the Protector of those who recognize Him and will not treat them in the hereafter in the same way as He treats those who deny Him, who are bereft of His guidance and have failed to obtain His protection. O Allah, You are the Protector of Islam and its people; make us firm in Islam until the day we meet You.

69 We agree with doing the prayer behind any of the People

of the *qibla* whether rightful or wrongful, and performing the funeral prayer for any of them when they die.

70 We do not say that any of them will categorically go to either the garden or the fire, and we do not accuse any of them of disbelief (*kufr*), associating partners with Allah (*shirk*), or hypocrisy (*nifaq*), as long as they have not openly demonstrated any of those things. We leave their secrets to Allah.

71 We do not agree with killing any of the Community of Muhammad, may Allah bless him and grant him peace, unless it is obligatory by Sharia to do so.

72 We do not accept rebellion against our Imam or those in charge of our affairs even if they are unjust, nor do we wish evil on them, nor do we withdraw from following them. We hold that obedience to them is part of obedience to Allah, the Glorified, and therefore obligatory as long as they do not order us to commit sins. We pray for their right guidance and ask for pardon for their wrongs.

73 We follow the *sunna* of the Prophet and the Congregation of the Muslims, and avoid deviation, differences and divisions.

74 We love the people of justice and trustworthiness, and hate the people of injustice and treachery.

75 When our knowledge about something is unclear, we say: "Allah knows best."

76 We agree with wiping over leather socks (in ablution) whether on a journey or otherwise, just as has come in the hadiths.

77 *Hajj* and *jihad* under the leadership of those in charge of the Muslims, whether they are right or wrong-acting, are continuing obligations until the Last Hour comes. Nothing can annul or controvert them.

78 We believe in the the noble angels who write down our actions, for Allah has appointed them over us as two guardians.

79 We believe in the Angel of Death who is in charge of taking the spirits of all the worlds.

80 We believe in the punishment in the grave for those who

deserve it, and in the questioning in the grave by Munkar and Nakir about one's Lord, one's religion and one's prophet, as has come down in the hadiths from the Messenger of Allah, may Allah bless him and grant him peace, and in reports from the Companions, may Allah be pleased with them all.

81 The grave is either one of the meadows of the garden or one of the pits of the fire.

82 We believe in being brought back to life after death and in being recompensed for our actions on the Day of Judgment, and the exhibition of works, and the reckoning, and the reading of the book, and the reward or punishments, and the Bridge, and the Balance.

83 The Garden and the fire are created things that never come to an end and we believe that Allah created them before the rest of creation and then created people to inhabit each of them. Whoever He wills goes to the garden out of His bounty and whoever He wills goes to the fire through His justice. Everybody acts in accordance with what is destined for him and goes towards what he has been created for.

84 Good and evil have both been decreed for people.

85 The capability in terms of divine grace and favor which makes an action certain to occur cannot be ascribed to a created being. This capability is integral with action, whereas the capability of an action in terms of having the necessary health and ability, being in a position to act, and having the necessary means, exists in a person before the action. It is this type of capability which is the object of the dictates of the Sharia. Allah the Exalted says: "*Allah does not charge a person except according to his ability*" (2:286).

86 People's actions are created by Allah but earned by people.

87 Allah, the Exalted, has only charged people with what they are able to do and people are only capable of doing what Allah has granted them to do. This is the explanation of the phrase: "There is no power and no strength except by Allah." We add to this that there is no stratagem or way by which anyone can avoid or escape disobedience to Allah except with Allah's help; nor does anyone have the strength to put obedience to Allah

into practice and remain firm in it, except if Allah makes it possible for him to do so.

88 Everything happens according to Allah's will, knowledge, predestination and decree. His will overpowers all other wills and His decree overpowers all stratagems. He does whatever He wills and He is never unjust. He is exalted in His purity above any evil or perdition and He is perfect far beyond any fault or flaw. *"He will not be asked about what He does, but they will be asked"* (21:23).

89 There is benefit for dead people in the supplication and alms-giving of the living.

90 Allah responds to people's supplications and gives them what they ask for.

91 Allah has absolute control over everything and nothing has any control over Him. Nothing can be independent of Allah even for the blinking of an eye, and whoever considers himself independent of Allah for the blinking of an eye is guilty of unbelief and becomes one of the people of perdition.

92 Allah is angered and He is pleased but not in the same way as any creature.

93 We love the Companions of the Messenger of Allah but we do not go to excess in our love for any one individual among them; nor do we disown any one of them. We hate anyone who hates them or does not speak well of them and we only speak well of them. Love of them is a part of Islam, part of belief and part of excellent behavior, while hatred of them is unbelief, hypocrisy, and rebellion.

94 We confirm that, after the death of Allah's Messenger, peace be upon him, the caliphate went first to Abu Bakr al-Siddiq, thus proving his excellence and superiority over the rest of the Muslims; then to Umar ibn al-Khattab; then to Uthman; and then to Ali ibn Abi Talib; may Allah be well pleased with all of them. These are the Rightly-Guided Caliphs and upright leaders.

95 We bear witness that the ten promised the garden, who were named by the Messenger of Allah, will be in the garden, as the Messenger of Allah whose word is truth, bore witness

that they would be. The ten are: Abu Bakr, Umar, Uthman, Ali, Talha, Zubayr, Sad, Said, Abd al-Rahman ibn Awf, and Abu Ubayda ibn al-Jarrah whose title was the Trustee of this Community, may Allah be pleased with all of them.

96 Anyone who speaks well of the Companions of the Messenger of Allah, may Allah bless him and grant him peace, and his wives and offspring, who are all pure and untainted by any impurity, is free from the accusation of hypocrisy.

97 The learned among the predecessors, both the first community and those who immediately followed: the people of virtue, the narrators of hadith, the jurists, and the analysts-they must only be spoken of in the best way, and anyone who says anything bad about them is not on the right path.

98 We do not prefer any of the saintly people among the Community over any of the prophets but rather we say that any one of the prophets is better than all the saints (awliya) put together.

99 We believe in what we know of the marvels (karamat) of the saints and in the authentic stories about them from trustworthy sources.

100 We believe in the signs of the Hour such as the appearance of the Antichrist (dajjal) and the descent of Jesus son of Mary, peace be upon him, from heaven, and we believe in the rising of the sun from where it sets and in the emergence of the Beast from the earth.

101 We do not accept as true what soothsayers and fortune-tellers say, nor do we accept the claims of those who affirm anything which goes against the Book, the sunna, and the consensus of the Muslim Community (umma).

102 We agree that holding together is the true and right path and that separation is deviation and torment.

103 There is only one religion of Allah in the heavens and the earth and that is the religion of Islam ("submission"). Allah says: "Surely religion in the sight of Allah is Islam" (3:19). And He also says: "I am pleased with Islam as a religion for you." (5:3)

104 Islam lies between going to excess and falling short,

between the likening of Allah's attributes to creation (*tash-bih*) and divesting Allah of attributes (*tatil*), between determinism and freewill, and between sureness and despair.

105 This is our religion and it is what we believe in, both inwardly and outwardly, and we renounce any connection, before Allah, with anyone who goes against what we have said and made clear.

We ask Allah to make us firm in our belief and seal our lives with it and to protect us from variant ideas, scattering opinions and evil schools of view such as those of the Mushabbiha, the Mutazila, the Jahmiyya, the Jabriyya, the Qadariyya, and others like them who go against the *sunna* and Sunnis and have allied themselves with error. We renounce any connection with them and in our opinion they are in error and on the path of destruction. We ask Allah to protect us from all falsehood and we ask His Grace and Favor to do all good.

1.2 MORE DEFINITIONS OF MAINSTREAM ISLAM

One who calls himself a mainstream Muslim today follows none other than the creed of Ashari and Maturidi. To adopt any other creed is innovation, just as to follow anyone other than the mainstream Imams in Sharia is to leave guidance for misguidance. Shaykh al-Islam Ibn Hajar al-Haytami (d. 974 A.H.) said:

> An innovator (*mubtadi*) is the person who does not have the belief conveyed unanimously by the Sunnis. This unanimity was transmitted by the two great imams Abu al-Hasan al-Ashari and Abu Mansur al-Maturidi. An innovator is one whose beliefs are different from the Sunni faith. And the Sunni faith is the faith of Abu al-Hasan al-Ashari, Abu Mansur al-Maturidi and those who followed them.[12]

---

12 Al-Haytami, *Fatawa hadithiyya* (Cairo: Halabi, 1970) p. 205.

Similarly, Imam Shihab al-Din Ahmad al-Qalyubi (d. 1069/1659 CE) wrote:[13]

> One who departs from what Abu al-Hasan al-Ashari and Abu Mansur al-Maturidi reported is not a Sunni. These two Imams followed the footprints of Allah's Messenger and his Companions.

Finally, Imam Abdullah ibn Alawi al-Haddad (d. 1132/1720 CE) said:

> If you look with a sound understanding into those passages relating to the sciences of faith in the Book, the *sunna*, and the sayings of the Salaf . . . you will know for certain that the truth is with the party called Ashari, named after the Shaykh Abu al-Hasan al-Ashari, may Allah have mercy on him, who systematized the foundations of the creed of the People of the Truth, and recorded its earliest versions, these being the beliefs which the Companions and the best among the followers agreed upon... The Maturidis are the same as the Asharis in the above regard.[14]

Thus, according to Haytami's definition, one may call oneself "Salafi," "Athari," "Hadithi." but unless one follows what he defines as "the faith of Ashari and Maturidi," such a person is an innovator.

According to al-Qalyubi, leaving the path of the Asharis and Maturidis is the same as leaving mainstream Islam. Finally, Imam al-Haddad calls Asharis "the People of Truth;" that is, the Saved Group (*al-firqa al-najiya*) mentioned in the Prophet's hadith already quoted.

"Salafis" say, "Those who call themselves Asharis today do not follow the way of Abu al-Hasan al-Ashari, and practice the figurative interpretation (*tawil*) of the attributes of Allah." In response it may be said that it was the way of many of the pious Salaf, including the mainstream Imams and the imams of hadith, to apply *tawil* in its proper place. This has been proven by scholars such as Ibn al-Jawzi al-Hanbali,[15] Qadi Iyad al-

---

13 Imam Shihab al-Din Ahmad al-Qalyubi, in the fourth volume of his commentary on Jalal al-Din al-Mahalli's book *Kanz al-raghibin sharh minhaj al-talibin*.

14 Imam Abdullah al-Haddad, *"The Book of Assistance,"* trans. Mostafa Badawi (London: Quilliam Press, 1989) p. 40-41.

15 Ibn al-Jawzi al-Hanbali, in his *Daf shubah al-tashbih*.

Maliki,[16] Ali al-Qari al-Hanafi,[17] and Imam Nawawi al-Shafii.[18] What follows is a presentation of their views on some of the relevant texts.

1.3 FIGURATIVE INTERPRETATION (*TAWIL*)
1.3.1. IMAM NAWAWI

No one doubts that the above scholars are among the most representative of the doctrine of mainstream Islam, although they practiced figurative interpretation (*tawil*). As Taj al-Din al-Subki and Imam al-Yafii said of Nawawi, "He was an Ashari." Sakhawi adds after quoting their views, "And he applied figurative interpretation (*tawil*) a great deal."[19] Suffice it to quote Imam Nawawi's words in *al-Majmu* touching the practice of *tawil* by the Salaf:

> The most well-known of the school of the theologians (*mutakallimin*) says that the divine Attributes are interpreted figuratively according to what befits them. Others say that they are not interpreted but that one refrains from speaking concerning their meaning, and defers its actual knowledge (*yuwakkilu ilmaha*) to Allah, all the while holding the belief that Allah is transcendent above all things and that the attributes of the created are negated concerning Him, It is thus said, for example: We believe that the Merciful is established over the Throne, and we do not know the reality of the meaning of this nor what is meant by it (*la nalamu al-haqiqata min dhalika wa al-murada bihi*), while we do believe that *"There is nothing like Him whatsoever"* (42:11) and that He is exalted far above the most elevated of created things. That is the way of the Salaf or at least their vast majority, and it is the safest because one is not required to probe into such matters. Therefore, if he believes in Allah's transcendence there is no need for

16 Qadi Iyad al-Maliki, in his commentary on Muslim.

17 Ali al-Qari al-Hanafi, in his commentary on Iyad's *al-Shifa*.

18 Imam Nawawi al-Shafii, in his commentary on Muslim.

19 The hafiz al-Sakhawi, *Kitab tarjimat shaykh al-islam, qutb al-awliya al-kiram wa faqih al-anam, muhyi al-sunna wa mumit al-bida Abi Zakariyya Muhyiddin al-Nawawi* (Biography of the Shaykh al-Islam, the Pole of the Noble Saints and the Jurist of Mankind, the Reviver of the *sunna* and the Slayer of Innovation Abu Zakariyya Muhyiddin al-Nawawi) (Cairo: Jamiyyat al-nashr wa al-talif al-azhariyya, 1354 / 1935) p. 36.

him to probe this nor to think about what is neither obligatory nor even needed to know. However, if there is a need for interpretation (*tawil*) in order to refute innovators and their like, then they (the Salaf) went ahead and applied interpretation. This is the correct understanding of what has reached us from the scholars concerning this subject, and Allah knows best.[20]

Nawawi repeats in many places[21] the unequivocal characterization of "the vast majority of the Salaf" or even "most or all of them" as people who applied figurative interpretation of the divine Attributes in the Quran and the *sunna* at the appropriate times and places. Nawawi rejects any division between the different methods, and shows that there is no difference in the intentions of the Salaf and theologians—Asharis—regarding the sound application of figurative interpretation, "If there is a need . . . in order to refute innovators and their like."

1.3.2. IMAM SUBKI

The conditional obligation of using theology (*kalam*) and figurative interpretation (*tawil*) to uphold sound belief is the position of the Asharis, as reported by one of their most eminent representatives, Taj al-Din al-Subki, in his *Tabaqat*:

> Bukhari was of those who used to say, "My pronunciation of the Quran is created." Muhammad ibn Yahya al-Dhuhli said, "Whoever claims my pronunciation of the Quran is created is an innovator whose company is shunned, and he who claims that the Quran is created commits disbelief."
>
> (Subki:) Muhammad ibn Yahya only meant—and Allah knows best—what Ahmad ibn Hanbal meant, namely to forbid from entering into that subject. He did not mean to contradict Bukhari. If he did mean to contradict him and to claim that the pronunciation which comes out of his own created lips is pre-eternal, that would be an enormity. One should think that he meant other than that and that both he, Ahmad ibn Hanbal, and other (anti-theology) imams only meant to prohibit people from entering into problems of dialectical theology (*kalam*).

20 Imam Nawawi, introduction to his *al-Majmu sharh al-muhadhdhab* (Cairo: Matbaat al-asima, n.d.) 1:25.

21 Nawawi, *Sharh sahih Muslim.*

For us, Bukhari's words are to be understood as a permission to mention *kalam* if it is needed, since the use of *kalam* in case of necessity is a legal obligation, and to keep silence about *kalam* in cases other than necessity is a *sunna*.

Understand this well, and leave the rantings of historians, and ignore once and for all the distortions of the misguided who think that they are scholars of hadith standing on the *sunna* when in fact they couldn't be further from it. How could anyone possibly think that Bukhari has anything in common with the position of the Mutazila when it has been authentically reported from him by al-Farabari and others that he said, "I hold as ignorant whoever does not declare the Jahmis to be disbelievers."[22]

Subki's rhetorical question is likely an allusion to Ibn Taymiyya and Ibn Qayyim, who had labeled the Asharis innovators, just as Bukhari had been accused with the same terms by followers of Imam Ahmad in his time.

As Nawawi and Subki show in so many words, the apprehension surrounding figurative interpretation (*tawil*) and the condemnation of theology (*kalam*) by Imam Ahmad was not because these opposed Quran and *sunna*, but because they were being used out of place by the ignorant or by opponents of mainstream Islam. It was a duty to refute these people, as it was with anthropomorphists and their literal interpretation of Allah's attributes were to be refuted. The Asharis stood in the forefront of both battles, as exemplified by Imam Ghazali, whose eloquent arguments against theology (*kalam*) did not preclude the fact that he, as Nawawi after him, interpreted Allah's attributes figuratively. Like their own Imam (al-Shafii) in his time, they wished to avoid the confusion that resulted when uneducated people delved into subjects they were unprepared to understand fully and correctly. Imam Nawawi cautioned laymen against probing into what was neither obligatory nor needed for their faith and practice, and to leave controversial subjects to the experts. This was encouraged "all the while negating anthropomorphism," as is made clear by Imam Ghazali in his words on the same subject.

22 Taj al-Din al-Subki, *Tabaqat al-shafiiyya al-kubra*, ed. Nur al-Din Shariba (Cairo: al-Halabi, 1373/1953) 2:241.

1.3.3. IMAM GHAZALI

Imam Ghazali compares the person who imagines Allah's "Hand" to be a limb of the body to an idol worshiper and states, "Whoever worships a body is a disbeliever according to the consensus of the Community."[23] Immediately preceding this comparison, Ghazali says:

> This is the way of the Salaf, which is the truth according to us: anybody among the uneducated dealing with one of the sayings of the Attributes is obligated to do seven things:
>
> °*taqdis*: believe Allah free from corporeality and the like.
>
> °*tasdiq*: believe that the Prophet (☺) was truthful in speaking these words, but in the manner in which he meant them.
>
> °*itiraf bi al-ajz*: admit that their understanding is beyond his capability.
>
> °*sukut*: remain silent and not ask questions about it, nor discuss it, knowing that it poses a danger to his faith, and that he may unwittingly commit disbelief by discussing it.
>
> °*imsak*: leave interpretation, not replacing the words which have appeared in the texts with any grammatical derivatives, nor translating them into another language.
>
> °*kuff*: hold himself back from pondering these words.
>
> °*taslim li ahlihi* defer all this to those who are qualified to deal with it.[24]

1.4. ORIGINS OF THE "SALAFIS" BELIEFS REGARDING ALLAH'S ATTRIBUTES

1.4.1. THE PEOPLE OF INNOVATION (AHL AL-BIDA)

Mainstream Islam has played a constant role in the intellectual battle against the enemies of true doctrine. These enemies are known as the People of Unwarranted Innovations and Idle Desires (*ahl al-bida wa al-ahwa*). This category includes all groups that have deviated from the practice and belief of the majority of Muslims, including: the Khawarij and Qadariyya

---

23 Imam Ghazali, in his *Iljam al-awam an ilm al-kalam* (Restraining the uneducated from the science of theology).

24 Hujjat al-Islam Abu Hamid al-Ghazali, *Iljam al-awamm an ilm al-kalam* (Istanbul : s.n., 1287/1870, repr. Istanbul: Waqf ikhlas offset, 1994) p. 4-5.

fought by the Companions; the Jahmiyya and Murjia fought by Ahmad ibn Hanbal; the Mutazila fought by al-Ashari; the Batiniyya and the philosophers fought by al-Ghazali; and others. While many of these groups played a role in early Islamic history and have since passed away, others, such as the Khawarij, are echoed in contemporary movements like that of the Wahhabis today. The great Hanafi scholar Ibn Abidin (1784-1836 CE) said:

> The name of Khawarij is applied to those who part ways with Muslims and declare them disbelievers, as took place in our time with the followers of Ibn Abd al-Wahhab who came out of Najd (in the Eastern Arabian peninsula) and attacked the Two Noble Sanctuaries (Makka and Madina). They (Wahhabis) claimed to follow the Hanbali school, but their belief was such that, in their view, they alone are Muslims and everyone else is a *mushrik* (polytheist). Under this guise, they said that killing *Ahl al-Sunna* and their scholars was permissible, until Allah the Exalted destroyed them in the year 1233 (1818 CE) at the hands of the Muslim army.[25]

Common to all groups of innovators (*ahl al-bida*) is deviation from the principles of law and jurisprudence codified by the great Sunni scholars. This deviation is based on their arbitrary reading of texts that admit some uncertainty with regard to their interpretation (*mutashabihat*). The Wahhabis, for example, used such verses to support anthropomorphist views and literal interpretation.[26] Another example is the Zahiri view that there is no interpretation (*mutashabihat*) in the Quran other than the abbreviated letters at the beginning of some *surahs* (*muqattaat*). This is not the view of the majority of Sunni scholars, but only that of Ibn Hazm al-Zahiri and some others.[27] Even Ibn Hazm calls the verses of the attributes "hidden things" (*ghuyubat*) in *al-Fasl fi al-milal*, which is interpretation (*mutashabihat*) by another name.

As Ghazali has shown in his *Mustasfa*, the correct view, and

---

25 Imam Muhammad Ibn Abidin, *Hashiyat radd al-muhtar ala al-durr al-mukhtar*, 3:309 *"Bab al-bughat"* [Chapter on Rebels].

26 For more on this topic see our *Doctrine of Ahl al-Sunna wa al-Jamaa Versus the "Salafi" Movement*.

27 Abu al-Aynayn Badran, *Usul al-fiqh al-islami* (Alexandria: Muassasat shabab al-jamia, 1402/1982) p. 416.

that of the majority of Sunni scholars, is that the unambiguous (*muhkam*) is that part of the Quran that is not open to conjecture, whereas the ambiguous (*mutashabih*) is. As for the question of whether acting upon the ambiguous (*mutashabih*) is permissible or not, there is disagreement, but the correct view is that no one may act upon it. This is so not because the ambiguous (*mutashabih*) has no meaning, but because the correct meaning is not known to any human being. There is no doubt that all the ambiguous (*mutashabihat*) verses have meaning, but it is known only to Allah, and we must not attempt to define His words where no indication is available to reveal the correct meaning to us.[28] This is confirmed by Nawawi's words, already cited, whereby the "actual knowledge" and "real meaning" of the verse of Allah's Establishment on the Throne are deferred to Him. Imam Malik had addressed the same verse similarly in his famous saying, "The establishment is known, its modality is inconceivable in the mind, and to inquire about it is an innovation."

Wahhabis and the so-called "Salafis," however, have made these texts their weapon of choice in cleaving the unity of the Muslim *umma*. Chief among their victims is the consensus concerning matters of faith and belief. Thus it is not uncommon to hear from "Salafis" charges that Muslims are divided in their doctrine, and that:

> The majority of Muslims from six hundred or one thousand years ago until today have deviated from the beliefs of the Pious Predecessors (*salaf as-salih*) and the correct doctrine (*aqida*) of the Sunnis by following the ideas of al-Ashari. Thus they have become like the Jahmiyya, the Khawarij and the Mutazila, falling out of the bounds of correct Islam.

Statements such as these, made by people who call themselves "scholars" of Islam, are among the most dangerous threat to Islamic unity today. What are the bases of these claims and why are they being put forward? Who is behind them and what is their view?

---

28 Ghazali, *al-Mustasfa min ilm al-usul* (Cairo: al-Maktaba al-tijariyya, 1356/1937) 1:68; Cf. Shawkani, *Irshad al-fuhul* p. 31-32.

1.4.2. THE "SALAFI" MOVEMENT

Although these innovators vehemently reject the term "Wahhabi" and prefer to be called "Salafi," their claims do no more than parrot the accusations Ibn Abd al-Wahhab leveled against the scholars of Islam over two centuries ago. They dislike being called "Wahhabi," claiming that such "labels" cause divisiveness among Muslims. Nonetheless, it is they who initiated any divisions through their incendiary accusations against Muslim scholars, like the statement that Muslims, "by following the ideas of al-Ashari . . . have become like the Jahmiyya." Obviously, they cared very little about Muslim unity at the time this statement was made, for it is plain that anyone who makes such claims is himself causing divisiveness and sedition. The doctrine of the Sunnis was formulated by no one other than the very Imams they attack. If they are not interested in Islamic unity, what then is their real purpose?

Before proceeding further, it is helpful to have some grasp of the application of the noun *salaf*, and its adjectival correspondent "Salafi." For example, scholars speak of the "Salafi school" of Quranic interpretation—a misnomer since it does not refer to the Pious Predecessors, but to scholars who came much later. The Sunni understanding of the term *salaf*, however, is firmly grounded in the words of the Prophet (ﷺ) that are pertinent to its meaning. In the well-known tradition recorded by Imams al-Bukhari and Muslim, the Prophet (ﷺ) said, when asked which age of mankind was best:

> The best age is this one; then the one that follows it; then the one that follows that one.

He also said:

> Good tidings in the hereafter (*tuba*) for those who see me, and good tidings in the hereafter for those who see those who saw me, and good tidings in the hereafter for those who see those who saw those who saw me.[29]

In other words, the best age of mankind is the one in which

---

29 Al-Hakim, *Mustadrak* 4:86; al-Dhahabi, *Mujam al-mashaikh* 1:160; Haythami declared it sound in *Majma al-zawaid* 10:20.

the Prophet (ﷺ) was sent—that is, the age of the Companions, the *sahaba*. The next best age is that of the Successors to the Companions, or *tabiun*. After the *tabiun* come the Successors to the Successors, or *tabi al-tabiin*. It is of these three generations that the scholars of Islam speak when they use the term *salaf*.

Contrary to the claims of the modern followers of Muhammad ibn Abd al-Wahhab, the way of the Salaf is not the way followed by them and their "referent scholars" (*maraji al-taqlid*), such as Ibn Taymiyya and Ibn Qayyim al-Jawziyya. The true Salaf were those scholars and followers of the Companions who lived from the time of the Tabiin to the third century, and who followed a certain way of interpreting the Quran. By no means can Ibn Taymiyya and Ibn Qayyim, tainted as they are with the confusion and scandal that attended their careers, be considered representative of the pristine ages of the Companions and the Successors.

1.4.3. IBN TAYMIYYA'S STRIFE

Taqi al-Din Ibn Taymiyya (661-728/1263-1328 CE) is often praised by modernists and orientalists as a reformer of Islam and a spiritual leader in the battle against non-believers. Yet, when his case is examined in the light of history, he is found guilty, on at least one occasion, of inciting war between Muslim leaders. Having caused bloodshed among Muslims in this manner, he proceeded to lay the foundation for the modern attack on Muslim unity. This is especially evident in his unrelenting assault upon the doctrines of mainstream Islam.

Let us begin with the physical assault on Muslim unity encouraged by Ibn Taymiyya's allowing Muslim to fight Muslim. An example is the case of Ghazan Khan, the governor of Khurasan. He was the ruler of the Mongols in the time of Ibn Taymiyya and is presented by the "Salafis" as a disbeliever. Their representation of Ghazan Khan helps the "Salafis" to present Ibn Taymiyya as a reformer and to justify the *fatawa*, or legal judgments he gave that permitted the ruler of Syria, al-Nasir, to fight Ghazan Khan and call himself a great leader of jihad.

In fact, Ghazan Khan was a firm believer in Islam. Al-

Dhahabi relates that he became Muslim at the hands of the Sufi shaykh Sadr al-Din Abu al-Majami Ibrahim al-Juwayni (d.720), one of Dhahabi's own shaykhs of hadith.[30] Ibn al-Athir says he was named Ghazan Mahmud. During Ghazan's rule, he built a huge mosque in Tabriz, as well as twelve Islamic schools (*madrasa*), a number of hostels (*khaniqa*), forts (*ribat*), a school for the secular sciences, and an observatory. He supplied Makka and Madina with many gifts. He followed one of the Sunni schools of law and was respectful of religious scholars. He had the descendants of the Prophet (ﷺ) mentioned before the princes and princesses of his house in the state records, and he introduced the turban as the court headgear.

Let us turn now to Ibn Taymiyya's assault on the doctrinal front. Here his efforts were aided by his disciple Ibn Qayyim al-Jawziyya (691-751, 1292-1350 CE). One ought not, by the way, confuse this Ibn Qayyim al-Jawziyya with the earlier Hanbali scholar, Ibn al-Jawzi of similar name. As will be seen, the latter provided testimony, within his own *madhhab*, of the danger of anthropomorphist trends that reached maturity only with Ibn Taymiyya's advent.

It is also of interest to note that while Ibn Taymiyya and his disciple are described as representatives of latter-day "Salafi" beliefs, they have little or nothing to do with the true Salaf insofar as the term is defined among Muslims. Only in recent times have they been called "Salafi," by 20th-century modernists like Rashid Rida, the disciple of Muhammad Abduh— who are both enemies of traditional Islamic education—and contemporary orientalists like the Frenchman Henri Laoust. If we take the term "Salafi" *stricto senso*, their use of it is found to be ahistorical and actually opposed to its true meaning.

Using their personal reasoning (*ijtihad*) Ibn Taymiyya and Ibn Qayyim derived legal rulings (*istinbat*) from the legal principles (*ahkam*) of Sharia. Both attributed their methods to principles (*usul*) of jurisprudence (*fiqh*) as laid down by Imam Ahmad Ibn Hanbal. *Ijtihad* has as its object the attainment of knowledge, which in turn pertains to three areas:

1. *aqaid*, touching on doctrines and beliefs

---

30 "*Al-shaykh al-qidwa Sadr al-Din Abu al-Majami al-Juwayni al-Khurasani al-Sufi al-Muhaddith. . . qadima ilayna bada ma aslama ala yadihi Ghazan maliku al-tatar bi wasitati naibihi Nurur.*" Dhahabi, *Mujam al-mashaikh* (Taif: Maktabat).

2. *ibadat*, concerning forms of worship and how they should be performed

3. *muamalat*, pertaining to affairs between men

There is no doubt that these two scholars had the ability to exercise *ijtihad* in the areas of *muamalat*. In fact, they provided many good edicts (*fatawa*) in this area. Moreover, they did not attempt to cause major changes in worship (*ibadat*), although they diverged substantially from the Sunnis in their *ijtihad*. However, they did pursue change in the area most crucial to Muslim unity and soundness of religion; they went astray in the area of *aqida* and completely left the pure teachings of the original scholars of the Salaf.

1.4.4. IBN TAYMIYYA AND IBN QAYYIM'S ANTHROPOMORPHISM (*TAJSIM*)

Evidence for this claim is found in Ibn Taymiyya's suggestion that Allah is a corporeal entity. This is to be found in his *al-Aqida al-hamawiyya, al-Aqida al-wasitiyya*, and *al-Tasis al-radd ala al-asas*. Here and in other works he indicates that Allah's "Hand," "Foot," "Shin," and "Face" are literal (*haqiqi*) attributes, and that He sits the Throne in person (*bi al-dhat*). Ibn Taymiyya's error was in believing that such attributes are literal, and in declaring that the Sunnis who believed them to be metaphorical were stripping Allah of His attributes (*muattila*). These are among the innovations in faith that Shaykh al-Islam Taqi al-Din al-Subki (683-756 A.H.) has refuted.[31]

Ibn Qayyim followed the same path in his infamous poem entitled, *al-Qasida al-nuniyya* (Ode rhyming in the letter n). This lengthy poem on the tenets of faith is filled with corrupt suggestions about Allah's attributes. The poem is also analyzed by Shaykh al-Islam Taqi al-Din Subki,[32] who gives the verdict that the anthropomorphic presentation of the divinity in the poem is beyond the pale of Islam. The poem could only be circulated secretly in Ibn al-Qayyim's lifetime, but it seems that

31 Taqi al-Din al-Subki, in his *Al-durra al-mudiyya fi al-radd ala Ibn Taymiyya* (The luminous pearl: a refutation of Ibn Taymiyya). Ed. Imam Kawthari (1284-1355 A.H.). Damascus: Matbaat al-taraqqi, 1929. And *Al-rasail al-subkiyya fi al-radd ala Ibn Taymiyya wa tilmidhihi Ibn Qayyim al-Jawziyya* (Subki's treatises in answer to Ibn Taymiyya and his pupil Ibn Qayyim al-Jawziyya) Ed. Kamal al-Hut. Beirut: Alam al-Kutub, 1983.

32 Taqi al-Din Subki, in his *Al-sayf al-saqil fi al-radd ala Ibn Zafil* (The burnished sword in refuting Ibn Zafil, i.e. Ibn Qayyim al-Jawziyya) Ed. Imam Kawthari. Cairo: Matbaat al-saada, 1937.

he never abandoned it, for the Hanbali historian Ibn Rajab heard it from Ibn al-Qayyim in the year of his death. Today, some "Salafi" followers quote this poem indiscriminately, heedless of the deviations it promotes. In his landmark translation of al-Misri's *Umdat al-salik*, Nuh Keller observed:

> [An] unfortunate peculiarity the poem shares with some of Ibn al-Qayyim's other works on Islamic faith is that it presents the reader with a false dilemma, namely that one must either believe that Allah has eyes, hands, a descending motion, and so forth, in a literal (*haqiqi*) sense, or else one has nullified (*attala*) or negated these attributes. And this is erroneous, for the literal is that which corresponds to an expression's primary lexical sense as ordinarily used in a language by the people who speak it, while the above words are clearly intended otherwise, in accordance with the Koranic verse, *"There is nothing whatsoever like unto Him"* (42:11), for if the above were intended literally, there would be innumerable things like unto Him in such as having eyes, hands, motion, and so forth, in the literal meaning of these terms. The would-be dilemma is also far from the practice of the early Muslims, who used only to accept such Koranic verses and hadiths as they have come, consigning the knowledge of what is meant by them—while affirming Allah's absolute transcendence above any resemblance to created things—to Allah Most High alone, without trying to determinately specify how they are meant (*bi la kayf*), let alone suggesting people understand them literally (*haqiqatan*) as Ibn al-Qayyim tried to do.
>
> While granting that his other scholarly achievements are not necessarily compromised by his extreme aberrances in tenets of faith, it should not be forgotten that depicting the latter as a "reform" or "return to early Islam" represents a blameworthy innovation on his part that appeared more than seven centuries after the time of the Prophet (ﷺ) (Allah bless him and give him peace) and his Companions. A particularly unsavory aspect of it is that in his attempts to vindicate the doctrine, Ibn al-Qayyim

casts aspersions upon the Islam of anyone who does not subscribe to it, at their forefront the Ashari school, whom his books castigate as "Jahmiyya" or "Muattila," implying, by equating them with the most extreme factions of the Mutazila, that they deny any significance to the divine attributes, a misrepresentation that has seen a lamentable recrudescence in parts of the Muslim world today.[33]

1.4.5. THE "SALAFI" MALIGNING OF ASHARIS AND OTHER FOLLOWERS OF MAINSTREAM ISLAM

As Shaykh al-Alawi al-Maliki said, "It is beyond us how Sunni Muslims can be considered equal with the most extreme faction of the Mutazila, the Jahmiyya."[34] Such misrepresentation nevertheless survived, due to to the Wahhabi heresy and its modern outgrowth, the "Salafi" movement. Present-day adherents of such views routinely attack Ashari scholars. Many examples are found in the booklet, *A Brief Introduction to the Salafi Dawah*,[35] whose first pages carry the words, "The Salafi is not of the Asharis, who deny Allah's attributes." Imagine calling Ibn Asakir or al-Khatib al-Baghdadi or Suyuti "deniers of Allah's attributes!! Another example is found in the tract, *Blind Following of Madhhabs*, which ends with the words, "Al-Ashari formulated a new doctrine by piecing together (*talfiq*) doctrines from different Muslim sects. . . Towards the end of his life he rejected this belief too and accepted the beliefs of Sunnis."[36] Consider this forgery passed in the name of the Renewer of the third Islamic century, whose influence has benefited almost every single renewer after him until the most recent of them, Imam Muhammad Zahid al-Kawthari (d. 1371/1952 CE).

This maligning can be traced back to Ibn Qayyim's extremism in referring to Asharis, who are historically the foremost

---

33 Nuh Ha Mim Keller, ed. and trans. *The Reliance of the Traveller* (Dubai: Modern Printing Press, 1991) p. 1058.

34 *Mafahimu yajibu an tusahhah* (Notions that should be corrected) 4th ed. (Dubai: Hashr ibn Muhammad Dalmuk, 1986), quoted in *Reliance* p. 1009.

35 *A Brief Introduction to the Salafi Dawah*, published by Jamiyyat ihya minhaj al-sunna.

36 Muhammad Al-Masumi al-Khajnadi, *Blind Following of Madhhabs* (Birmingham: al-Hidayah, 1993) p. 80.

group among the Sunnis to strive in defense of sound Islamic
belief. Ibn Qayyim's positions are themselves inherited from
his teacher Ibn Taymiyya. Ibn Taymiyya, not content with
merely charging the theologians (*mutakallimun*) of the Asharis
and Maturidis with innovation, lumps them together with the
Mutazila and the Jahmis and places them all into the category
of pre-Islamic idol-worshippers, who, although they believed in
Allah as the Creator of all things, still worshiped other than
Him:

> The theologians . . . have fallen short of the
> knowledge of the rational proofs which Allah men-
> tioned in His Book, so they strayed from them and
> went into different, innovated directions, which due
> to the falsehoods contained in them, they went out of
> some of the truth which they and other than them
> share in believing; and they entered into some of the
> innovated falsehoods, and they have taken out from
> the Islamic doctrine of monotheism (*tawhid*) what
> belongs to it, for example, *tawhid al-ilahiyya* and the
> establishment of the literalness of Allah's Names and
> Attributes.
>
> They did not know of *tawhid*, other than the
> *tawhid al-rububiyya* which consists in affirming that
> Allah is the Creator of all things, and this tawhid was
> affirmed by those who associated partners to Allah
> (*mushrikun*), about whom Allah said: "*If thou
> shouldst ask them: Who created the heavens and the
> earth? They would answer: Allah*" (31:25), and He
> said: "*Say: Who is Lord of the seven heavens, and Lord
> of the Tremendous Throne? They will say: Unto Allah
> all that belongeth*" (23:6-87), and He said of them:
> "*And most of them believe not in Allah except that they
> attribute partners unto Him*" (12:106). Similarly when
> the group that is from the belief of the early genera-
> tions (i.e. "Salafis" who claim that they alone follow
> the belief of early Muslims) say to them (the theolo-
> gians): who has created the heavens and the earth?
> they say: Allah. Yet they worship other than Him [!]
> at the same time. For verily the *tawhid* which Allah
> has ordered unto His servants is the "*tawhid al-
> uluhiyya*" which comprises the "*tawhid al-rubu-*

biyya," and is that they worship Allah and not attribute anything as partner to Him, in order that religion belong in totality to Allah.[37]

When the Imam of Asharis and Shaykh al-Islam Abu Bakr al-Baqillani died in 403, al-Hanbali went barefoot to his funeral with others of the Hanbali school, and ordered a herald to shout the words, "This (al-Baqillani) is the Supporter of the *sunna* and the Religion! This is the Imam of Muslims!" (*hadha nasir al-sunna wa al-din hadha imam al-muslimin*).[38] It is ironic and rather unfortunate that, under the pen of Ibn Taymiyya and his student, the doctrine of the "supporter of the sunna," is represented as innovation and pre-Islamic idol-worship.

1.4.5.1. ASHARIS OF YESTERDAY AND TODAY

Other Asharis, besides Shaykh al-Islam al-Baqillani, have been targeted by Ibn Taymiyya and the disrespect of today's "Salafis." Asharis are Allah's Victorious Party and the Saved Group spoken of by the Prophet (ﷺ). Their names shine in the firmament of the people of truth:

• *Hafiz* Abu Sulayman al-Khattabi (d. 386)
• Shaykh al-Islam al-Qadi al-Baqillani (d. 403)
• *Imam* Abu Bakr Ibn Furak (d. 406)
• *Hafiz* Abu Ishaq al-Isfaraini (d. 418)
• *Imam* Abu Mansur al-Baghdadi (d. 429)
• *Imam* al-Sumnani (d. 444)
• *Hafiz* al-Bayhaqi (d. 458) (with Ghazali the renewer of the 5th century)
• *Hafiz* al-Khatib al-Baghdadi (d. 463)
• *Imam* al-Qushayri (d. 464)
• *Imam* al-Haramayn al-Juwayni (d. 478)

---

37 Ibn Taymiyya, *Minhaj ahl al-sunna al-nabawiyya fi naqd kalam al-shia wa al-qadariyya* (The open road of the prophetic *sunna* in the criticism of the sayings of Shias and predestinarians) (Bulaq: al-Matbaa al-kubra al-amiriyya, 1321/1904) 2: 62.

38 On Baqillani look up al-Khatib al-Baghdadi, *Tarikh Baghdad* 5:379-383; al-Qadi Iyad, *Tartib al-madarik*, published in the Cairo edition of Baqillani's *Tamhid* (1366/1947) p. 242-259; Ibn Asakir, Tabyin (Damascus 1347/1929) 217-226; and Ibn Imad, *Shadharat*, a. 403 (3:168-170).

•*Imam* Ghazali (d. 505) (with Bayhaqi the renewer of the 5th century)
•al-Turtushi (d. 521)
•Ibn Tumart (d. 524)
•al-Qadi Iyad al-Maliki (d. 544)
•*Imam* Shahrastani (d. 548)
•*Hafiz* Abu al-Qasim Ibn Asakir (d. 571)
•*Imam* al-Fakhr al-Razi (d. 606) (renewer of the 6th century)
•*Faqih* Fakhr al-Din Abu Mansur Ibn Asakir (d. 620)
•*Imam* Sayf al-Din Al-Amidi (d. 631)
•Shaykh al-Islam al-Izz ibn Abd al-Salam (d. 660)
•*Imam* al-Qurtubi (d. 671)
•Shaykh al-Islam al-Nawawi (d. 676) (with Ibn Daqiq al-Id the renewer of the 7th century)
•al-Qadi al-Baydawi (d. 685)
•Ibn Abu Jamra (d. 695)
•*Imam* al-Nasafi (d. 701)
•*Imam* al-Khazin (d. 725)
•Shaykh al-Islam al-Izz ibn Jamaa (d. 733)
•Ibn Juzayy (d. 741)
•*Imam* Abu Hayyan al-Nahwi al-Andalusi (d. 744)
•Shaykh al-Islam Taqi al-Din al-Subki (d. 756) (with Bulqini the renewer of the 8th century)
•Shaykh al-Islam Taj al-Din al-Subki (d. 771)
•Shaykh al-Islam al-Bulqini (d. 805) (with Subki the renewer of the 8th century)
•*Imam* al-Sharif al-Jurjani (d. 816)
• al-Fayruzabadi (d. 817)
•*Imam* Taqi al-Din Abu Bakr al-Hisni (d.829)
•Shaykh al-Islam Ibn Hajar al-Asqalani (d. 852) (with Suyuti the renewer of the 9th century)
•*Hafiz* al-Sakhawi (d. 902)
•Shaykh al-Islam al-Suyuti (d. 911) (with Asqalani the renewer of the 9th century)
•Shaykh al-Islam Zakariyya al-Ansari (d. 926)
•Abu al-Hasan al-Bakri (d. 952)
•Shaykh al-Islam Ibn Hajar al-Haytami (d. 974)
•*Imam* al-Shirbini al-Khatib (d. 977)
•*Imam* al-Qalyubi (d. 1069)

•*Imam* Ibn Alawi al-Haddad (d. 1132) (the renewer of the 12th century)
•Hasanayn Muhammad Makhluf (Founding member of the Muslim World League and former mufti of Egypt)
•Abdullah Kanun al-Hasani (Founding member of the Muslim World League and President of the Scholars of Morocco Institute)
•Muhammad ibn Ahmad al-Khazraji (Minister of Justice and Islamic Affairs, United Arab Emirates)
•Muhammad al-Shazili al-Nayfar (Founding member of the Muslim World League and Dean of al-Zaytuna University, Tunis)
•Al-Husayni Abd al-Majid Hashim (President of al-Azhar University, Egypt and Secretary-General of the Research Institute in Makka)
•Muhammad Fal al-Banani (Secretary-General of Muslim Scholars in Mauritania and founding member of the Muslim World League)
•Muhammad Salim ibn Adud (Minister of Culture and Islamic Affairs in Mauritania, President of the Supreme Islamic Court, and founding member of the Institute of *fiqh* in Makka)
•Ahmad Kuftaro (Mufti of Syria, founding member of the Muslim World League)
•Yusuf ibn Ahmad al-Siddiq (Chief Judge of the Islamic Court in Bahrain and founding member of the Muslim World League)
•Muhammad Rashid Kabbani (Mufti of Lebanon and present member of the Muslim World League)
•Muhammad Malik al-Kandahlawi (shaykh of hadith, University of al-Ashrafiyyah, Lahore)
•Sayyid Muhammad Abdul Qadir Azad (President of the Islamic Scholars Society of Pakistan)
•Dr. Abdul Razzaq Iskandar (Principal of the Islamic University of Karashi)
•**and innumerable others**.

1.4.6. IBN TAYMIYYA'S TWO *TAWHID*S

It was shown in the translation of the Iraqi scholar Jamil al-Zahawi's *al-Fajr al-sadiq* how the tendency to compare Muslims to idol-worshippers became the trademark of Muhammad ibn Abd al-Wahhab and his followers, and caused bloodshed and discord among Muslims.[39] What is of even greater interest here is Ibn Taymiyya's departure from the single *tawhid* taught by the Prophet (ﷺ) and practiced by the Companions.[40] Ibn Taymiyya actually devised two forms of monotheism while Allah and His Prophet (ﷺ) ordered but one, according to the sound hadith, "I order you to believe in Allah alone. Do you know what belief in Allah alone is? It is to bear witness that 'There is no god but Allah and that Muhammad is the Messenger of Allah?'" Ibn Taymiyya obviously did not mean to deny the consensus whereby if the disbeliever says, "There is no god but Allah and Muhammad is the Messenger of Allah," he enters Islam. However, his manipulation of the Prophet's terms for *tawhid* allowed him to misrepresent Muslims as pre-Islamic idol-worshippers. This, in turn, formed the basis of Ibn Abd al-Wahhab's method.

Imam Ahmad ibn Hanbal, to whom Ibn Taymiyya claimed his affiliation, never said that *tawhid* consisted of two parts; one being *tawhid al-rububiyya* and the other *tawhid al-uluhiyya*. Nor did he ever say, "Whoever does not know *tawhid al-uluhiyya*, his knowledge of *tawhid al-rububiyya* is invalid because the idolaters also had such knowledge." Nor did any of the followers of the Followers (*taba al-tabiin*) ever say such a thing to their contemporaries, nor any of the Followers (*tabiin*) to theirs, nor any of the Companions of the Prophet (ﷺ) to theirs. Nor is it related in the *sunna*, which is the exposition of the Book of Allah, in the *sahih*, the *sunan*, the *masanid*, or the *maajim*, that the Prophet (ﷺ) ever said that *tawhid* consisted of two parts.

Indeed the books of the *sunna* of the Prophet (ﷺ) overflow with proof that the Prophet's call to the people unto Allah was

---

39 See the author's translation in *Doctrine of Ahl al-Sunna wa al-Jamaa versus the "Salafi" Movement* (As-Sunnah Foundation of America, 1996).

40 For more on this topic see Ibn Marzuq's *al-Tawassul bi al-nabi wa bi al-salihin* (Istanbul: Hakikat kitabevi, 1993) p. 25-101 and Hasan Ali al-Saqqaf's *Al-tandid bi man addada al-tawhid* (Slander of him who counts several *tawhid*s), in print.

such that they witness that "There is no god except Allah alone and that Muhammad is the Messenger of Allah," in order that they repudiate idol-worship. One of the most famous illustrations of this is the narration of Muadh ibn Jabal when the Prophet (繁) sent him to Yemen and said to him, "Invite them to the witnessing that 'There is no god but Allah.'" It is narrated in five of the six books of authentic traditions, and Ibn Hibban declared it sound, that a Bedouin Arab reported the sighting of the new moon to the Prophet (繁), and the latter ordered the people to fast without asking this man other than to confirm his witness that "There is no god except Allah alone and that Muhammad is the Messenger of Allah." According to Ibn Taymiyya, it would have been necessary for the Prophet (繁) to call all people to the *tawhid al-uluhiyya* of which they were ignorant, for as for *tawhid al-rububiyya* they knew it already; and he should have said to Muadh: "Invite them to *tawhid al-uluhiyya*" and He should have asked the Bedouin who had sighted the new moon of Ramadan, "Do you know *tawhid al-uluhiyya?*"

Allah never ordered such a thing in the Quran as *tawhid al-uluhiyya* for His servants; nor did He ever say, "whoever does not know this *tawhid*, his knowledge of *tawhid al-rububiyya* is not taken into account." Rather, He ordered the witness of absolute Oneness (*kalimat al-tawhid mutlaqa*), for He said to His Prophet (繁), "Know that there is no other god except Allah alone." He spoke in the same way in all Quranic verses about Oneness mentioned in the Quran, including *Surah al-Ikhlas*, which is equivalent to one third of the Quran. If Ibn Taymiyya was believed, for the moment, and Allah's servants all knew about *tawhid al-rububiyya* and not about *tawhid al-uluhiyya*, Allah would have made this explicitly clear. Instead, according to Ibn Taymiyya, Allah misguided his servants and punished them for their ignorance of half of *tawhid*; He should not have said to them, *"Today I have perfected for you your religion and I have completed My blessing upon you and I have accepted for you Islam as your religion"* (5:3)!

1.4.7. IBN TAYMIYYA'S FALSE REPENTANCE AND PRETENSE OF BEING AN ASHARI

Two telling examples of how Ibn Taymiyya's mind worked are, first, his show of repenting the doctrine of the anthropomorphism of Allah, and second, his pretense of being an Ashari at his trial in Cairo. This is despite the fact that his writings are replete with attacks on Asharis, and disavowals, like the one above, that they even belong to the Muslim fold. Ibn Hajar al-Asqalani writes in his *al-Durar al-kamina*:

> An investigation [of his views] was conducted with several scholars [in Cairo] and a written statement was drawn, in which he said: "I am an Ashari," and his handwriting is found with what he wrote verbatim, namely: "I believe that the Quran is a meaning which exists in Allah's Essence, and it is an Attribute from the pre-eternal Attributes of His Essence, and that it is uncreated, and that it does not consist in the letter nor the voice, and that His saying: *The Merciful established Himself over the Throne*" (20:4) is not taken according to its external meaning (*laysa ala zahirihi*), and I don't know in what consists its meaning, nay only Allah knows it, and one speaks of His "descent" in the same way as one speaks of His "establishment."

It was written by Ahmad ibn Taymiyya and they bore witness to him that he had repented of his own free will of which he was accused. This took place on the 25th of Rabi al-Awwal of the year 707 and it was witnessed by a huge array of scholars and others.[41]

In stark contrast to Imam Ahmad, who suffered imprisonment and lashing in defense of mainstream beliefs, Ibn Taymiyya resorted to lying about his own beliefs in order to avoid prosecution. Ibn Taymiyya is but one of many who have been castigated by their fellow Hanbalis for upholding anthropomorphist beliefs as early as the time of Ibn al-Jawzi.

---

41 Ibn Hajar, *Al-durar al-kamina fi ayan al-miat al-thamina* (The hidden pearls: notable people of the eighth century] (Hyderabad: Dairat al-maarif al-uthmaniyya, 1384 H) 1:148.

1.4.8. IBN JAWZI AL-HANBALI ON LIKENING ALLAH TO HIS CREATION (*TASHBIH*)

Imam Abd al-Rahman Ibn al-Jawzi (508-597), the foremost Hanbali scholar of his generation, noted the prevalence of scholars who claimed to be followers of Ahmad ibn Hanbal in a remarkable book that opens with the words:[42]

> I have seen among the followers of our school (Hanbalis) some who held unsound discourses on doctrine. Three in particular have applied themselves to write books in which they distort the Hanbali school of law: Abu Abd Allah ibn Hamid,[43] his friend al-Qadi (Abu Yala),[44] and Ibn al-Zaghuni.[45]

Scholars have been particularly harsh with the most important of these individuals, Abu Yala ibn al-Farra. . . Ibn al-Athir relates that Abu Muhammad al-Tamimi said of him that he had stained the Hanbalis with such distortion and disgrace that the waters of the sea will never wash them clean.[46] Al-Qadi Abu Bakr ibn al-Arabi says:

> One of my shaykhs whom I consider trustworthy has related to me that Abu Yala used to say in relation to the external meanings of Allah's attributes: "No matter what arguments to the contrary you give me, I consider it necessary for Him to possess everything in the way of attributes, except a beard and genitals."[47] One of the imams of the People of Truth [*Ahl al-Sunna*] said: "This is foul apostasy and a mockery of Allah, and the one who said such a thing has no knowledge of Allah, he must not be followed nor even looked at, nor does he adhere in any way to the Imam whose school he claims to follow and under whose cover he disguises himself; rather, he is a partner of

42 Ibn al-Jawzi, *Daf shubah al-tashbih bi akuff al-tanzih*, ed. Hasan al-Saqqaf (Amman: dar al-imam Nawawi, 1412/1991).

43 Abu Abd Allah al-Hasan ibn Hamid al-Baghdadi al-Warraq al-Hanbali (d. 403), Abu Yala's teacher.

44 The author of the *Tabaqat al-hanabila*, al-Qadi Abu Yala ibn al-Farra al-Hanbali (d. 458).

45 Abu al-Hasan Ali ibn Ubayd Allah al-Zaghuni al-Hanbali (d. 527), author of al-*Idah* and one of Ibn Jawzi's teachers.

46 Ibn al-Athir, *al-Kamil* 10:52.

47 This is also the view of the anthropomorphist (*mujassim*) Dawud al-Jawaribi according to Abd al-Qahir al-Baghdadi in *al-Farq bayn al-firaq*.

polytheists in their idol-worship, for he neither worships Allah nor does he know Allah: he has merely drawn in his own mind an image to be worshiped. Exalted is Allah far above what the heretics and deniers proclaim!"[48]

1.4.9. THE PREVALENCE OF THE ANTHROPOMORPHISTS (*MUJASSIMA*) IN THE HANBALI SCHOOL OF LAW

Ibn al-Jawzi's phrase "the followers of our school" is an insider's acknowledgment of the prevalence of anthropomorphists among those who claim to follow Imam Ahmad ibn Hanbal. This phenomenon was not limited to 6th-century Baghdad. The *hashwiyya*, or vulgar anthropomorphists, teemed in many parts of the Muslim world in preceding centuries as well. In Sijistan for example, Ibn Hibban (d. 354) was exiled for refusing to assert limits to Allah, and Tabari (d. 310) was attacked for rejecting the view that Allah sat the Prophet (ﷺ) next to Him. Also, Bukhari (d. 256) was expelled from Bukhara for declaring that the pronunciation of the Quran was created.[49] In all these cases, the persecutors were followers of Imam Ahmad ibn Hanbal.[50]

The shaykh of hadith Ibn al-Salah (d. 643) said, "Two imams have been severely tried because of their followers although they themselves are innocent: Ahmad ibn Hanbal was tried with the anthropomorphists (*mujassima*), and Jafar al-Sadiq was tried with the rejectionists (*rafida*)."[51]

Ibn al-Jawzi continues:

> I have seen them (al-Warraq, Abu Yala, and al-Zaghuni) descend to the level of popular belief, construing the divine attributes according to the requirements of what the human senses can perceive. They have heard that "Allah created Adam according to his

---

48 Abu Bakr ibn al-Arabi, *al-Awasim* 2:283.

49 See the pages below for the description of all three incidents.

50 Abd Allah ibn Muhammad al-Harawi, Yahya ibn Ammar and their companions in Ibn Hibban's case, Muhammad ibn Yahya al-Dhuhli and his in Bukhari's. See relevant sections below for references.

51 Ibn al-Salah as quoted by Taj al-Din al-Subki in his *Qaida fi al-jarhi wa al-tadil*, ed. Abd al-Fattah Abu Ghudda, 5th ed. (Aleppo and Beirut: Maktab al-matbuat al-islamiyya, 1404/1984) p. 43.

likeness and form (*ala surahtihi*)'" so they affirm that
Allah has a form and a face in addition to His essence,
as well as two eyes, a mouth, an uvula, molar teeth, a
physiognomy, two hands, fingers, a palm, a little fin-
ger, a thumb, a chest, thighs, two legs, two feet. They
say: "We have not heard about the head itself." They
also say: "He can touch and can be touched, and His
servant can approach His Essence." One of them says:
"And he breathes." Then they placate the common
people by adding: "But not as we think."

Similarly, Imam Kawthari mentions two dissensions (*fitna*)
that took place in Baghdad in the 4th and 5th centuries involving the propagation of some of the heresies mentioned by Ibn
al-Jawzi that were being spread by al-Barbahari and other
Hanbalis:

The matter of the Barbahari dissension (*fitna*)
became a serious threat in 323 AH. They were led by
Abu Muhammad al-Hasan ibn Ali ibn Khalaf al-
Barbahari al-Hanbali in Baghdad, the year the
Qarmatiyya (anthropomorphists) plucked out the
Black Stone from the Noble Kabah and compelled
people to assent to their beliefs at sword's point. The
Caliph al-Radi then issued an edict against them as
documented in the *History of Ibn al-Athir* for that
year, in which he said: 'You mention the "hand" (of
Allah) and the "fingers" and the 'two feet' and the
"two gilded sandals" and the "short and curly hair"
and the "climbing" to heaven and the "descending" to
the world—exalted is Allah far above what the
oppressors and rejecters say of Him! The Amir of the
believers swears an oath before Allah by which he
binds himself, that unless you put an end to your vile
belief and crooked way, to destroy you to the last man
by sword and by fire inside your very houses.
In the mid-fifth century the matter of this *fitna*
rose again in Baghdad, until Abu Ishaq al-Shirazi,
Abu Bakr al-Shashi and others of the Shafii imams
had to write against them to Nizam al-Mulk in the following terms: "A rabble, a riffraff calling themselves
Hanbalis have disseminated unspeakable innovations

in Baghdad of the kind not even a heretic (*mulhid*) can be forgiven for, let alone a Muslim (*muwahhid*), and they have charged with disbelief and oppression whoever declares that Allah is transcendent above defects and faults, or denies that He possesses the attributes of created objects or similarities with them, or declares Him to be beyond incarnation, extinction, and mutability from one state to another. They refuse to say other than Allah has feet and teeth and uvula and fingertips, and that he speaks with a voice like thunder or like a wild horse!" It is related in the *hafiz* Ibn Asakir's book *Tabyin kadhib al-muftari ala al-Imam Abi al-Hasan al-Ashari* (The exposition of the fabricators' lies against the Imam al-Ashari).[52]

The recurrence of such incidents through history teaches us, time and again, that the "Salafis," like the Wahhabis and Ibn Taymiyya before them, do not create their own positions. Instead, they take many of them from previous anthropomorphists, like the Barbaharis and Karramis of Baghdad who lived in the 4th, 5th and 6th centuries, and who were put down each time by scholars such as Abu Ishaq al-Shirazi, Fakhr al-Din al-Razi, and Ibn al-Jawzi.

More of Ibn al-Jawzi's text:

They have applied the apparent meanings with regard to divine Names and Attributes. Thus, they give the divine Attributes a wholly innovative and contrived name for which they have no evidence either in the transmitted texts of Quran and *sunna* or in rational proofs based on reason. They have paid attention neither to texts that steer one away from the apparent sense towards the meanings required for Allah, nor to the necessary cancellation of the external meaning when it attributes to Allah the distinguishing marks of creatures. They are not content to say, "attribute of act" (*sifatu fil*) until they end up saying, "attribute of essence" (*sifatu dhat*). Then, once they affirmed them to be "attributes of essence," they claimed, we do not construe the text according to the directives of the Arabic language. Thus they refuse to construe "hand" (*yad*) as meaning "favor" and

---

52 Imam Kawthari, in his *Maqalat* p. 348-349.

"power"; or "coming forth" (*maji*) and "giving" (*ityan*) as "mercy" and "favor"; or "shin" (*saq*) as "tribulation." Instead they said, We construe them in their customary external senses, and the external sense is what is describable in terms of well-known human characteristics, and a text is only construed literally if the literal sense is feasible. Then they become vexed when imputed with likening Allah to His creation (*tashbih*) and they express scorn at such an attribution to themselves, clamoring, 'We are Sunnis!' Yet their discourse is clearly couched in terms of *tashbih*. And some of the masses follow them.

I have advised both the follower and the leader and said, "Colleagues! You are adherents and followers of our school of law (*madhhab*). Your greatest Imam is Ahmad ibn Hanbal, may Allah have mercy on him, who said while under the lash of the Inquisition, 'How can I say what was never said?' Beware of innovating in his *madhhab* what is not from him! Then, you said regarding the hadiths (of the Attributes), 'They must be taken in their external sense.' Yet the external sense of *qadam* ("foot") is a bodily limb![53] And when it was said concerning Jesus (ﷺ): 'Allah's spirit' (*ruh Allah*) the Christians thought that Allah possessed an attribute named His Spirit which had entered Mary!

"Whoever says, 'He is established on His throne in His Essence (*bi al-dhat*),' has made Allah an object of sensory perception. It behooves one not to neglect the means by which the principle of religion is established and that is reason. For it is by virtue of reason that we have known Allah and judged Him to be Eternal without beginning. If you were to say, 'We read hadiths but we are silent,' no one would have any objection against you. However, your interpretation of the apparent sense is morally repugnant and disgusting. Do not introduce into the school of law (*madhhab*) of this man of the Salaf, Ahmad Ibn Hanbal, what his thought does not contain.

A few remarks are in order here before proceeding with the rest of Ibn al-Jawzi's text. In Islam there is no contradiction between reason and belief. Allah has addressed His servants in

---

53 A reference to the hadith whereby Allah places his foot (*qadam*) in the fire, discussed further below by al-Khattabi, Ibn Hazm, and others.

many places in the Quran, "*O you who possess understanding*" (cf. 65:10), alerting them to the fact that knowledge of the realities of religion is an obligation only of those possessing minds. Similarly, the obligation to carry out the duties of Islam falls away when mental capacity is absent. The position of Ibn al-Jawzi and that of mainstream Islam is that Allah first gave mankind reason, then He sent revelation. Thus it is possible for us to recognize and heed Allah's description of Himself and His commands.

As Zahawi pointed out, it was an innovation for Ibn Abd al-Wahhab to have made principles based on narration (*naql*) prior to calling on reason (*aql*).[54] This allowed him to suspend the role of reason in matters of belief at will. Ibn Taymiyya's positions regarding the age of the world[55] and Allah's use of sensory perception[56] are similar. Based on the argument that *naql* establishes nothing to the contrary, he concludes that the created world, like Allah, is eternal and without beginning, and that Allah is not necessarily different from a body, though unlike created bodies. Some of these aberrations were refuted in Ibn Taymiyya's time by Shaykh al-Islam Taqi al-Subki,[57] and in a later time by the Yemeni scholar al-Sanani (d. 1768 CE).[58] Imam al-Kawthari, in editions of Subki's refutations of Ibn Taymiyya and in other places, illustrated Ibn Taymiyya's position regarding some of these topics.

Let the reader be warned not to be deceived by the dis-

54 Zahawi, in his *al-Fajr al-sadiq.*

55 Ibn Taymiyya, *Bayan muwafaqat sahih al-manqul wa sarih al-maqul* (The exposition of the conformity of sound transmitted proof-texts with what is evidently reasonable), published in the margin of the 1930 edition of the *Minhaj al-sunna* and recently re-edited by Muhammad al-Sayyid al-Julaynid and Abd al-Sabur Shahin as *Dar taarud al-aqli wa al-naql* (The prevention of contradiction between reason and transmitted texts) (Cairo: Muassasat al-ahram, 1409/1988).

56 Ibn Taymiyya, *al-Tasis fi radd asas al-taqdis.*

57 Taqi al-Din al-Subki, *Al-rasail al-subkiyya fi al-radd ala Ibn Taymiyya wa tilmidhihi Ibn Qayyim al-Jawziyya,* ed. Kamal al-Hut (Subki's treatises in Answer to Ibn Taymiyya and his pupil Ibn Qayyim al-Jawziyya). Beirut: Alam al-Kutub, 1983.

58 Muhammad ibn Ismail al-Sanani, *Risala sharifa fi ma yataallaqu bi kam al-baqi min umr al-dunya* (Precious treatise concerning the remaining age of the world) ed. al-Wasabi al-Mathani. Sana: Maktabat dar al-quds, 1992; and *Raf al-astar li-ibtal adillat al-qailin bi-fana al-nar* (Exposing the nullity of the proofs of those who claim that the fire will pass away), ed. Albani. Beirut: al-Maktab al-islami, 1984.

claimer invoked by some of Ibn Taymiyya's admirers, which suggests that he did not really hold all these beliefs but merely quoted them in his review of the positions of those he criticized.[59]

1.4.10. IBN TAYMIYYA ATTACKS ASHARIS FOR PRECLUDING A BODY AND A LIMIT FOR ALLAH

Kawthari states in extremely strong terms that Ibn Taymiyya's position on Allah's attributes is tantamount to disbelief and apostasy because it reduces Allah to a corporeal body. He shows that there is seamless continuity between the defenders of mainstream Islam in the time of Ibn al-Jawzi and in later times, and a consistency among the proponents of anthropomorphism and their manner of accusing mainstream Muslims and Asharis of being Mutazili and other non-Sunnis, if they rejected anthropomorphism. Here are some of his comments taken from *Maqalat al-Kawthari*:

How much did the Hanbalis Ibn Aqil and Ibn al-Jawzi suffer at their hands, and how much was the former falsely summoned to repent from being a Mutazila whereas they were both only declaring Allah's transcendence! Then there was the story of Ibn al-Qudwa al-Karrami against Imam Fakhr al-Din al-Razi . . . Then there was the sedition of Abd al-Ghani al-Maqdisi al-Hanbali—it can be found in the addendum to Abu Shama's *al-Rawdatayn*. Then came the seditions of Ibn Taymiyya in Damascus which have become known far and wide. They are detailed in *al-hafiz* Taqi al-Din al-Husni's *Dafu shubahi man shabbaha wa tamarrad wa nasaba dhalika ila al-sayyid al-jalil al-imam Ahmad* (Repelling the sophistries of the rebel [Ibn Taymiyya] who likens Allah to creation, then attributes this position to Imam Ahmad) . . .[60] In the *al-Tasis*

---

59 Cf. Julaynid and Shahin in their introduction to *Dar taarud al-aqli wa al-naql*, chapter entitled "Ibn Taymiyya between *tashbih* and *tanzih*" p. 53, and Mashhur Ibn Hasan al-Salman in the book he wrote against Imam Nawawi entitled *al-Rudud wa al-taaqqubat ala ma waqaa li al-imam al-nawawi fi Sharh Sahih Muslim min al-tawil fi al-sifat wa ghayriha min al-masail al-muhimmat* (Riyad: Dar al-hijra, 1413/1993) p. 20-23.

60 Taqi al-Din al-Husni's *Dafu shubahi man shabbaha wa tamarrada wa nasiba dhalika il al-sayyid al-jalil al-imam Ahmad* (Cairo: Dar ihya al-kutub al-arabiyya, 1350/1931).

fi radd asas al-taqdis (The laying of the foundation: refutation of al-Razi's "The Foundation of Allah's Sanctification") he says:

> *Al-arsh* (the Throne) in language means *al-sarir* (elevated seat or couch), so named with respect to what is on top of it, just as "the roof" is so named with respect to what is under it. Therefore, if the Quran attributes a throne to Allah, it is then known that this throne is, with respect to Allah, like the elevated seat is with respect to other than Allah. This makes it necessarily true that He is on top of the Throne.

So then the Throne is, for Ibn Taymiyya, Allah's seat (*maqad*)—Exalted is He from such a notion! He also says:

> It is well-known that the Book, the *sunna*, and the consensus nowhere say that all bodies (*ajsam*) are created, and nowhere say that Allah Himself is not a body. None of the imams of the Muslims ever said such a thing. Therefore if I also choose not to say it, it does not expel me from religion nor from Sharia.

These words are complete impudence. What did he do with all the verses declaring Allah to be far removed from anything like unto Him? Does he expect that the feeble thought that every single idiot can come up with—be addressed with a specific text? Is it not enough that Allah the Exalted said: "*There is nothing whatsoever like Him*" (42:11)? Or does he consider it permissible for someone to say: Allah eats this, and chews that, and tastes the other thing, just because no text mentions the opposite? This is disbelief (*kufr*) laid bare and pure—anthropomorphism (*tajsim*). In another passage of the same book he says:

> You (Asharis) say that He is neither a body, nor an atom (*jawhar*), nor spatially bounded (*mutahayyiz*), and that He has no direction, and that He cannot be pointed to as an object of sensory perception, and that nothing of Him can be considered distinct from Him, and you have asserted this on the grounds that Allah

is neither divisible nor made of parts and that He has
neither limit (*hadd*) nor end (*ghayat*), with your view
thereby to forbid one to say that He has any measure
(*hadd*) or dimension (*qadr*), or that He even has a
dimension that is unlimited. But how do you allow
yourselves to do this without evidence from the Book
and the *sunna*?[61]

The reader's intelligence suffices to comment on these
heretical statements. Can you imagine for an apostate to be
more brazen than this, right in the midst of a Muslim society?
In another place of the same book he says, "It is obligatorily
known that Allah did not mean by the name of 'the One' (*al-
Wahid*) the negation of the Attributes." He is here alluding to
all that entails His "coming" to a place and the like. He continues, "Nor did He mean by it the negation that He can be perceived with the senses, nor the denial of limit and dimension
and all such interpretations which were innovated by the
Jahmiyya and their followers. Negation or denial of the above
is not found in the Book nor the *sunna*." And this is on an equal
footing with what came before with regard to pure anthropomorphism and plain apostasy.

In another book of his, *Muwafaqat al-maqul*, which is in the
margin of his *Minhaj*, Ibn Taymiyya asserts that things occur
newly in relation to Allah and that He has a direction according to two kinds of conjecture.[62]

And you know, O reader, what the Imams say concerning him who deliberately and intently establishes
that Allah has a direction, unless his saying such a
thing is a slip of the tongue or a slip of the pen. Then
there is his establishing that the concept of movement
applies to Allah, along with all the others who establish such a thing. Then his denial that there is an
eternal sojourn in hellfire has filled creation, and so
has his saying on the variety of eternity without
beginning (*al-qidam al-nawi*). His words pertaining to

---

61 These passages are from Ibn Taymiyya's *al-Tasis* 1:101.
62 Ibn Taymiyya, *Muwafaqat al-maqul*. on the margins of *Minhaj al-sunna* (Bulaq:
al-Matbaa al-kubra al-amiriyya, 1321/1904) 2:75, 1:264, 2:13, 2:26.

this latter point are in his criticism of Ibn Hazm's book on consensus.[63]

Imam Kawthari's frank condemnation of Ibn Taymiyya has been dismissed by the latter's supporters as excessive, but they have failed to show in what. Kawthari provides enough excerpts from the books of Ibn Taymiyya himself, to reveal—beyond a shadow of a doubt—the leanings of his views. Shahrastani reports that Ibn Karram used to say, "Allah is firmly seated on the throne and he is in person (*dhatan*) on the upper side of it."[64] It is remarkable how much closer Ibn Taymiyya is to the views of this 3rd-century *mujassim* than to Imam Ahmad's position. The latter is, with respect to declaring Allah free of boundaries, location, and direction, not a Taymiyyan, but very much an Ashari. Indeed, Shahrastani (d. 548) reports that Imam Ahmad and his school were so abhorred by likening Allah to His creation (*tashbih*), that they used to say, "Whoever moves his hand while reciting the verse 'I created with My Hand,' or gestures with his fingers when narrating the hadith 'The heart of the believer is between two fingers of the Merciful,' cut their hands or fingers off!"[65]

Ibn Taymiyya should also have cried out, "You Hanbalis claim that He cannot be pointed to as an object of sensory perception . . ." It is clear, at any rate, that his own peculiar thinking harkens back to the *hashwi* Hanbalis and the anthropomorphist school fought by Ibn al-Jawzi in the 4th and 5th centuries, and not the Sunni school of Imam Ahmad.

1.4.11. IBN HIBBAN EXILED BY THE ANTHROPOMORPHISTS FOR PRECLUDING LIMITS FOR ALLAH

The trend of attributing limits to Allah was also dominant in Khorasan and Sijistan, whence Ibn Hibban (d. 354) was expelled for refusing to assert limits to Allah. Taj al-Din al-Subki[66] relates that Ismail al-Harawi asked "one of the anthropomorphists," identified as Yahya ibn Ammar, about Ibn

---

63 See , *Naqd maratib al-ijma* p. 169. Muhammad Zahid Kawthari, *Maqalat al-Kawthari* (Riyadh: Dar al-ahnaf, 1414/1993; Cairo: al-Maktaba al-azhariya li al-turath, 1415/1994) p. 350-353.

64 Shahrastani, *al-Milal wa al-nihal* (Cairo, 1317) p. 145.

65 *Op. cit.* p. 137-138.

66 Taj al-Din al-Subki, in his *Tabaqat* and *Qaida fi al-jarh wa al-tadil*.

Hibban as a narrator. Ibn Ammar said, "He was very learned but had little religion. He came to us and denied that Allah had a limit, so we expelled him from Sijistan." Suyuti mentions that they had almost decided to kill him.[67] The Hanafi hadith master al-Alai comments, "O wonder, by Allah! Who is more deserving of being expelled and declared an innovator lacking in religion?" Subki declares, after relating the exchange and before citing al-Alai's words, "Look at the ignorance of this critic of hadith scholars! I truly wonder who deserves criticism more: the one who asserts limits for His Lord, or he who denies them!"[68]

It is useful to note that the Ismail al-Harawi mentioned here is no other than the great Sufi shaykh al-Harawi al-Ansari (d. 481). Subki says of him, "The anthropomorphists call him Shaykh al-Islam."[69] As much as he excelled in his books on the sciences of self-purification, or *tasawwuf*, his hatred for Asharis led him to excesses, illustrated in the voluminous *Dhamm al-kalam wa ahlih* (Blame of theology and its practitioners)—the only one of his works that is read by the "Salafis" and the worst. Sakhawi relates that his teacher Ibn Hajar read this book to his students as an example of how not to write and only for their information. After, he would forbid them from transmitting it.[70] As Abd al-Fattah Abu Ghudda explained, their reading of it in the first place was only "for the record, not for reliance" (*li al-tasjil la li al-tawil*).[71]

The tribulations of Ibn Hibban, reminiscent of those endured by Bukhari, who was exiled from his home and died in exile, and Tabari, who found himself confined inside his house, are not a thing of the past. Even today mainstream Islamic scholars are being hounded and banished by those who would deny unity and doctrine. The renewer of the 14th century Hijra, Muhammad Zahid al-Kawthari, for example, was expelled from Istanbul by the Kemalist regime and died in exile in Cairo. A living example before our eyes is the *muhaddith* of Makka and son of its greatest recent orator,[72] al-Sayyid

67 Suyuti, *Tadrib al-rawi sharh taqrib al-nawawi* (al-Maktaba al-ilmiyya, 1379) p. 54.
68 Subki, *Tabaqat* (Halabi ed.) 3:132; also his *Qaida fi al-jarh wa al-tadil*, p. 30-32.
69 Subki, *Tabaqat* 3:132.
70 Sakhawi, al-*Ilam bi al-tawbikh li man dhamma ahl al-tawrikh* (Damascus: Matbaat al-taraqqi, 1349; repr. Baghdad: Matbaat al-Ani, 1382) p. 65.
71 Abu Ghudda, commentary on al-Subki's *Qaida*, p. 63.
72 Alawi ibn Abbas al-Maliki (1909-1971 CE).

Muhammad ibn Alawi al-Maliki al-Hasani, whom the Wahhabis have tried more than once to expel from his native homeland to no avail.

1.4.12. DHAHABI'S LACK OF COMMITMENT AGAINST ANTHROPOMORPHISM AND IBN HAJAR'S REJECTION OF DHAHABI'S REASONING

Although al-Alai and al-Subki found it obvious who was at fault and who was blameless, and exonerated Ibn Hibban, Dhahabi labels both positions, Ibn Hibban's and the *mujassima*'s, "meddlesome" (*fudul*), but stops short of specifically condemning either.[73] This is a virtual exoneration of the anthropomorphists. Herein lies the symptom of Ibn Taymiyya's influence on him, since Dhahabi places on the same level those who declare Allah to be a limited body and those that declare Him free of limit. Dhahabi's excuse is the same as Ibn Taymiyya's excuse for refusing to preclude limbs and limits for Allah: it is not said in the Quran and *sunna* (he claims) that Allah has no limits! These are Dhahabi's words:

> I say, Ibn Hibban's denial of a limit for Allah and the others' assertion of limits are both a kind of meddlesome discourse, and it would have been better for both parties to say nothing. For there is no text for either the denying or the asserting, and there is nothing like Allah whatsoever. Therefore, whoever asserts limit to Allah is told, "You have given limits to Allah by your view without proof from a text, and he who has limits is created, exalted is Allah high above this" while the one who asserts limit says to the other: "You have reduced your Lord to a non-existent thing, for there is no limit to the non-existent." Therefore whoever declares Allah's transcendence and keeps silent, he is safe and has followed the road of the Salaf.[74]

The reactions against Dhahabi's mode of reasoning go to the heart of the matter. Ibn Hajar comments in his *Lisan al-*

---

73 Dhahabi, in his *Mizan.*
74 Dhahabi, *Mizan al-itidal fi naqd al-rijal* (Cairo: al-Halabi, 1382) 3:507.

mizan, "Dhahabi's words, 'the one who asserts limit says to the other: You have reduced your Lord to a non-existent thing, for there is no limit to the non-existent' are untrue. It is not granted that to deny limit to Allah is tantamount to reducing Him to the non-existent after the certitude of His existence. The truth is Ibn Hibban was right."[75]

1.4.13. ALAI'S AND SUBKI'S DENUNCIATION OF DHAHABI'S BIAS FOR ANTHROPOMORPHISTS

Subki reprimands his master in much more severe terms than Ibn Hajar with regard to non-commitment against *tajsim*: "Here our shaykh al-Dhahabi may Allah have mercy on him with all his learning and piety, displays an excessive bias against Sunnis; therefore it is not permitted to follow him in this opinion . . ." He proceeds to cite al-Alai's denunciation of Dhahabi's favor of anthropomorphists and bias against Asharis, and then condemns his shaykh for "reaching a risible level of excessive partisanship":

> . . . I have copied from a text written in the hand of the hadith master Salah al-Din Khalil ibn Kikaldi al-Alai, may Allah have mercy on him, the following:
>
> I do not doubt the shaykh and hadith master al-Dhahabi's piety, great fear of Allah, and vast erudition in the sayings of scholars. However, the school of affirming the attributes (*madhhab al-ithbat*), aversion for figurative interpretation (*munafarat al-tawil*), and neglect for affirming transcendence (*al-ghafla an al-tanzih*) have gotten the better of him. It has influenced his personality so much that he shows, on the one hand, strong animosity against the people of transcendence, and on the other, strong inclination towards the people of affirmation of the attributes. When he writes the biography of one of the latter, he draws up all that has been said of his merits, sings his praise, turns a blind eye on his faults, and gives them the best rendering he is capable of. But when he cites someone from the other side, such as, for example, Imam al-Haramayn or al-Ghazali and their likes,[76] he does not sing their praise, but accumulates the

75 Ibn Hajar al-Asqalani, *Lisan al-mizan* (Hyderabad: Dairat al-maarif al-nizamiyya, 1329) 5:114.

76 i.e. Asharis and those who apply figurative interpretation.

sayings of those who have criticized them, reiterates those sayings and demonstrates them considering it a pious action without a second thought looks away from their ample merits and does not make their list, and whatever fault of theirs he is able to cite he cites it. He does the same with the people of our time. And whenever he finds no saying against one of them, he will say in his biography: "May Allah reform him," or something like it. The reason for all this is his disagreement in doctrine.

There is far more to say to the detriment of al-Dhahabi than what al-Alai has described, although he is my master and teacher, but the truth is more deserving of being followed. And the truth is that he has reached a risible level of excessive partisanship, and I fear for him on the Day of Resurrection on the part of the majority of Muslim scholars and their imams who have been the standard-bearers of the prophetic law for us: for they are Ashari for the most part, and when he criticized an Ashari he was unsparing and unrelenting. For myself, I believe they will be his opponents on the Day of Resurrection, and perhaps the least one among them will be worthier of Allah's regard than him. I ask Allah that He lighten his punishment and inspire them to disregard his offenses against them and intercede for him. . .

He has too frequently attacked the people of piety (I mean the *fuqara* who are the best of creation),[77] set his tongue loose on many of the imams of the Shafiis and Hanafis, showed prejudice against Asharis and excessive bias for anthropomorphists, and this is the foremost among hadith masters and a venerable leader! What do you think will be the case of the common writers of biographies?[78]

Subki further denounces Dhahabi for including the masters of jurisprudence, al-Razi and al-Amidi, among the men of weak narration in his book only because they are Ashari—although neither are narrators and have never been faulted for a weak narration. Despite the exaggerated tone and content of Subki's comments, his stern warning must be heeded (see Appendix 2).

---

77 i.e. Sufis.
78 Subki, *Qaida* p. 32-37, 59-60.

1.4.14. THE SOURCES OF
IBN TAYMIYYA'S IDEAS

The resemblance of Kawthari's censure of Ibn Taymiyya to Ibn al-Jawzi's censure of the anthropomorphizing Hanbalis of his time is striking. It comes as no surprise, therefore, that Ibn Taymiyya in fact took his own materials from a related group. As Kawthari says, "Ibn Taymiyya replicates part and parcel what is found in Uthman ibn Said al-Darimi's *al-Radd ala al-jahmiyya,* and the *Kitab al-sunna* attributed to Abd Allah ibn Ahmad ibn Hanbal, and Ibn Khuzayma's *al-Tawhid wa sifat al-rabb.*" Here is a look at these three of Ibn Taymiyya's sources:

1.4.14.1. UTHMAN IBN SAID AL-DARIMI AL-SAJZI

Uthman Ibn Said al-Darimi al-Sajzi (d. 280 not to be confused with Abd Allah ibn Abd al-Rahman al-Darimi, author of the *Sunan,* who died in 255), is said by some biographers to have studied with Ahmad, al-Buyuti, Yahya ibn Main, and Ibn al-Madini. However, he is never mentioned in the Six Books of traditions, which suggests problems concerning his person, in view of the teachers with which he is said to have studied.

He wrote his books against Bishr al-Marisi and the Jahmiyya at large. In his fervor to refute their excessively figurative interpretations, he fell into the opposite extreme of anthropomorphism.[79] One also wonders why Ibn Taymiyya would take up arguments originally meant for Jahmis, who were heretics, and redirect them to the Asharis, who are the Sunni. Here are some examples of what his book *al-Naqd ala al-jahmiyya* (The critique of the Jahmis) contains:[80]

> The Living, the Self-Subsistent, does what He wills, moves if He so wills, descends and ascends if He wills, collects and spreads and rises and sits if He wills, for the distinguishing mark between the living and the dead is movement: every living thing moves without fail, and every dead thing is immobile without fail. (p. 20)

---

[79] This is illustrated by the excerpts of *Kitab al-sunna* quoted after the section below.

[80] Uthman ibn Said al-Darimi, *Kitab al-naqd ala al-jahmiyya* (Cairo, 1361/1942).

In this phrase the author has compared Allah to every living thing, although nothing is like Him whatsoever.

> Those who object claim that Allah has no limit, no boundary, and no end, and this is the principle upon which Jahm has built all of his heresy and from which he has carved his falsehoods; these are statements that we have never heard anyone say before him... Allah certainly has a limit... and so has His place, for He is on His Throne above the heavens, and these are two limits. Any person who declares that Allah has a limit and that His place has a limit, is more knowledgeable than the Jahmis. (p. 23).

In these statements it is seen that al-Darimi considers Imam al-Shafii a Jahmi, since al-Shafii explicitly stated,

> Know that limit and finiteness do not apply to Allah."[81]Those who revived the views of al-Darimi in later times, like Ibn Taymiyya, and in modern times, like those who call themselves "Salafis," could not be farther from the doctrine of the true Salaf. Does any rational person doubt that anyone who declares "Allah has a limit" is worshipping an idol? As Abd al-Qahir al-Baghdadi said, it is obligatory to declare as unbeliever someone who says that Allah has limits.[82]

Although today's "Salafis" do not show the same openness as al-Darimi in ascribing limits to the Creator, this belief is couched in their repeated denial that Allah is everywhere. Wahhabis and "Salafis" believe that the only alternative to the claim that "Allah is in every place" is their claim that "He is in one place only; above His throne."

Each claim is as worthless as the other since both ascribe spatial location to Allah, Exalted is He above anything they may claim. Both are equally false in devising for Him dispersion in an infinity of places, and limitation in a single place. Both are disbelief according to Imam Abd al-Ghani al-

81 al-Shafii, *al-Fiqh al-akbar fi al-tawhid li al-imam Abi Abd Allah Muhammad ibn Idris al-Shafii*, 1st ed. (al-Azbakiyya, Cairo: al-matbaa al-adabiyya, 1324/1906 or 1907) p. 8. The original manuscript of this work is kept at the Zahiriyya Library in Damascus, Ms. #Q-2(3).

82 Abd al-Qahir al-Baghdadi, in *al-Tabsira al-baghdadiyya, al-Asma wa al-sifat, and al-Farq bayn al-firaq* Cited in Kawthari's *Maqalat* p. 314.

Nabulusi's clear statement, "Whoever believes that Allah permeates the heavens and the earth, or that He is a body sitting
on His Throne, is a disbeliever, even if he thinks he is a
Muslim."

>He created Adam by touching him (*masisan*) (p.
>25).

>If He so willed, He could have settled on the back
>of a gnat and it would have carried Him thanks to His
>power and the favor of His lordship, not to mention
>the magnificent Throne (p. 75).

This is a dangerous, ugly, astonishing combination of
tajsim, takyif, tashbih, and *tamthil*. In a word, the author's
premise for inferring that the object of his worship can settle on
top of a gnat is his understanding that Allah physically settles
on the Throne. One of the greatest indications of Ibn
Taymiyya's anthropomorphist views is that in advocating the
interpretation of *istiwa* as *istiqrar* or settling—which is
absolutely condemned by the Salaf—he does not hesitate to
reproduce the above statement verbatim. It is ironic that he
does so in his *Tasis*, an attack on al-Razi for a book written in
refutation of anthropomorphists.[83]

>He is distinguished from His creation and above
>His Throne with a patent distance in between the two,
>with the seven heavens between Him and His crea-
>tures on earth. (p. 79)

>If the Lord sits on the chair or foot-stool (*kursi*), a
>kind of groaning is heard similar to that of the new
>camel saddle. This is because the pressure of
>Allah's Essence on top of it. (p. 92 and 182)

The latter view also held by Abu Yala is but another illustration of the aberrations of the *hashwiyya*, or populist anthropomorphists. As Ibn al-Jawzi and Kawthari mentioned, if the
hadith of the groaning is authentic, it is a foremost case of figurative interpretation (*tawil*) whereby the groaning stands for

---

83 Ibn Taymiyya, *al-Tasis fi al-radd ala asas al-taqdis* 1:568. See Appendix 1.

the submission of the chair or footstool of the Creator. However, the authenticity of the hadith has been questioned. Ibn al-Jawzi mentioned the weakness of two of its narrators and Ibn Asakir wrote a whole monograph entitled *Bayan al-wahm wa al-takhlit fi hadith al-atit* (The exposition of error and confusion in the narration of the groaning). Concerning its meaning Ibn al-Jawzi said, after citing al-Khattabi:

The meaning of the groaning of the *kursi* is its impotence before Allah's majesty and greatness, as it is known that the groaning of the camel saddle under the saddle's rider is a indication of the power of what sits on top of it, or its impotence to bear it. The Prophet (ﷺ) drew this kind of simile for Allah's greatness and majesty in order to teach the Arab who had sought Allah's intercession with the Prophet (ﷺ) that the One whose greatness is overwhelming is not to be sought as an intercessor with those under His station. As for al-Qadi Abu Yala's words, "The groaning is because of the pressure of Allah's Essence on it," this is overt anthropomorphism.[84]

> Who told you that the top of the mountain is not closer to Allah than its bottom? . . . The top of the minaret is closer to Allah than its bottom. (p. 100)

According to this logic, the tall man is closer to Allah than the short one, and the one who flies a plane closer than those on the ground. The nearest to Allah would then be the astronauts. However, this is contrary to the teaching of Islam, whereby Allah's servant is closest to Him when in prostration,[85] and prostration is abasement, not elevation. Allah explicitly equated prostration with proximity to Him when He ordered, *"Prostrate and draw near"* (96:19). The Prophet (ﷺ) revealed that no Muslim uses the Prophet Jonah's prayer, *la ilaha illa anta subhanaka inni kuntu min al-zalimin* (21:87) except it is answered; yet Jonah spoke it in the belly of the whale, deep under the sea.[86] Besides this, Muslims remove

---

84 Ibn al-Jawzi, *Daf shubah al-tashbih* p. 268.

85 *Aqrabu ma yakunu al-abdu min rabbihi wa huwa sajidun fa akthiru fihi al-dua,* related by Muslim, Salat #482, Abu Dawud, Salat #875, al-Nisai 2:226, and Ahmad in the Musnad 2:421.

86 *Dawatu dhi al-nuni idha daa rabbahu wa huwa fi batni al-hut... lam yadu biha rajulun muslimun fi shayin qattu illa istajaba allahu lah,* related by Tirmidhi (#3500), al-Nisai in *Amal al-yawmi wa al-layla* (#656), al-Hakim 1:505 and 2:383. The latter declared it sound (*sahih*) and Dhahabi confirmed him.

Allah from any place, whether high or low. For them His elevation (*uluw*) is loftiness of rank not spatial height, just as his
greatness (*azama*), has nothing to do with bulk.

The author's influence on Ibn Taymiyya is undeniable, as
Ibn Taymiyya formulates, a few centuries later, the exact same
view put forth by Darimi. As Ibn Taymiyya explicitly declares
in his *Tasis*, itself written in refutation of Karrami anthropomorphists:[87] "The Creator, Glorified and Exalted is He, is
above the world and His being above is literal, not in the sense
of dignity or rank."[88] Ibn Taymiyya is far removed from the
position of mainstream Islam in this respect. As Ibn Hajar al-
Asqalani stated in *Fath al-bari*:

Al-Kirmani (d. 786) said:

> The external meaning of "in the heaven" (*fi al-
> sama*) is not meant (in the Prophet's hadith: 'Do you
> not trust me who am trusted by the One in the heav-
> en?'), for Allah is transcendent above incarnation in a
> place; but because the direction of elevation is nobler
> than any other direction, Allah predicated it to
> Himself to indicate the loftiness of His Essence and
> Attributes."

Others besides Kirmani addressed in similar terms the
expressions that came down concerning elevation and similar
topics.[89]

> We do not concede that all actions are created. We
> have agreed by consensus that the movement, the
> descent, the walking, the running (*al-harwala*), and
> the establishment on the Throne and to the heaven
> are eternal without beginning (*qadim*). (p. 121)

The consensus of scholars says the exact reverse. Ibn Hazm
al-Zahiri (d. 456) explicitly states in his *al-Fasl fi al-milal wa
al-ahwa wa al-nihal*, "If the establishment on the Throne is
eternal without beginning, then the Throne is eternal without
beginning, and this is disbelief."[90] It is not only the false refer-

---

87 This was written against *al-Razas Asas al-taqdis* (The foundation of declaring
Allah transcendent).

88 Ibn Taymiyya, *al-Tasis al-radd ala asas al-taqdis* 1:111. This passage is quoted
in full below, in the section on Ibn Taymiyya's conception of Allah's "descent."

89 Ibn Hajar al-Asqalani, *Fath al-Bari* 13:412.

90 Ibn Hazm, *al-Fasl fi al-milal wa al-ahwa wa al-nihal* 2:124.

ence to consensus that is unsettling in these statements, nor their utter lack of foundation in the Quran and the *sunna*. Rather, the author should have begun by questioning the logic of attributing eternity without beginning to the establishment on the Throne and to the heaven, when the Throne and the heaven themselves are not eternal and without beginning! This has been pointed out by Kawthari and others.

1.4.14.2. ABD ALLAH IBN AHMAD IBN HANBAL (D. 290)

Misunderstanding Imam Ahmad's opinion, Abd Allah ibn Ahmad ibn Hanbal wrote a book that he entitled *Kitab al-sunna*, but whose stand in relation to the *sunna* and anthropomorphism can be judged by the following excerpts:[91]

> Is *istiwa* other than by sitting (*julus*)? (p. 5)
> He saw Him on a chair of gold carried by four angels: one in the form of a man, another in the form of a lion, another in that of a bull, and another in that of an eagle, in a green garden, outside of which there was a golden dais.

This is taken almost verbatim from the Bible's Book of Revelation (4:2-7):

> There was someone on the Throne . . . from it issued lightning, voices, and thunder . . . in its midst and around it stood four angels . . . the first was like a lion, the second like a young bull, the third has the face of a man, and the fourth is like an eagle in flight.

Kawthari appropriately calls this "the grossest idol-worship (*al-wathaniyya al-kharqa*) to which they ("Salafis") are calling the *umma* today."

> "Allah spoke to Moses with His lips," (*mushafa-hatan*), that is: upper lip against lower lip.

Kawthari mentions that this same text is found in Abu Yala's *Tabaqat*, in his biography of al-Istakhri, and falsely attributed to Imam Ahmad.

---

91 Abd Allah ibn Ahmad Ibn Hanbal, *Kitab al-sunna* (Cairo: al-Matbaa al-Salafiya, 1349/1930).

Verily Allah did not touch with His hand except Adam, whom He created with His own hand, Paradise, the Torah, which He wrote with His own hand, and a pearl which He wrought with His own hand, then dipped into it a stick to which He said: Stretch thyself as far as I please and bring out what is in thee with My leave, and so it brought out the rivers and the vegetation. (p. 68)

If the Lord sits on the chair or foot-stool (*kursi*), a kind of groaning is heard similar to that of the new camel saddle. (p.70)[92]

Allah sits on the kursi and there remains only four spans vacant. (p. 71)

He showed part of Himself. (p. 149)

And His other hand was empty without anything in it. (p. 164)

This is a commonplace of the *hashwiyya*. Al-Khallal (d. 310), one of Imam Ahmad's companions, repeats it countless times in his *Kitab al-sunna*, attributing it to Mujahid, and declaring anyone who denies it to be a *jahmi kafir zindiq*.[93] Ibn al-Qayyim endorses it unreservedly in his *Badai al-fawaid*.[94] The grammarian and commentator Abu Hayyan al-Andalusi relates the same about Ibn Taymiyya:

I have read in a book by our contemporary Ahmad ibn Taymiyya written in his own hand and which he entitled *Kitab al-arsh* (The Book of the Throne): 'Allah the Exalted sits (*yajlisu*) on the *kursi*, and He has left a space vacant for the Prophet (ﷺ) to sit with Him.' Taj al-Din Muhammad ibn Ali al-Barnibari tricked him into thinking that he was supporting him until he obtained that book from him and we read this in it.[95]

It is related that the commentator of Quran and historian al-Tabari (d. 310) was nearly killed for questioning the above interpretation, as Ibn Hibban was nearly killed for questioning

---

92 Ibn Said al-Darimi also endorses this, the previous, and the next view in his book.

93 al-Khallal, *al-Sunna* p. 215-216.

94 Ibn Qayyim al-Jawziyya, *Badai al-fawaid* (Misr: al-Matbaa al-muniriya, 1900?) 4:39-40.

95 Abu Hayyan, *Tafsir al-nahr al-madd min al-bahr al-muhit* (The commentary of the river extending from the ocean) 1:254 (*Ayat al-kursi*).

that Allah had a limit. The Hanbalis asked about the purported hadith of the Prophet's sitting on the Throne next to Allah. This hadith is traced to Layth, who is supposed to have related it from Mujahid. According to some Hanbalis, the hadith helps to explain the verse, "Perhaps your Lord shall raise you to an exalted station" (*asa an yabathaka rabbuka maqaman mahmuda*) (17:79). Tabari replied, "It is absurd" and said, "Glory to Him who has no comrade" means nor 'one-who-sits-next-to-Him' on the Throne" (*subhana man laysa lahu anis wa la lahu fi arshihi jalis*). When the Hanbalis heard this, they threw their inkwells at Tabari and he withdrew to his house. Suyuti mentions some of this,[96] and Ibn al-Jawzi relates, in *al-Muntazam*, that Thabit ibn Sinan mentions in his *History*, "I hid the truth about this because the mob had gathered and forbidden the visit of Tabari in the daytime, and said that he was a rejectionist (*rafid*) and a heretic (*mulhid*).[97]

Al-Khallal, Ibn al-Jawzi's offenders, Ibn Hibban and Tabari's would-be killers, Ibn Qayyim, and Ibn Taymiyya together form the party that maintains that Allah sits on the Throne, places His feet on the kursi as one would on a footstool, and that the Prophet (ﷺ) sits on the throne by His side. As a contemporary scholar remarked, all this seems to reflect another passage of the Bible; namely what is found in the Gospel of Mark (19:16): "Then the Lord [Jesus], after he spoke to them, was raised to the heaven, and sat at the right of God."[98] Yet these anthropomorphists claim that their views represent the way of the Salaf, and that to depart from it is to leave Islam. What is clear, on the contrary, is that to follow the views of Ibn Taymiyya and the persecutors of mainstream Muslims in ascribing a body to Allah, is to commit disbelief. To leave the views of Ibn Taymiyya and the persecutors of mainstream Muslims is a sign that one follows the Salaf.

1.4.14.3.IBN KHUZAYMA (D. 311)

He wrote a large volume that he named *Kitab al-tawhid*

---

96 Suyuti, in *Tahdhir al-khawass min akadhib al-qussas* (The warning of the elect against the lies of story-tellers).

97 See the introduction to Ibn Jarir al-Tabari's *Kitab ikhtilaf al-fuqaha* (The differences among jurists), ed. Frederik Kern, Egypt 1902.

98 Quoted in Saqqa *op. cit.*

(Book of the declaration of oneness),[99] and he later regretted having authored, as established by two reports cited by Bayhaqi with their chains of transmission.[100] Imam Fakhr al-Din Razi was so repelled by Ibn Khuzayma's book that he renamed it *Kitab al-shirk*[101] (Book of associating partners to Allah), just as Kawthari later renamed Abd Allah ibn Ahmad's book *Kitab al-zaygh* (Book of aberration).[102]

Ibn Khuzayma cites, as proof for establishing that Allah has a foot and other limbs, the verse, *"Have they feet wherewith they walk or have they hands wherewith they hold, or have they eyes wherewith they see, or have they ears wherewith they hear?"* (7:195). This contravenes the sound position of the Salaf expressed by al-Muqri and related by Abu Dawud in his *Sunan*, "'Allah hears and sees' means: He has the power of hearing and seeing [not the organs]."[103]

Kawthari points out that Ibn Khuzayma's understanding is identical to that of the anthropomorphists of Tabaristan and Isfahan. These are mentioned by al-Saksaki as saying,[104] "If He does not have eyes, nor ears, nor hand, nor foot, then what we are worshipping is a watermelon!" They claim, in support of their views, that in the Quran Allah has derided those who lacked limbs by saying, *"Have they feet wherewith they walk?"*[105]

Ibn al-Jawzi says the following about him:

> I saw that Abu Bakr Ibn Khuzayma compiled a book on Allah's attributes and divided it into chapters such as: "Chapter of the Asserting of His hand"; "Chapter of His Holding the Heavens on His fingers"; "Chapter of the Asserting of His foot, in spite of the Mutazila." Then he said, Allah said, *"Have they feet wherewith they walk or have they hands wherewith they hold, or have they eyes wherewith they see, or*

99 Muhammad ibn Ishaq ibn Khuzayma, *Kitab al-tawhid wa-ithbat sifat al-rabb allati wasafa biha nafsahu..* . (Cairo: Idarat al-tibaa al-muniriyya, 1354/1935).

100 Bayhaqi, *al-Asma wa al-sifat*, ed. Kawthari, p. 267.

101 Razi, *al-Tafsir al-kabir* 14:27 (#151).

102 Kawthari, *Maqalat*, p. 355.

103 Abu Dawud, *Sunan*, *Kitab al-Sunna*, ch. 19, last hadith.

104 Al-Saksaki, in his *al-Burhan fi marifat aqaid ahl al-adyan* (The demonstration concerning the knowledge of the doctrines of the people of religion).

105 Kawthari, *Maqalat*, p. 361.

have they ears wherewith they hear?" (7:195); then he informs us that he who has no hand and no foot is like cattle.

I say, verily I wonder at that man, with all his lofty skill in the science of transmission of hadith, saying such a thing, and asserting for Allah what he vilifies the idols for not having, such as a hand that strikes and a foot that walks. He should have asserted the ear also. If he had been granted understanding, he would not have spoken thus, and he would have understood that Allah reviled the idols in comparison to their worshippers (i.e. not to Him). The meaning is, You have hands and feet, how then do you worship what lacks them both?

Ibn Aqil al-Hanbali (d. 515) said:[106]

Exalted is Allah above having an attribute which occupies space this is anthropomorphism itself! Nor is Allah divisible and in need of parts with which to do something. Does not His order and His fashioning act upon the fire? How then would He need the help of any part of Himself, or apply Himself to the fire with one of His attributes, while He is the one Who says to it: *"Be coolness and peace"* (21:69)? What idiotic belief is this, and how far remote it is from the Fashioner of the dominions and the firmaments! Allah gave them the lie in His book when He said, *"If these had been gods, they would never have gone down to it"* (21:99); how then can they think that the Creator goes down to it? Exalted is Allah above the ignorant pretenses of the *mujassima!"*[107]

These, then, are the sources for Ibn Taymiyya's stand on ascribing a body and a direction to the Creator. As seen above, these sources have little to do with the established position of Imam Ahmad on the same issues. On the contrary, it is certain that Imam Ahmad irrevocably condemned the slightest ascription of a body to Allah, whether or not the speaker added, "but not like other bodies." In *Manaqib Ahmad*, al-Bayhaqi relates that Imam Ahmad said, "A person commits an act of disbelief

---

106 One of the great early authorities of the Hanbali school.
107 Ibn al-Jawzi, *Daf shubah al-tashbih* p. 172-174.

(*kufr*) if he says Allah is a body, even if he says, Allah is a body but not like other bodies." He continues:

> The expressions are taken from language and from Islam, and linguists applied "body" to a thing that has length, width, thickness, form, structure and components. The expression has not been handed down in Sharia. Therefore, it is invalid and cannot be used.[108]

Given that the correct followers of the school of law of Imam Ahmad in the 4th and 5th centuries stand firmly on the side of mainstream Islam, it should not be surprising that they would reject proponents of likening Allah to creation (*tashbih*) both then and later. Indeed, such views were contained and prevented from being disseminated until Ibn Taymiyya threw the full weight of his learning and skill behind them. In repayment for his efforts he was duly arrested more than once in his career.

1.4.15. IBN TAYMIYYA'S LITERAL REPRESENTATION OF ALLAH'S "DESCENT"

Something may be understood of the contemporary scholar's impression of Ibn Taymiyya from the *Tuhfat al-nuzzar* or "Travels" of Ibn Battuta, who relates:

> When I went to Damascus there was a man called Ibn Taymiyya speaking about religious science, but there was something strange in his mind . . . One day he was giving the Friday sermon and he said, "Our Lord descends to the nearest heaven thus," then he went down two steps on the minbar and he said "like my descending" (*ka nuzuli hadha*).

This well-known incident is confirmed both internally through Ibn Taymiyya's own writings, and externally as related in Ibn Hajar's *Durar*:

> (Najm al-Din Sulayman ibn Abd al-Qawi) al-Tufi (al-Hanbali) said, 'They ascertained that he had blurt-

---

108 al-Bayhaqi, *Manaqib Ahmad*. Unpublished manuscript.

ed out certain words concerning doctrine which came out of his mouth in the context of his sermons and legal decisions, and they mentioned that he had cited the hadith of Allah's descent, then climbed down two steps from the minbar and said: "Just like this descent of mine" and he was categorized as an anthropomorphist."[109]

Ibn Taymiyya's conception of Allah's bodily descent is also stated in his own writings, as in the following excerpt, written in refutation of Imam al-Razi, who was a fierce enemy of the Karramiyya and other anthropomorphists:

> The Creator, Glorified and Exalted is He, is above the world and His being above is literal, not in the sense of dignity or rank. It may be said of the precedence of a certain object over another that it is with respect to dignity or rank, or that it is with respect to location. For example, respectively, the precedence of the learned over the ignorant and the precedence of the imam over the one praying behind him. Allah's precedence over the world is not like that, rather, it is a literal precedence (i.e. in time). Similarly the elevation above the world could be said to be with respect to dignity or rank, as for example when it said that the learned is above the ignorant. But Allah's elevation over the world is not like that, rather He is elevated over it literally (i.e. in space). And this is the known elevation and the known precedence.[110]

It should be clear that the above in no way represents the position of Imam Ahmad or his school. As Ibn al-Jawzi reported in his *Daf shubah al-tashbih*: Ali ibn Muhammad ibn Umar al-Dabbas related to us that Rizq Allah ibn Abd al-Wahhab al-Tamimi said: "Ahmad ibn Hanbal did not attribute a direction to the Creator."[111]

1.4.16. IBN TAYMIYYA COMPARES ALLAH TO THE MOON

In his infamous *Aqida wasitiyya*, Ibn Taymiyya establishes

109 Ibn Hajar, *al-Durar* 1:153.
110 Ibn Taymiyya, *al-Tasis al-radd ala asas al-taqdis* 1:111.
111 Ibn al-Jawzi, *Daf shubah al-tashbih* p. 135.

a clear-cut case of *tamthil*, or similitude, for Allah and His attributes by comparing Him to the moon in his interpretation of the verse 57:4, *"He is with you wherever you are"*:

> The phrase "and He is with you" does not mean that He blends into creation ... Nay the moon ... one of the smallest of Allah's creations, is both placed in the heaven (*mawduun fi al-samaa*) and present with the traveler and the non-traveler wherever they may be. And the Exalted is above (*fawq*) the Throne, as a watchful guardian of His creatures and their protector Who is cognizant of them.[112]

Ibn Taymiyya's admirers may claim that he represents the Sunni doctrine, but all know that none of the Sunnis ever compared Allah to the moon, or Allah's knowledge to the moon's rays. Exalted is Allah high above the fancies of those who offer such parallels for Him. Today we still find the same type of aberration passing for Islamic education. For example, in books like Ibn al-Uthaymin's *Sharh al-aqida al-wasitiyya* (addressed below). The author, dissatisfied with Ibn Taymiyya's moon, turns to comparing Allah to the sun instead.

As a consequence for having taken such strange positions, Ibn Taymiyya was imprisoned by agreement of the Muslim scholars of Egypt and Syria, who wished to prevent the dissemination of his ideas. His imprisonment, it should be stressed, came as a result of the consensus of the scholars of his time and not, as it is claimed by his admirers, a massive conspiracy against him. He was not jailed by a tyrannical ruler, nor was he jailed due to the jealousy of his contemporaries, as is supposed today by those who claim to follow his teachings. It is feared that the authorities made him something of a martyr instead, and stimulated interest in his otherwise pedestrian observations on Divine attributes. More of Ibn Taymiyya's deviations are discussed further below. Let us close this section with a recapitulation of Ibn Taymiyya's deviations and his unmitigated condemnation by al-Haytami.

---

112 Ibn Taymiyya, *al-Aqida al-wasitiyya Salafiyya*, ed. 1346 / 1927, p. 20.

1.4.17. IBN HAJAR AL-HAYTAMI'S SCATHING CONDEMNATION OF IBN TAYMIYYA

Shaykh al-Islam Ahmad ibn Muhammad Abu al-Abbas Shihab al-Din al-Haytami, known as Ibn Hajar al-Haytami (909-974/ 1504-1567), was the Shafii Imam of his time. He was a brilliant scholar of in-depth applications of Sharia, and represents, with Imam Ahmad al-Ramli, the foremost resource for legal opinion (*fatwa*) in the entire late Shafii school. Al-Haytami was educated at al-Azhar, but later moved to Makka, where he authored major works in Shafii jurisprudence, hadith, tenets of faith, education, hadith commentary, and formal legal opinion. His most famous works include: *Tuhfat al-muhtaj bi sharh al-minhaj* (The gift of him in need, an explanation of "the road"); a commentary on Nawawi's *Minhaj al-tal-ibin* (The seeker's road), whose ten volumes represent a high point in Shafii scholarship; the four-volume *al-Fatawa al-kubra al-fiqhiyya* (The major collection of legal opinions); and *al-Zawajir al-iqtiraf al-kabair* (Deterrents from committing enormities). This last work, with its detailed presentation of evidence from the Quran and hadith and masterful legal inferences, remains unique among Muslim works treating fear of Allah (*taqwa*) and is even recognized by Hanafi scholars like Ibn Abidin as a source of authoritative legal texts (*nusus*) that are valid in their own school.[113]

He writes in his *Fatawa hadithiyya*:

> Ibn Taymiyya is a slave who Allah has forsaken and misguided and blinded and deafened and debased. That is the declaration of the imams who have exposed the corruption of his positions and the mendacity of his sayings. Whoever wishes to pursue this must read the words of the *mujtahid* imam Abu al-Hasan (Taqi al-Din) al-Subki, of his son Taj al-Din Subki, of the Imam al-Izz ibn Jamaa and others of the Shafii, Maliki, and Hanafi shaykhs . . .
>
> In short, his words are not given any importance whatsoever; rather they are thrown aside into every wasteland and rocky ground, and it must be considered that he is a misguided and misguiding innovator

---

113 Very slightly adapted from Nuh Keller's biographical notice on Haytami in his *Reliance of the Traveller* p. 1054.

(*mubtadi dall mudill*) and an ignorant who brought evil (*jahilun ghalun*) whom Allah treated with His justice, and may He protect us from the likes of his path, doctrine, and actions, *Amin* . . .

Know that he has differed from people on questions about which Taj al-Din al-Subki and others warned us. Among the things Ibn Taymiyya said which violate the scholarly consensus are:

• He who violates the consensus commits neither disbelief (*kufr*) nor transgression (*fisq*).

• Our Lord is subject to created events (*mahallun li al-hawadith*) glorified, exalted, and sanctified is He far above what the wrong-doers and rejecters ascribe to Him!

• He is complex or made of parts (*murakkab*), His Essence standing in need similarly to the way the whole stands in need of the parts (*taftaqiru dhatuhu iftiqara al-kulli li al-juz*), elevated is He and sanctified above that!

• The Quran is created in Allah's Essence (*muhdath fi dhatillah*),[114] elevated is He above that!

• The world (*al-alam*) is of a pre-eternal nature (*qadim bi al-naw*) and that it existed with Allah from pre-eternity (*wa lam yazal ma Allah*) as an everlasting created object (*makhluqan daiman*), thus making it necessarily existent in His Essence (*fa jaalahu mujaban bi al-dhat*) and not acting deliberately (*la failan bi al-ikhtyar*), elevated is He above that![115]

• Sayings about Allah's "corporeality," "direction," "displacement," (*al-jismiyya wa al-jiha wa al-intiqal*), and that He fits the size of the Throne, being neither bigger nor smaller, exalted is He from such a hideous invention and wide-open disbelief (*kufr*), and may He forsake all his followers, and may all his beliefs be scattered and lost!

• Saying that the fire shall go out (*al-nar tafni*)[116]

• Saying that the prophets are not free from sin (*al-anbiyaa ghayru masumin*),[117]

---

114 The Jahmis believed that the Quran was created.

115 These are of the crassest expressions of *kalam* and speculation in which one could possibly indulge.

116 This was refuted by Sanani in *Raf al-astar*.

117 This is a logical corollary of his belief that contradicting the *ijma* on matters of belief and law is neither *kufr* nor *fisq*.

• Saying that the Prophet (☀) has no particular status before Allah (*la jaha lahu*)[118] and must not be used as a means (*la yutawassalu bihi*),[119]

• Saying that the undertaking of travel (*al-safar*) to him in order to perform his visit (*al-ziyara*) is a disobedience (*masiya*) in which it is unlawful to shorten the prayers,[120] and that it is forbidden to ask for his intercession in view of the Day of Need,

• Saying that the words (*alfaz*) of the Torah and the Gospel were not substituted, but their meanings (*maani*) were.

Some said, "Whoever looks at his books does not attribute to him most of these positions, except that whereby he holds the view that Allah has a direction, and that he authored a book to establish this, and forces the proof upon the people who follow this school of thought that they are believers in Allah's corporeality (*jismiyya*), dimensionality (*muhadhat*), and settledness (*istiqrar*)." That is, it may be that at times he used to assert these proofs and that they were consequently attributed to him in particular. But whoever attributed this to him from among the imams of Islam upon whose greatness, leadership, religion, trustworthiness, fairness, acceptance, insight, and meticulousness there is agreement - then they do not say anything except what has been duly established with added precautions and repeated inquiry. This is especially true when a Muslim is attributed a view which necessitates his disbelief, apostasy, misguidance, and execution. Therefore if it is true of him that he is a disbeliever and an innovator, then Allah will deal with him with His justice, and other than that He will forgive us and him.[121]

---

118 A reference to Ibn Taymiyya's manner of answering questions specific to the Prophet with generalities about all human beings.

119 The scholars' refutation of this heresy innovated by Ibn Taymiyya is detailed in the second volume of the present work.

120 Ibn Hajar says in *Fath al-bari* (1993 ed. 3:66) about Ibn Taymiyya's prohibition to travel in order to visit the Prophet: "This is one of the ugliest matters ever reported from Ibn Taymiyya." Yet even today the "Salafi" scholar Bin Baz persists in saying that it is forbidden to travel with the intention of visiting the Prophet and comments that this was not an ugly but a correct thing for Ibn Taymiyya to say!

121 Ibn Hajar al-Haytami al-Makki's *Fatawa hadithiyya* (Cairo: Halabi, 1390/1970) p. 114-117.

2. Mainstream Islam's Method Toward the Divine Attributes

It should, by now, be sufficiently clear in what way Ibn Taymiyya deviated from the doctrine of the mainstream. Thus it is unjustified for him and those who follow his ideas to be properly described as "Salafi." This section highlights the method of the true Salaf with regard to interpreting ambiguous verses of the Quran, and how the Khalaf, or scholars of later generations, applied the Salaf method to satisfy the needs of their times. The Khalaf expanded the details of the Salaf method but retained its priorities, preserving the paramount belief that there is nothing like Allah whatsoever. Present-day "Salafis" attack the Khalaf and insist that present-day scholars should keep to the way of the Salaf. However, the "Salafis" are closer in spirit to those whom the Salaf and Khalaf fought, namely, the anthropomorphists.

As stated earlier, the arbitrary reading of texts that admit some uncertainty regarding their interpretation is common to all groups of innovators. There are, in fact, two types of verses in the Quran. On the one hand, there are verses called *muhkamat*, which convey firm and unequivocal meaning. On the other hand, there are the *mutashabihat*, which are less clear in their meaning. It is in the attempt to interpret the latter that innovators come to the fore.

2.1. The Ambiguities (*MUTASHABIHAT*) In the Quran and Hadith

Let us begin with the definition of the word *mutashabih*. A verse or a hadith is called *mutashabih* if: it has more than one meaning in Arabic, and its meaning or interpretation is not explicit.

The *muhkam* is a verse that has one explicit meaning. An example of the *mutashabih* is the verse: *al-rahmanu ala al-arsh istawa*. (20:5). This is sometimes translated as *"The Merciful is established on the Throne,"* but the word *istawa* has over fifteen meanings in Arabic, including:

1 To settle (*istaqarra*), as in verse 11:44: *"And the ship came to rest (istawat) upon al-Judi."* The anthropomorphists apply this to verse 20:5, as stated by Ibn Battal and Abu Bakr Ibn al-Arabi.[1]

2 To ascend or rise (*irtafaa*). Al-Baghawi says that this is the meaning of 20:5, according to Ibn Abbas and most of the commentators of Quran.[2]

3 To rise above or tower above (*ala*). This is the meaning given by Mujahid for 20:5 in *Sahih al-Bukhari*, and Ibn Battal declares it to be "the true position and saying of Sunnis."[3]

4 To be steadfast, as in verse 48:29, *"And it stands firm (istawa) upon its stalk."*

5 To attain maturity, as in verse 28:14, *"And when he reached his full strength and was ripe (istawa)."*

6 To subdue (*qahara*), conquer (*istawla*), and prevail or overcome (*ghalaba*), as in the poet's saying concerning Bishr ibn Marwan's conquest of Iraq: *istawa bishrun ala al-iraq* .

On his boasting: *idha ma alawna wa istawayna alayhim jaalnahum mara li nisrin wa tairin:* When we tower over them

---

1 Ibn Hajar, *Fath al-bari* (Beirut 1989 ed.) 13:500; Ibn al-Arabi, *Aridat al-ahwadhi* 2:236.

2 Ibn Hajar, *Fath al-bari* 13:500. *"Tawhid"* ch. 22.

3 *Sahih Bukhari*, *"Tawhid"* ch. 22, title; Ibn Hajar, *op. cit.*

and overcome them, we shall make them a pasture for eagles and other birds. Ibn Battal and Abu Mansur al-Baghdadi attribute the interpretation of 20:5 *as istawla* chiefly to the Mutazila.[4]

7 To mount (*saida*), as in verse 23:28, "*And when you are on board (istawayta) the ship*" and 43:13, "*That they may mount (li yastawu) upon their backs.*" With regard to 20:5 this is worse than *istaqarra*.

8 To attain the end-point of an act like growth, as in verse 28:14 already cited, or like creation (*intiha khalqihi ilayh*), as in verse 41:11, "*Then turned He to the heaven when it was smoke.*" This is the interpretation of Ibn Hazm, who explains *istiwa* as "an act pertaining to the Throne, and that is the termination of His creation at the Throne, for there is nothing beyond it."[5]

"To rise," "ascend," and "rise above" must be understood in the sense of rank and lordship, not in the sense of physical elevation or displacement. Among the most befitting meanings of verse 20:5 are also "subdue" (*qahara*) and "conquer" (*istawla*). By this it is understood that Allah praises Himself as the Irresistible (*al-qahhar*) and declares that even the greatest of all creations, the Throne, lies subject to Him. This in no way suggests, as one objection goes, that subduing and conquering infer prior opposition before the Creator; no more than do the attributes of Irresistible (*qahhar*) or Omnipotent (*qahir*) presuppose any resistance or power on anyone's part. This is confirmed by the verses, "*He is the Omnipotent (qahir) over His slaves,*" (6:18, 6:61) and, "*Allah prevails (ghalib) in His purpose*" (12:21). To those who object to *istawla* on the grounds that it supposes prior opposition, Ibn Hajar remarked that the objection is invalidated by the verse, "*Allah was ever Knower, Wise*" (4:17), which the commentators, he says, have explained to mean "He is ever Knower and Wise."[6]

One never tires of saying, "*There is nothing like Him whatsoever*" (42:11). The best explanation of any verse is its

---

4 Ibn Hajar, *op. cit.*; al-Baghdadi, *Usul al-din* (Istanbul: Dar al-funun fi madrasat al-ilahiyyat, 1928) p. 112.

5 Ibn Hazm, *al-Fasl fi al-milal wa al-ahwa wa al-nihal* 2:125.

6 Ibn Hajar, *op. cit.*

recitation; leaving it as it was revealed and unexplained. This was the way of Malik, al-Shafii, al-Awzai, Ahmad, and the rest of the Salaf with regard to this verse. However, due to the influence of those who have continued to impose physical limitations on the Creator since the time of the Salaf, it has been and still is an obligation of Muslims to clarify the ambiguities that may otherwise be used to lead believers astray. This has been the position of mainstream scholars since Bukhari, al-Khattabi, Ibn Battal, and Ibn al-Jawzi, through the time of Nawawi, Subki, and Ibn Hajar, as the present book abundantly makes clear.

2.2. THE METHOD OF THE TRUE SALAF REGARDING AMBIGUITIES

The scholars of the true Salaf—that is, the pious Muslims in the first three centuries after the Hijra—used to interpret the *mutashabihat* in the following way. They refuted the unacceptable interpretations, but did not specify which one of the acceptable meanings was the true meaning of the verse or hadith.

When Imam Malik, al-Shafii, and others were asked about the interpretation of the verse: *al-rahman ala al-arsh istawa* and other verses, they used to say, "Accept these verses and hadith as they were given without believing that they have meanings which pertain to a manner, such as images, descriptions related to creations, and the like." Imam Ahmad Ibn Hanbal said, "Allah mentioned Establishment (*al-istiwa*), and Establishment is only what Allah mentioned about it, not what humans imagine about it." From these quotations it is clear that the Salaf, including Imam Ahmad, rejected any meanings that implied a mode or manner (*kayf*) of "establishment," because specifying the manner implies a resemblance to created things.

Thus it is seen that the way of the Salaf was to simply accept expressions based on faith, and to not question how they are meant, not add, subtract, or substitute potential synonyms, and to stress Allah's absolute transcendence beyond the characteristics of created things. To suggest that they added the terms "sitting," "in person" (*bi al-dhat*), "sitting in person," or "literally" (*haqiqatan*), is to deny their insistence on rejecting the *kayf* of Allah's establishment.

When expressing their opinions on this subject, "Salafis" are fond of quoting not the *bila kayf* (no-modality) opinions of the great Imams, but that of the anthropomorphists who opposed them. Some of them have already been mentioned, like the Hanbalis Abu Yala and al-Zaghuni condemned by Ibn al-Jawzi, and the Hanbalis Abdullah ibn Ahmad, Ibn Said al-Darimi, and Ibn Khuzayma, who were denounced by al-Razi and Kawthari. As said before, their assertion that the only alternative to the Jahmi belief that "Allah is in every place" is that "He is in one place only, above His throne," is just as false as saying, "He is in every place, for Allah exists without place." Yet, the belief that He exists in a place is what anthropomorphists of yesterday and today pass as having been the opinion of the Salaf. However, just because someone lived in the first three centuries does not mean that he represented the doctrine of the Salaf. It will be clear from the opinions of the Salaf and Khalaf, noted below, that the mainstream Islamic position never adds "in person" or "literally" to the mention of Allah's establishment on the Throne. To do so would be to specify a modality, to suggest space, and thus to leave Islam.

2.3. The Methodology of the Khalaf

The Khalaf scholars are those who came in succeeding generations after those of the first three Hijri centuries. They are named for their successorship of the inheritance of the Prophet (ﷺ), having acquired the knowledge and understanding of religion. An example of their method is in the interpretation of the verse: *yad Allahi fawqa aydihim* (48:10) "*Allah's Hand is over their hands.*"

Khalaf scholars usually offer an explicit meaning to such verses. This is acceptable insofar as there is a fear that people will otherwise interpret such verses anthropomorphically, likening Allah to his creations (*tashbih*) and speaking of His "Hand" as a literal (*haqiqi*) attribute in the manner of Ibn Taymiyya, Ibn Qayyim, and the early Hanbali anthropomorphists discredited by Ibn al-Jawzi. Thus the Khalaf scholars here explain the words: *yad Allah* (Allah's hand) in this verse as referring to *ahd Allah*; that is, "the Covenant with Allah." Similarly, in the verse: *lima khalaktu bi yadayy*, which is literally "for what I created with My two Hands," they interpreted the word *yadayy* (Allah's two hands) as "care" (*al-inaya*).

The explanation of this word in other verses confirms the above meanings. The scholars have pointed out that, among the Arabs, *al-yad* also signifies strength (*al-quwwa*). The verse, "*We have built the heaven with (Our) hands*" (51:47) is cited in al-Hafiz al-Zabidi's massive dictionary of Arabic as an illustration that "hands" may mean "strength."[7] Allah says, "*And make mention of our bondmen, Abraham, Isaac and Jacob, men of parts (literally of two hands) and vision*" (38:45), meaning "men possessing strength." The word also means ownership (*al-mulk*), as Allah said, "*Lo! The bounty is in Allah's hand*" (3:73). It also means favor, as it is said, "So-and-so has a hand over so-and-so," to mean that he owes him a favor. It also means a kind of link, as Allah said, "*Or he agrees to forego it in whose hand is the marriage tie*" (2:237).

As Nawawi said in a passage already quoted from his commentary on Muslim, that many of the Salaf applied similar figurative interpretation (*tawil*) of Allah's "Hand." This is shown in the explanation of *aydin* (Hands) as meaning "strength" in the verse: "*We have built the heaven with (Our) hands*" (51:47).

Ibn Jarir al-Tabari said in his *Tafsir* that Ibn Abbas said, "It means, with strength." He reports an identical position from Mujahid, Qatada, Mansur, Ibn Zayd, and Sufyan al-Thawri.[8] This is also Imam al-Ashari's explanation, according to Ibn Furak, in his recension of Ashari's school.[9]

These interpretations are all acceptable and do not imply the slightest denial of any of Allah's Attributes, about which there is consensus. It is obligatory to believe, however, that the word *yad* (hand) does not mean an organ as we know it, in accordance with the verse already cited, "*There is nothing like Him whatsoever*" (42:11), and that the word *yad* does not imply a resemblance to creatures.

If the Prophet's saying, "The Black Stone is Allah's right

7 *Taj al-arus* (10:417).
8 Ibn Jarir al-Tabari, *Tafsir* 7:27.
9 Abu Bakr ibn Furak, *Mujarrad maqalat al-Ashari* (Beirut, 1987) p. 44.

hand," is established as true, the mind witnesses that Allah is not spatially confined anywhere and is not divisible. The senses witness that the Black Stone is not literally the right hand of Allah; rather, it is seen that it consists in prosperity and blessing.[10] Yet the excesses of the anthropomorphists are at work here also. Ibn Rajab relates[11] that Ibn al-Faus al-Hanbali gave the hadith a literal meaning; "He used to say, 'The Black Stone is Allah's Right Hand,' literally (*haqiqatan*)."[12] Ashari's biographer, Abu Bakr ibn Furak, writes that he embarked on a study of *kalam* (theology) because of this hadith.[13]

2.4. AL-KHATTABI ON THE PRIORITY OF AVOIDING LIKENING ALLAH TO HIS CREATION (*TASHBIH*)

As shown in the excerpts of Nawawi and Subki concerning the avoidance of, and the recourse to, figurative interpretation among both the Salaf and the Khalaf, the priority was to repel false understandings and prevent the pitfall of attributing to Allah the characteristics of creation. Again and again, the paradigm that is the entire foundation for understanding Allah and His attributes is, *"There is nothing like Him whatsoever."* This paradigm becomes even more essential, if such a thing is possible, in times when there is an increase in heretical views. The great hafiz Abu Sulayman al-Khattabi (d. 386) addresses this priority in clear and direct terms in his Commentary on Abu Dawud's *Sunan*:

> Abu Ubayd (d. 222)[14] used to say, "As for us we narrate those hadiths but we do not smear them with meanings." Abu Sulayman says, "It is even more relevant for us not to be forward in that from which those who have more knowledge, antiquity, and seniority than us stood back."

10 This hadith on the authority of Ibn Abbas and others is related by Ibn Abi Umar al-Madani in his *Musnad*, Tabarani, Suyuti in his *Jami al-saghir* 1:516 (#3804-3805), Ibn Asakir in *Tarikh Dimashq* 15:90, 92, and others. It is considered *daif* (weak) by Ibn al-Jawzi, Ibn Adi, and Albani. Ibn Qutayba in *Gharib al-hadith* (3:107(1)) says that it is a saying of Ibn Abbas.

11 Ibn Rajab, in *Dhayl tabaqat al-hanabila*.

12 *Ibid*. 7:174-175.

13 al-Subki, *Tabaqat al-shafiiyya* 3:53.

14 Abu Ubayd al-Qasim ibn Sallam.

However, the people of the time in which we live have joined two parties. The first [the Mutazila and Jahmiyya] altogether disavow this kind of hadith and declare them forged to begin with, which implies their giving the lie to the scholars who have narrated them, that is, the imams of our religion and the transmitters of the prophetic ways, and the intermediaries between us and Allah's Messenger. The second party [the Mushabbiha] gives its assent to the narrations and applies their outward meanings literally in a way bordering anthropomorphism.

As for us we steer clear from both views, and accept neither as our school. It is therefore incumbent upon us to seek for these hadiths, when they are cited and established as authentic from the perspectives of transmission and attribution, an interpretation (*tawil*) extracted according to the known meanings of the foundations of the religion and the schools of the scholars, without rejecting the narrations to begin with, as long as their chains are acceptable and narrators trustworthy.[15]

2.5. AL-IZZ IBN ABD AL-SALAM ON THE OBLIGATION OF RESORTING TO FIGURATIVE INTERPRETATION TO REFUTE INNOVATION

Shaykh al-Islam Izz al-Din Abd al-Aziz ibn Abd al-Salam al-Sulami al-Shafii (578-660) gave the following edict concerning interpretation of the divine Attributes:

Q. What is the meaning of the Prophet's saying, "The heart of the believer is between two fingers of the Merciful, He turns it over as He wishes?"[16] Does one contravene his obligation if he says, "I do not say anything concerning the verses and the hadiths on the attributes. Rather I hold the same belief concerning them as the Pious Salaf held. To speak about them is an innovation (*bida*), and I let them pass according to their external sense," or is interpretation necessary?

A. The meaning of the Prophet's saying, "The heart of the believer is between two fingers of the

15 Al-Khattabi, *Maalim al-sunan ala sunan Abi Dawud* (Hims ed.) 5:95. Cited in al-Buti, *al-Salafiyya marhalatun zamaniyyatun mubarakatun la madhhabun islami* (Damascus: Dar al-fikr, 1408/1988) p. 140.

16 Muslim (#2654), Ahmad (2:168), Ajurri, Sharia (p. 316).

Merciful," is that Allah exerts His custody of it with His power and determination as He wills, changing it from disbelief to belief and from obedience to disobedience, or the reverse.

It is like His saying, *"Blessed is He in Whose hand is the sovereignty"* (67:1) and, *"O Prophet! Say unto those captives who are in your hands"* (8:70). It is understood that the captives were not left in the physical hands of the Muslims but that they were subdued and conquered by them. The same applies to the expressions, "Specific and non-specific matters are in the hand of so-and-so," and "The slaves and the animals are in the hand of so-and-so." It is understood that all these mean that they are in his control (*istila*) and disposal and not in his physical hand. Similarly, Allah's saying, *"Or he agrees to forgo it in whose hand is the marriage tie"* (2:237). The marriage tie is not in his physical hand, but the hand is only an expression of his empowerment and his ability to dispose of the matter.

For one to say, "I believe in this matter what the Salaf believed" is a lie. How does he believe what he has no idea about, and the meaning of which he does not know?

Nor is speaking about the meaning a reprehensible innovation, but rather an excellent, obligatory innovation (*bida hasana wajiba*) (in cases where something dubious appears). The only reason the Salaf kept from such discourse is that in their time no-one construed the words of Allah and those of His Prophet (ﷺ) to mean what it is not permissible to construe them to mean. If any such dubiousness had appeared in their time they would have shown it to be a lie and rejected it strenuously. Thus did the Companions and the Salaf refute the Qadariyya when the latter brought out their innovation, although they did not use to address such matters before the Qadariyya appeared on the scene. Nor did they reply to the individuals who mentioned them. Nor did any of the Companions relate any of it from the Prophet (ﷺ) since there was no need for it. And Allah knows best."[17]

---

17 al-Izz ibn Abd al-Salam, *Fatawa*, ed. Abd al-Rahman ibn Abd al-Fattah (Beirut: Dar al-marifa,1406/1986) 55-57.

2.6. Al-Buti's Recapitulation of the Two Methods: The Non-Specific Figurative Interpretation of the Salaf, the Specific Figurative Interpretation of the Khalaf, and the Impermissibility of Imposing One Over the Other

In his landmark study of the "Salafi" innovation, Dr. Muhammad Said Ramadan al-Buti recapitulates the essential similarity of the methods of the Salaf and Khalaf, and reiterates that they are both centered in the priority of Allah's transcendence.[18] He shows that both the Salaf and the Khalaf applied figurative interpretation, but while the Salaf applied an implicit, non-specific form of figurative interpretation that he calls *tawil ijmali*, the Khalaf applied an explicit, specific form that he calls *tawil tafsili*.

We have already shown that the consensus in place regarding these texts is the refraining from applying to them any meaning which establishes a sameness or likeness between Allah and His creatures, and the refraining from divesting their established lexical tenor.

The obligatory way to proceed is either to explain these words according to their external meanings which conform with Allah's transcendence above any like or partner, and this includes not explaining them as bodily appendages and other corporeal imagery. Therefore it will be said, for example: He has established Himself over the Throne as He has said, with an establishment which befits His Majesty and Oneness; and He has a hand as He has said, which befits His Divinity and Majesty; etc.

Or they can be explained figuratively according to the correct rules of language and in conformity with the customs of speech in their historical context. For example: the establishment is the conquering (*istila*) and dominion (*tasallut*), Allah's

---

18 Muhammad Said Ramadan al-Buti, *al-Salafiyya marhalatun zamaniyyatun mubarakatun la madhhabun islami* (The Salafiyya is a blessed historical period, not a school of law in Islam).

hand means His strength in His saying: *"Allah's hand is over their hand"* (48:10) and His generosity in His saying, *"Nay, both His hands are spread wide, and He bestows as He wills"* (5:64).[19]

Now, to proceed to any one of these two types of commentary is not devoid of interpretation (*tawil*) in either case. However, the first type of commentary is a non-specific interpretation, while the second is a specific interpretation.

In the case of the first type of commentary, it is plain to see that the lexical meaning of the hand, face, and eye, is not other than the familiar bodily organs and appendages used by all creatures. Such a meaning is negated for Allah's Essence in all cases and in both types of commentary. This is the non-specific interpretation. This is what they express when they say, "He has a hand which befits His majesty as He has said, and eyes which befit His majesty, as He has said."

But is it obligatory to stop at this non-specific point of interpretation, as most of the Salaf have tended to do, or is it allowed to go beyond non-specific interpretation and treat aspects of the metaphors, figurative meanings, and other usages which are found in abundance in Allah's book and the hadith of His Prophet (ﷺ)?

The way that we advocate and have made known does not demand from the Muslim researcher a preference for either one of these two methods. What is important is to not attribute to Allah a bodily appendage in the process of your understanding of the word "hand" which He has attributed to Himself, and to not divest of its meaning the lexical evidence established by Allah's own speech in your desire to assert His transcendence, and to steer clear of the perils of worshipping another together with Him.

This is the belief in which those who stubbornly claim the name of "Salafi" for themselves differ with us, substituting their purported affiliation with the pious Salaf, to the method (*manhaj*) upon whose perfection in every single doctrinal principle and juridical method there is complete and general agreement. The bases of their arguments against us are, first, that the Salaf of this Community, who are the best of Muslims,

---

19 Ibn al-Jawzi interpreted the former verse as Allah's favor (*nima*) and power (*qudra*), and the latter, according to Hasan al-Basri, as His kindness and goodness. Ibn al-Jawzi, *Daf shubah al-tahsbih* p. 115.

showed no tendency for specific interpretation whatsoever, nor added anything beyond what Allah established for Himself in the texts, together with His transcendence above all that does not befit His lordship and divinity and loftiness above any kind of partner or rival. The second argument they use against us is that any inroad one makes into the words whose lexical sense Allah has linked to Himself, any probing of their import as figures, or metaphors, or similitudes, is necessarily, in one way or another, a form of divestiture (*tatil*)!

We say, relying upon Allah for our success, that we consider neither one of the above two "arguments" binding upon us, for they are both unacceptable and inapplicable, and, in addition, they are not real, even though they may imagine them to be so. It is not true that none of the Salaf tended to apply specific interpretation in commenting on the verses of the divine attributes. Even if we were to suppose hypothetically that that were true, it is not true that interpreting these attributes in conformity with the principles of religion, the rules of the Arabic language, and in accordance with their Quranic contexts, constitutes a form of divestiture.

In refutation of their first claim we say, we know that countless numbers of the actual Salaf of this Community (the Muslims of the first three centuries, whom the Prophet (ﷺ) himself said were the best of all people), applied specific interpretation in commenting upon the verses of the attributes and the hadiths related to them—the same kind of interpretation which displeases those who call themselves "Salafis" today. Examples:

• Imam Ahmad's authentic interpretation of Allah's coming in the verse "*And thy Lord shall come with angels, rank on rank*" (89:22) as referring to the coming of His order (*amr*) according to the verse, "*Wait they aught save that thy Lord's command (amr) should come to pass?*" (16:32)[20]

• The Prophet's saying, "Allah smiled/laughed last night at the good deed of both of you . . ." which is part of a longer hadith about the Ansari who hosted a guest of the Prophet's while he himself remained hungry with his wife. Bukhari and Muslim extracted it through various chains. Al-Bukhari

---

20 The full bibliographic references are given below.

interpreted Allah's smile or laughter as His mercy, and he did not stop and content himself to say, "Let it pass without asking how."[21]

• Bayhaqi in his *al-Asma wa al-sifat* related Hammad ibn Zayd's interpretation of Allah's descent to the nearest heaven, in the hadiths of descent, as His drawing near to His servants.[22]

• Ibn Taymiyya related Jafar al-Sadiq's interpretation of Allah's "face" in His saying, *"Everything will perish save His face"* (28:88) as meaning religion; and al-Dahhak's interpretation of the face in the same verse as meaning: Allah's essence, paradise, the fire, and the Throne. As for Ibn Taymiyya himself, he interprets the face as meaning direction (*jiha*), so that the meaning would be for him: Everything will perish save that by which Allah's direction is sought. Then he adds, "This is what the vast majority of the Salaf have said."[23]

• Al-Bayhaqi relates that al-Muzani reported from al-Shafii the following commentary on the verse, *"To Allah belong the East and the West, and wheresoever you turn, there is Allah's face"* (2:115): "It means—and Allah knows best—there is the face towards which Allah has directed you." Bayhaqi continues, "The *hafiz* Abu Abd Allah and the *hafiz* al-Qadi Abu Bakr ibn al-Arabi have related to us . . . from Mujahid that he said regarding this verse, 'It means Allah's *qibla*, therefore wheresoever you may be, East and West, do not turn your faces except towards it.'"[24]

Ibn Hajar in *Fath al-bari* and al-Baghawi in his *Tafsir* related that Abd Allah ibn Abbas and the majority of the commentators have interpreted *istawa* in Allah's saying *"The Merciful is established on the Throne"* (20:4) as meaning He rose above it (*irtafaa*). Similar to it is what Ibn Hajar related

21 Bukhari ("Tafsir Surah 59" and *Manaqib al-ansar* Ch. 10 #3798) and Bayhaqi in *Shuab al-iman* (3:259 #3478) have: "Allah wondered (*ajiba*) or laughed/smiled (*dahika*)"; Muslim (Ashriba Ch. 32 #172-173): "Allah wondered"; Ibn Abi al-Dunya and Bayhaqi in the *Sunan*: "Allah laughed/smiled."

22 Bayhaqi, *al-Asma wa al-sifat* p. 456. Ibn al-Jawzi spoke to this effect in his *Daf shubah al-tashbih* (p. 196): "Since you understand that the one who descends towards you is near to you, content yourself with the knowledge that he is near you, and do not think in terms of bodily nearness."

23 Ibn Taymiyya, *Majmuat al-fatawa* 2:428.

24 Bayhaqi, *al-Asma wa al-sifat* p. 309.

in his long commentary on that verse, from Ibn Battal: "The commentary on *istawa* as meaning He towers above it (*ala*) is correct and the true position and the saying of Sunnis."[25]

Those are some of the Attributes of Names and the Attributes of Action that have been mentioned in the Book of Allah and in the authentic *sunna* of the Prophet (ﷺ) and interpreted specifically by many of the men of the Salaf in detail. They did not stop at the general interpretation which is expressed in their saying, "Take their outward meaning without how." Numerous other examples of what we have mentioned can be found in books such as in Bayhaqi's *al-Asma wa al-sifat*, al-Khattabi's *Maalim al-sunan*, al-Baghawi's *Tafsir*, and other references.

Perhaps what you have seen of Ibn Taymiyya's doing in searching for an acceptable interpretation for Allah's "Face" in His saying, *"All that is on it will perish, but the face of thy Lord full of Majesty, Bounty and Honor will abide"* (44:26-27) should put an end to all misconceptions and cut off the source of all arguments and differences in this subject, since he is the one who heaps criticism on the Khalaf for their interpretation of such verses. We reject the double standard of those who are looking to excuse away Ibn Taymiyya's clear case of interpretation or give it a preference or a special right over others, claiming, "The face in that verse does not neccessarily refer to an attribute, and therefore such interpretation is different from other interpretations, therefore there is nothing wrong with plunging into this form of figurative interpretation (*tawil*)."

We say, this kind of talk is unacceptable for it is a manipulation of the meaning of *tawil*. What made the *wajh* "not neccessarily refer to one of the attributes" is precisely the *tawil* for which Ibn Taymiyya has allowed us to open the door. Were it not for such *tawil* which is being investigated here, it would not have occurred to anyone's mind that the face is anything but one attribute among the other attributes of Allah's names (*asma wa al-sifat*) which Allah has asserted for His essence in the way that He wills and as befits the majesty of His face and the greatness of His sovereignty. If it were at all acceptable to rely on such an excuse (as what "Salafis" bring up for Ibn

---

25 Ibn Hajar, *Fath al-bari* 13:500 (Beirut 1989 ed.); Baghawi, *Tafsir Surah 20:4.*

Taymiyya) for interpreting the verses and hadiths of attributes, then this excuse can be used by any interpreter and it would not be allowed for Ibn Taymiyya to use it alone!

It is significant that none of the interpretations that we have transmitted from the Salaf—including the one adopted by Ibn Taymiyya for the face ("religion"), after one of the Salaf whom he has mentioned (Jafar al-Sadiq)—necessitates any divestiture of meaning (*tatil*) nor any misapplication of language and usage. On the contrary our interpretations are fully supported by the principles of doctrine and the rulings of Sharia, in full conformity with the rules of grammar and the evidence of language. No better proof illustrates all this than that adopted by Imam Ahmad in interpreting the "coming" in the verse *"And thy Lord shall come with angels, rank on rank"* (89:22) as: *"The command of thy Lord cometh,"* in the light of the verse: *"Wait they aught save that thy Lord's command (amr) should come to pass?"* (16:32). Indeed, the best commentary on the Quran is the Quran itself. This is explained in detail further down.

Let us now proceed to refute the second claim of the "Salafis" against the Sunnis, namely their saying that "forcibly interpreting any of these phrases, which Allah has asserted in their lexical sense as attributes of His essence, as figurative or metaphorical or similes, is none other than a form of divestiture (*tatil*)."

We say, the examples that we have shown are enough to discredit this claim. Indeed, the true Salaf that interpreted the texts which we have mentioned, bringing them out of their literal sense into the metaphorical, were not divesters of meaning —far be it for them to be labeled with such a name! Therefore, if there were in their interpretations any form of divestiture, or any discrepancy within viewpoints, or any misunderstanding, they would not have forwarded such interpretations in the first place.

Nevertheless, let us hypothetically set aside this kind of interpretation and suppose that it has not been said and does not exist. Let us also suppose that none of the righteous Salaf has given himself the right to assert more than what Allah

Himself has asserted of His essence, leaving all further knowledge and details to Allah. Even so: this would by no means provide a proof for the claim of "Salafis" that holding a different viewpoint than theirs is absolutely forbidden! For the refraining of the true Salaf from exerting effort (*ijtihad*) to find the meanings of these phrases or attributes may have a number of reasons.

1 Among these reasons may be their fear of probing something for which they did not consider themselves qualified, not because of ignorance or lack of knowledge, but only, in the likelier and greater number of cases, as a result of the extreme fear and awe of Allah and His majesty in their hearts.

2 Another reason would be their general circumstances and the conditions they were in, as they did not find in their surroundings anything that called them to force their way into these dangers to torment themselves over something for which there was no need.

3 Yet another reason for their lack of interest in interpretation could be the conclusion of their own *ijtihad*, which is not binding on any other than themselves. Least of all would it be binding on those who possess the scholarly wherewithal that qualifies them for investigation, and personal effort of qualified legal reasoning (*ijtihad*). We are among those who believe that the legal method or school (*madhhab*) of a Companion is not a legal proof in itself; how then could we consider that of the Successors and their Successors?

All the above causes are possible, so to consider the view of the "Salafis" as an evidence on the basis of the possibility that there might be another cause (namely, the prohibition of *tawil* and the obligation to stop at the outward meaning of these attributes while declaring Allah's transcendence and Oneness) is illogical, because this position is by now worthless and unacceptable, since it relies on a proof that is more comprehensive than what is being claimed, and it is known that speculation precludes the probative force of a conclusion.

Yet the measuring-scale that cannot be ignored in any case is the arbitration of the Arabic language in which the Book of Allah has been revealed and through the medium of which the purified *sunna* of the Prophet (ﷺ) has reached us. Such arbitration can only be achieved by applying the rules of grammar and language pertaining to what is literal, what is metaphorical, what makes figurative interpretation obligatory, and what makes it forbidden. No one is capable of applying the above unless he has a firm understanding of this language and possesses a fully matured gift of knowledge in the roots or methodology of Islamic law and the doctrines of Islam (to an extent that qualifies him for *ijtihad*), together with self-discipline proceeding from Godwariness, uprightness, and truthfulness in religion. The long hadith that Ibn Taymiyya tried to use to extract his interpretation of *wajh* (face) as *jiha* (direction), making use of language, its derivations, and the varieties of its literal and metaphorical meanings, is nothing but a practical application of this model.

This, however, is not the place to discuss Ibn Taymiyya's interpretation of *wajh* as "direction" from a linguistic standpoint or that of its Quranic meaning, nor comparing his opinion in this matter to that of those who interpreted it as Allah's Essence; this is not the point we are presently making. All we want to clarify for now is that *ijtihad* in interpreting these words complies fully with the parameters of lexical evidence and the rules pertaining to it, and falls completely within all the requirements of Islamic belief and the principles pertaining to it which are agreed upon by the Sunnis; and that such *ijtihad* is an accepted type of *ijtihad* because it evolves within the circle of the Way (*manhaj*) that is agreed upon without violating it or deviating from it in the least.

Therefore, as long as that Way is firmly adhered to, then literal conformity with the *ijtihad* of the Salaf and their views regarding the verses of the Attributes and others, is neither obligatory nor binding. For reasons and circumstances may differ between one *mujtahid* and another, in addition to the natural differences which arise between one historical period and another. This was mentioned more than once and in many occasions by such imams as Hammad bin Zayd, al-Khattabi, and al-Bayhaqi.

An illustration of what I just said was given in what Bayhaqi related from al-Khattabi, after the latter cited the hadith of Anas ibn Malik narrated by Bukhari and Muslim:

> The Gehenna will keep asking: is there more? until the Lord of Might places His *qadam* (lit. "foot") in it. Then it will say: 'Enough! Enough!' Then it will gather up its parts together. And there will still remain room in paradise until Allah gives rise to a creation which He will then place in the remainder of paradise.

After mentioning what has been said about Allah's *qadam* and *rijl* (lit. "leg") through different chains of transmission Bayhaqi said:

> Abu Sulayman al-Khattabi said: "It is likely that those who mentioned *al-qadam* and *al-rijl* without attributing it to Allah (i.e. by saying: "Allah's *qadam*" etc.) did so because of their great fear, and to avoid misinterpretation in the matter. Abu Ubayd used to say. . .[26]
>
> Abu Sulaiman said: "The meaning of the *qadam* here is possibly a reference to those whom Allah has created of old or "sent forth" for the fire in order to complete the number of its inhabitants. Everything that is "sent forth" is a *qadam*, in the same way that the verbal noun of demolishing (*hadama*) is a *hadm* or ruin, and that of seizing (*qabada*) is *qabd* or a seizure. Likewise Allah said: *"They have a sure foundation (qadam sidq) with their Lord"* (10:2) with reference to the good works which they have sent forth. This explanation has been transmitted to us from al-Hasan al-Basri.
>
> It is supported by the Prophet's saying in the aforementioned hadith: "As for Paradise, Allah will create for it a special creation." Both meanings (i.e.

---

26 See the continuation of this passage above, in the section entitled "al-Khattabi" on the Priority of Avoiding *tashbih* For Both the Salaf and the Khalaf.

respectively pertaining to the Fire and Paradise) are in agreement with the sense that Paradise and hell-fire will be provided with an additional number of dwellers to complete their respective numbers, at which point they will be full.[27]

The reader knows that al-Khattabi (d. 386) is one of the Khalaf who is closest to the Salaf and one of the most attached to them. He is one of the most distinguished scholars of mid-fourth century, and you may ponder his just and objective discourses on this topic, in which he combines his appreciation for the Salaf, his respect and acknowledgement for their merit and precedence, together with appreciation for changing times and the cropping up of unexpected situations that require the muj-tahid to act appropriately or, as he puts it: "according to the known meanings of the foundations of the religion and the schools of the scholars."

His pursuit of what the situation demands "according to the meanings of the foundations of the religion" shows clearly his agreement with those who shun *tawil* and assert what Allah has asserted about His essence without interpretation nor modality whenever there is evidence to support it and lack of evidence to support interpretation. It also shows his disagreement with them whenever there is strong evidence to prove that the meaning of the word is different from its outward sense, relying in both cases on his scholarly insight.

An example of his position in the first case is his position regarding the numerous confirmed, authentic hadiths of Allah's "descent." He says in his book *Maalim al-sunan*: "This is the kind of knowledge in the outward sense which we have been commanded to believe without attempting to uncover its inner meaning, and it belongs to the *mutashabbih* that Allah has mentioned in His book."[28]

An example of his position in the second case is what he said in his commentary on the hadith of Abu Dawud narrated by Jubayr ibn Mutam from his father from his grandfather who said:

An Arab came to Allah's Messenger and said, O

---

27 al-Khattabi, *Maalim al-sunan* (Hims ed.) 5:95.
28 al-Khattabi, *Maalim al-sunan* (Hims ed.) 5:101.

Messenger of Allah, people are in distress, the children are hungry, the crops are withered, and the animals are perishing, so Ask Allah to grant us rain, for we seek you as our intercessor with Allah, and Allah as our intercessor with you." The Prophet (ﷺ) said: "Woe to you! Do you know what you are saying?" Then the Prophet (ﷺ) declared Allah's glory and he went on until the effect of his speech showed on the faces of his Companions. He then said: "Woe to you! Allah is not to be sought as intercessor with anyone. Allah's state is greater than that. Woe to you! Do you know Allah's greatness? Verily, His Throne is on His Heavens like this" and he formed with his fingers something like a dome over him, "and it groans on account of Him like a saddle groans because of its rider." Ibn Bashshar added in his version: "Allah is above His Throne and His Throne is above His Heavens."[29]

Al-Khattabi comments:

If this discourse is taken in its outward sense, then it suggests modality (*kayfiyya*), which does not apply to Allah and His Attributes. It is therefore understood that the import of the hadith is not to attribute modality to Him or suggest boundaries to Him in this manner. Rather, it consists in words spoken roughly in order to give an idea of the greatness of Allah and make understandable to the questioner what is beyond his level of understanding, for he was an uneducated bedouin unversed in the minutiae of language and the subtleties of speech which elude the mind.

In this discourse, we find ellipsis and allusiveness. Thus the meaning of his saying: "Do you know what Allah is?" means: Do you know Allah's greatness? and his saying: "It groans under him" means that it is unable to carry His Majesty and Greatness. Thus it groans under him for it is known that the reason a camel saddle groans under the rider is because

29 Abu Dawud, *Sunan*, "*Kitab al-Sunna*," ch. 19 (4:232 #4726), al-Bazzar (1:29 #39), Tabari in his *Tafsir* (3:10), Abu Yala in his *Musnad*, as mentioned by Haythami in *Majma al-zawaid* (10:159), and Ibn Abi Asim in his *Sunna* (#252). Abu Dawud adds: "This tradition with the chain of Ahmad ibn Said is sound." However, the authenticity of the hadith has been questioned. Ibn al-Jawzi mentioned the weakness of two of its narrators and Ibn Asakir wrote a monograph entitled *Bayan al-wahm wa al-takhlit fi hadith al-atit* (The exposition of error and confusion in the narration of the groaning). See above, section on Uthman al-Darimi's excerpts.

of the weight of what is on it and its inability to carry it. By drawing this kind of similitude he illustrates the meaning of Allah's Greatness and Might and the height of His Throne in order for it to be known that the holder of lofty rank, mighty status, and exalted name, is not to be made an intercessor with one who is lesser in position and below Him in degree.[30]

Notice the difference between Khattabi's first and second positions regarding the same subject. This is the *mutashabih* Allah has mentioned in the Quran. This is the very subject which, until today, prompts some people to devise a barrier between the "school" of the Salaf and the "school" of the Khalaf. Then they substitute what they have called "the school of the Salaf" (*madhhab al-salaf*) to the one and only method (*manhaj*) that is agreed upon in understanding these texts and explaining them.

However, the opposite is true in the matter as we have seen in some of the positions taken by this Imam whom we have quoted extensively, and he is, as we have previously stated, closer to the Salaf than to the Khalaf. Despite that, he uses for his guiding light in the positions which he takes on these texts and phrases what he calls "the meanings of the foundations of the Religion and the schools of the scholars." He did not take for his guide the partial *ijtihad*s made by many of the scholars of the Salaf. Therefore the matter is, as he has put it, dependent upon the situations at hand, changing circumstances, and the methods of teaching which, no doubt, vary greatly between uneducated bedouins and educated researchers examining the issues with the light of the arts of the Arabic language and its standards of eloquence at a time when the scientific methods of knowledge in general and the explanations of texts in particular has reached completion.

We can see the self-same flexibility even in the positions of the Salaf themselves, and we have already stated many examples in this regard. Whoever wishes to refer to the Imam al-Tabari's commentary on the verses of Allah's attributes will find many more examples in addition to those we have already mentioned.

30 al-Khattabi, *Maalim al-sunan* (Hims ed.) 5:101.

This concludes our exposition of the fact that the *ijtihad* of the Salaf and Khalaf in the explanation of the verses of Allah's Attributes and other of the *mutashabihat* that may pertain to the attributes is not, in itself, considered a textual evidence or a binding method which all are obligated to follow, whether the purported obligation be to abide by the *ijtihad* of the Salaf to their closeness to the time of the Prophet (ﷺ), or whether to abide by that of the Khalaf for their involvement in the era of knowledge, culture and literary achievements.

Rather, the only proof binding upon both the Salaf and the Khalaf is that dictated by the principles of the derivation of rulings from the evidences and the general principles of belief which are agreed upon.

It may be that, based on *ijtihad*, some disagreement has taken place in the course of conforming to this immutable proof. Such disagreements happened quite often between the scholars of the Salaf as well as those of the Khalaf. As was seen earlier, the scholars of the Salaf were divided into three groups in understanding the meaning of *wajh* (face) in Allah's statement, *"Everything will perish except His Face"* (28:88). One group believed that the meaning was the outward sense without interpretation or modality; another group interpreted the Face as Allah Himself; yet another group interpreted it as the direction, and Ibn Taymiyya, as we said, leans towards the third opinion.[31]

What is important to know is that even if the scholars of the Salaf and the Khalaf were divided among themselves, and even if the former disagreed with the latter in the varying views of their *ijtihad* in this matter: nevertheless, no opinion from any one of these groups forms by itself and to the exclusion of the others, a standard measure of truth and falsehood. It is not permissible, therefore, to consider an opinion based on *ijtihad* as a

---

31 Ibn Hazm al-Zahiri considered baseless and impermissible the interpretation of the Face as meaning Allah Himself due to lack of evidence; however, he considered the face to be "none other than Allah" as elucidated by the verse, *"We feed you for the sake of Allah's face"* (76:9), on which he comments: "It is therefore correct with certainty that they do not intend other than Allah. As for His saying: *"Wheresoever you turn there is Allah's face"* (2:115). Its meaning is only: there is Allah with His knowledge and His acceptance for whomever turns towards Him." Ibn Hazm, *al-Fasl fi al-mila* 1 2:166. Ibn Taymiyya quotes the following commentaries for *wajh*: Ali: Allah's face is the truth (*al-haqq*); Mujahid: it is He Himself; Al-Dahhak: everything perishes except Allah, paradise and the fire; Ibn Kaysan: it is His sovereignty. (Ibn Taymiyya, *Majmuat al-fatawa* 2:428).

pointer to the one true *madhhab* and turn it into a tool for tearing asunder and dividing the community of Muslims. Muslims are held together by the guidance of Allah's Book, the clinging to the *sunna* of Allah's Messenger, and the upholding of the firm rules this congregation has agreed upon concerning the principles of the derivations of lexical meanings and the method of knowledge.

What we have said is not contradicted by the possibility that any one of us may, after studying and examining the matter, eventually incline towards the opinion of one of the two groups or to believe a part of what either group says to the exclusion of the other. Indeed, this is the business of *ijtihad* and the examination of what is dictated by context and coherence as well as the principles of deriving rulings from the evidence - as long as the *ijtihad* is done within the boundaries of the rules and principles (*usul*) that have been agreed upon by consensus.

Nor can this difference in *ijtihad* ever be viewed as a sign of division among Muslims into groups that quarrel and oppose each other on which way is righteous and which way is false. This way of thinking is one of the most dangerous kinds of innovations (*ibtida*) in the religion of Allah . . . For divergences of opinion that have no right-or-wrong solution do not cause, *al-hamdu lillah*, misguidance or deviation from the truth to any of the parties involved (if one may call them parties) and do not tear apart their ranks, by Allah's grace, nor destroy their encompassing unity.[32]

---

32 Muhammad S. Ramadan al-Buti, a*l-Salafiyya marhalatun zamaniyyatun mubarakatun la madhhabun islami* (Damascus: dar al-fikr, 1408/1988) p. 132-144.

3 SAYINGS OF MAINSTREAM SALAF AND KHALAF SCHOLARS ON THE UNDERSTANDING OF ALLAH'S ATTRIBUTES

3.1. ALLAH'S ESTABLISHMENT OVER THE THRONE (*ISTIWA ALLAH ALA AL-ARSH*)

The positions of Sunni scholars will continue to be listed in an effort to establish a sound understanding about the attributes mentioned in the Quran and *sunna* and to refute any unsound understanding.

Umm Salama, the Prophet's wife, said the following about *istiwa*: "The establishment is not unknown (*ghayr majhul*) and its modality is inconceivable in the mind (*ghayr maqul*); one does not ask "how" about Him; "how" is inapplicable to Him."[1]

Sufyan al-Thawri (d. 161) forwarded Imam al-Haramayn al-Juwayni's (d.478)[2] interpretation of *istiwa* in verse 20:4 as "a command concerning the Throne" (*amrun fi al-arsh*), as quoted by al-Yafii in his book *Kitab marham al-ilal al-mudila fi daf al-shubah wa al-radd ala al-mutazila* (Book of the resolution of difficult problems for the removal of doubts and the refutation of the Mutazila):

1 Ibn Hajar, *Fath al-bari* 13:406-407 (Beirut 1989 ed.).
2 Imam al-Haramayn al-Juwayni, in his *al-Irshad ila qawati al-adilla fi usul al-itiqad* (The guidance to the decisive proofs in the foundations of belief).

The understanding of *istiwa* as Allah's turning to a particular command concerning the Throne is not far-fetched, and this is the *tawil* of Imam Sufyan al-Thawri, who took as corroborating evidence for it the verse, *"Then turned He (istawa) to the heaven when it was smoke"* (41:11).[3]

Imam Abu Hanifa (d. 150) says in his *Wasiyya*:

Had He been in a place and needing to sit and rest before creating the Throne, then the question "Where was Allah?" would have applied to Him, which is impossible . . . We assert that Allah is established on the throne without His need (*haja*) nor settlement (*istiqrar*) upon it, for He it is Who preserves the Throne and other than it without needing any of them.[4]

He said in his *al-Fiqh al-akbar*:

Allah has no limits, nor any rivals . . . He who says, "I do not know if my Lord is in the heavens or on the earth" is a disbeliever, and he who says, "He is on the Throne, and I do not know whether the Throne is in the heaven or on the earth," he is also a disbeliever.

Imam Abu Mansur al-Maturidi explained this in saying, "The reason is that by such words he suggests a place for Allah and this is idolatry."[5]

A man asked Imam Malik (d. 179), "How did Allah make *istiwa* on the throne?" Imam Malik inclined his head and was silent until the sweat of fever covered his brow, then he looked up and said, *"Istiwa* is not unknown (*ghayru majhul*), the modality of it is inconceivable in the mind (*al-kayfu minhu ghayru maqul*); but belief in it is obligatory, and inquiring

---

3 In al-Yafii, *Marham al-ilal al-mudila*, ed. E. Denison Ross (Calcutta: Asiatic Society of Bengal, 1910) p. 245.

4 Abu Hanifa, *Wasiyyat al-imam al-azam Abu Hanifa*, ed. Fuad Ali Rida (Beirut : Maktabat al-Jamahir, 1970) p. 10.

5 Abu Hanifa, *Kitab al-fiqh al-akbar bi sharh al-Qari* (Cairo: Dar al-kutub al-arabiyya al-kubra, 1327/1909) p. 16; cf. al-Maturidi, *Sharh al-Fiqh al-akbar in Majmuat rasail* (Hyderabad: Matbaat majlis dairat al-Maarif al-Nizamiyya, 1321/1903).

about it is a heretical innovation. You are an innovator." And he gave orders for him to be taken out.[6]

Imam Shafii (d. 204), in his small treatise entitled *al-Fiqh al-akbar* said, "Whoever says, '*al-Rahmanu ala al-arsh istawa*,' it is said to him, 'This verse is one of the ambiguous verses (*mutashabih*) concerning which one is perplexed to give an answer, and the same is said regarding similar verses.'"[7]

Others who list the verse of *istiwa* among the *mutashabihat* are Imam Malik ibn Anas, the *fuqaha* of Madina, and al-Asmai according to Abu Mansur Abd al-Qahir al-Baghdadi in *Usul al-din*.[8]

The Imam of Sunnis, Abu al-Hasan al-Ashari (d. 324), says in his *Al-ibana fi usul al-diyana*:

> Allah is above the heavens, above the Throne, above everything, with a loftiness (*fawqiyya*) which does not make Him any closer to the Throne or the heavens, just as it does not make Him any further from the earth. He is close to everything in existence, He is closer to the servant than his jugular vein, and He is a Witness over all things.

He also says, as reported by Abu Mansur al-Baghdadi in *Usul al-din*:

> Allah's establishment on the Throne is an action He has created named *istiwa* and related to the Throne, just as He has created an action named *ityan* (coming) related to a certain people; and this implies neither descent nor movement.[9]

Hafiz Abu Hatim Ibn Hibban al-Busti (d. 354) flatly denied that Allah had limits and was expelled from Sijistan under threat of death by the anthropomorphists, as mentioned above.

Ibn Jarir al-Tabari (d. 310) said in his *Tafsir*, "Allah made Himself exalted over the heaven with the exaltation of sovereignty and power, not that of displacement and movement."[10]

6 Ibn Abi Zayd al-Qayrawani, *al-Jami fi al-sunan wa al-adab wa al-maghazi wa al-tarikh*, ed. M. Abu al-Ajfan and Uthman Battikh (Beirut: Muassasat al-risala; Tunis: Al-maktaba al-atiqa, 1402/1982) p. 123.

7 al-Shafii, *al-Fiqh al-akbar* p. 17.

8 al-Baghdadi, *Usul al-din* p. 112-113.

9 al-Baghdadi, *Usul al-din* p. 113.

10 Ibn Jarir al-Tabari, *Tafsir al-Tabari* 1:192.

Imam Abu Mansur Abd al-Qahir al-Baghdadi (d. 429) in *Usul al-din* says:

> The correct position according to us is the inter-
> pretation of the Throne in this verse to mean the sov-
> ereignty (*al-mulk*), as if He meant that the sovereign-
> ty has not been established for any but Him. This
> interpretation is taken from the saying of the Arabs,
> "So-and-so's throne has toppled" if he lost his power.

He then cites three examples from poetry illustrating this.[11] He says about the characteristics of mainstream Muslims in his *al-Farq bayn al-firaq* (The differences between the sects), "Sunnis are in consensus (*ajmau*) that Allah, the Flawless, the Exalted, is not bounded by location." He then reports the saying of Ali ibn Abi Talib, "Allah created the Throne as an indication of His power, not for taking it as a place for Himself."[12]

Imam al-Haramayn al-Juwayni (d. 478) said in his *al-Irshad*:[13]

> Care must be taken to show the vulgar anthropo-
> morphists (*hashwiyya*) the verses upon which they do
> practice *tawil* so that when they invoke as proof of
> their belief in Allah's "settling" (*istiqrar*) the external
> meaning of *"The Merciful is established on the
> Throne"* (20:4), ask them for the meaning of *"And He
> is with you wheresoever you are"* (57:4). If they take
> the latter according to its external sense also, then
> they annul the external sense of His being estab-
> lished on the Throne which they claim, and they also
> proclaim the disgrace of their beliefs for all reason-
> able persons to see. However, if they understand it as
> referring to His encompassing us with His knowl-
> edge, then they have applied *tawil*, and it is no longer
> forbidden for us to do the same in interpreting His
> establishment as "subduing" (*qahara*) and "prevailing
> over" (*ghalaba*), as is permitted by the Arabic lan-
> guage . . . Moreover, *istiwa* in the sense of *istiqrar*, or
> settling, presupposes a prior state of disturbance, and
> to hold this is disbelief (*kufr*) . . .

11 al-Baghdadi, *Usul al-din* p. 112-113.
12 al-Baghdadi, *al-Farq bayn al-firaq* (Beirut: dar al-kutub al-ilmiyya, n.d.) p. 256.
13 Quoted by al-Yafii in the latter's book *Kitab marham al-ilal al-mudila*.

> If they ask, "Why don't you let the verse pass according to its external sense without interpreting it, and only say that it is among the *mutashabihat*, whose meaning only Allah knows?" We respond, "If the questioner wants to let *istiwa* pass according to the external sense it commonly suggests, which is physical settlement, then such a sense drives us to anthropomorphism, but if that is explicitly shown to be impossible, then the external sense ceases . . . at which time it is not far-fetched to understand the verse rightly and reasonably according to the demands of the Divine Law and the obligation to avoid *tawil*, lest wrong belief results."[14]

Imam Abu Hamid Ghazali (d. 505) says almost the same thing as Abu Mansur al-Baghdadi in the *Ihya*,[15] and something related in the *Iljam* which was excerpted above.

The grammarian al-Raghib (d. 507) says:

> The expression *istawa ala* has the meaning of *istila* or holding mastery over something, as in the verse of the Quran, *al-rahmanu ala al-arsh istawa* . . . It means that everything is alike in relation to Him in such manner that no one thing is nearer to Him than another thing, since He is not like the bodies that abide in one place exclusive of another place.[16]

Imam Fakhr al-Din Razi (d. 606)[17] says in his commentary to verse 19:93:

> Since it is affirmed by this verse that "All those in the heavens and the earth must come to Allah as His slave," and since it is obligatory that Allah is clear of being a slave, He is therefore clear of being in a place or direction, or on the Throne or the Chair.

Imam Abu Mansur Ibn Asakir (d. 620) says in his *aqida*, "It must not be said: When was He, or where was He, or how was He. He exists without a place."

Ibn al-Jawzi said:

---

14 Imam al-Haramayn in al-*Yafii*, Marham al-ilal p. 245.
15 Section on *qawaid wa aqaid* (principles and doctrines).
16 Al-Sayyid al-Zabidi, *Taj al-arus*, s.v. s-w-y.
17 Imam Fakhr al-Din Razi, in his *al-Tafsir al-kabir*.

Whoever says, He is established on the Throne "in person" (*bi dhatihi*), has diverted the sense of the verse to that of sensory perception. Such a person must not neglect that the principle is established by the mind, by which we have come to know Allah, and have attributed pre-eternity to Him decisively. If you said, We read the hadiths and keep quiet, no one would criticize you; it is only your taking them in the external sense which is hideous. Therefore do not bring into the school of this pious man of the Salaf—Imam Ahmad—what does not belong in it. You have clothed this *madhhab* with an ugly deed, so that it is no longer said "Hanbali" except in the sense of "anthropomorphist" . . .

Then they say, "We take them according to their external senses." O wonder! What is the "external sense" of what Allah alone knows? Is the "external sense" of *istiwa* other than sitting down? and is the "external sense" of *nuzul* other than displacement? . .

They said, He is established on the Throne "in person." But this addition is not related by anyone! It is only what they understood with their senses, namely, that one is not established other than with his own person . . . [18]

Imam al-Izz ibn Abd al-Salam (d. 660) was asked in his *Fatawa*: "What do you say about Abu Zayd al-Qayrawani al-Maliki's (d. 386) saying, "Allah is above His exalted Throne in person (*bi dhatihi*), and He is in every place with His knowledge": Does such an affirmation attribute a direction to Allah or not? And is the one who holds such belief declared a disbeliever (*kafir*) or not?" He replied, "The apparent meaning of what Ibn Abi Zayd said attributes direction for Allah, because he has made a difference between Allah's being on the Throne and His being with His creation. As for the second question, the more correct position is that the one who holds belief in Allah's direction is not declared a disbeliever, because the scholars of Islam did not bring such as these out of Islam, rather, they adjudicated inheritance from Muslims for them, burial in Muslim grounds, sanctity of their blood and property, and the obligation to pray over their remains. The same is true of all the uphold-

18 Ibn al-Jawzi, *Daf shubah al-tashbih* p. 102, 104, 127-128.

ers of innovations; people never ceased to apply to them the rulings that apply to Muslims. Pay no attention to what the common people claim about their disbelief."[19]

Imam Nawawi (d. 676) said in *Sharh al-muhadhdhab*:

> It is said, we believe that the Merciful is established over the Throne, and we do not know the reality of the meaning of this nor what is meant by it (*la nalamu haqiqata mina dhalika wa al-murada bihi*), while we do believe that "There is nothing like Him whatsoever," and that He is exalted far above the most elevated of created things. That is the way of the Salaf or at least their vast majority, and it is the safest because one is not required to probe into such matters.[20]

Ibn al-Humam al-Hanafi (d. 681) said in *al-Musayara*:

> It is obligatory to believe that Allah is established on the Throne while negating any likeness to creation. As for saying that His establishment (*istiwa*) is a conquering (*istila*), it is permissible but not obligatory since there is no evidence for it specifically . . . However, if it is feared that the common people will not understand *istiwa* without conceiving of contact and other corporeal characteristics, and if they do not negate the latter, then there is no harm in directing their understanding to *istila*, as its usage and meaning for *istiwa* is established in language from the poet's saying, "Bishr has conquered (*istawa ala*) Iraq" and "When we towered above them and conquered them (*istawayna alayhim*).[21]

Shaykh Abd al-Ghani al-Nabulusi (d. 1143) said, as already quoted, "Whoever believes that Allah permeates the heavens and the earth, or that He is a body sitting on His Throne, is a disbeliever, even if he thinks he is a Muslim."

Al-Dhahabi disavowed the term "in person;" "There is no need for this expression, and it disturbs the soul."[22]

19 Al-Izz ibn Abd al-Salam, *Fatawa* p. 151, 153.

20 Nawawi, *al-Majmu* 1:25.

21 Ibn al-Humam, *al-Musayara fi ilm al-kalam wa al-aqaid al-tawhidiyya al-munjiya fi al-akhira* (Cairo: al-matbaa al-hamawiyya, 1348/1929) p. 18.

22 Al-Dhahabi, *Siyar alam al-nubala* 19:607.

Ibn Hajar also rejected the statement that Allah is on the Throne "in person," as being equally preposterous as saying that He is everywhere:

> Some of the Mutazila have claimed that Allah was everywhere on the basis of the hadith, "If one of you stands in prayer, let him not spit in front of him for Allah is in front of him." This is evident ignorance, because the hadith then states that he should spit under his foot, which invalidates their principle. The hadith also constitutes a refutation of those who say that Allah is on the Throne "in person."[23]

Even Sulayman ibn Abd Allah ibn Muhammad ibn Abd al-Wahhab (d. 1817 CE), the Wahhabi founder's grandson, declared an unbeliever anyone who used the term "in person" in relation to Allah being in a place, whether one or many:

> Whoever believes or says, Allah is in person (*bi dhatihi*) in every place or in one place, he is a disbeliever (*kafir*). It is obligatory to declare that Allah is distinct from His creation, established over His throne without modality or likeness or examplarity. Allah was and there was no place, then He created place and He is exalted as He was before He created place.[24]

3.2. INTERPRETING ALLAH'S WORDS, "*HE WHO IS IN THE HEAVEN* (*MAN FI AL-SAMA*)"

Allah's saying, "*Have you taken security from Him Who is in the Heaven that He will not cause the earth to swallow you?*" (67:16) indicates that everything elevated is called "Heaven." The commentaries say that Allah said this to the idolaters in response to their claim that the gods on earth were idols, and that Allah the Exalted owned only the heavens. Allah's response means, "Have you taken security from Him Who is on high with the highness of loftiness and sublimity;" in the same way as it is said, "the *sultan* is higher than the *amir*," even though they may both sit on the same dais.

---

23 Ibn Hajar, *Fath al-bari* (1989 ed.) 1:669.

24 Sulayman ibn Abd Allah b. Muhammad b. Abd al-Wahhab, *al-Tawdih an tawhid al-khallaq fi jawab ahl al-Iraq* (1319/1901) p. 34. New ed.: al-Riyad : Dar tibah, 1984.

Similarly, in His saying, *"He is the Omnipotent over His slaves"* (6:18, 6:61), pre-eminence or increased stature here signifies pre-eminence in importance and rank. Pharaoh described himself as pre-eminent over the Banu Israil by saying, "Verily we are omnipotent over you." It is understood that his intention is not to infer a physical or geographic height above them. Al-Tabari said in his *Tafsir*, "Allah made Himself exalted over the heaven with the exaltation (*uluw*) of sovereignty and power, not that of displacement and movement."[25]

Another meaning for 67:16 is mentioned in Zamakhshari's *Kashshaf*. It reads, "Have you taken security from Him whose sovereignty is in the Heaven (*amintum man malakutihi fi al-sama*). When "whose sovereignty" (*malakutihi*) is omitted, the pronoun "Him" (*man*) remains instead. There are many instances of this turn of speech in the Quran. For instance, "And ask the town" (*wasal al-qaryat*); that is, "And ask the people of the town;" *"And your Lord came"* (*wa jaa rabbuka*); that is, *"And your Lord's order came"* (*wa jaa amru rabbika*).

Concerning the last verse, Imam Ahmad said, "It means His command." The authenticity of Imam Ahmad's comment is verified by Bayhaqi, who said, "Its chain of transmission is impeccable."[26] This is related verbatim in Ibn Kathir who adds, "Imam Ahmad's words signify negation of likening Allah to creation."[27]

It is not believed that Ibn Kathir would have suffered the argument of some of today's "Salafis," who say that al-Bayhaqi may have misunderstood the wording of the original text and misphrased it! Nor are such baseless hypotheses accepted. It is true that Imam Ahmad said those words as they came to us, with a faultless chain of transmission, whether or not they satisfy the "Salafis'" expectations of Imam Ahmad. Ibn Hazm, in *al-Fasl fi al-milal*, confirms that Imam Ahmad interpreted Allah's "coming" as His command.[28] Al-Khallal himself reports that Imam Ahmad interpreted *Surah al-Baqara* figuratively, to mean "Allah's reward," as in the hadith of Muslim, "On the Day of the Rising, *al-Baqara* and *Al Imran* will come . . ."[29]

25 Al-Tabari, *Tafsir Ibn Jarir* 1:192.
26 Bayhaqi, in his book *Manaqib al-Imam Ahmad*.
27 Ibn Kathir's *al-Bidaya wa al-nihaya* 10:327.
28 Ibn Hazm, *al-Fasl fi al-milal* 2:173.
29 Al-Khallal, in his book *Al-Sunna*.

Similarly, Bayhaqi relates that Imam Bukhari interpreted Allah's "laughter" to mean his mercy; Al-Khattabi confirmed it.[30]

Allah says, in *Surah al-Mulk*: "*He it is Who hath made the earth subservient unto you. . .*" (67:15). "*Have ye taken security from Him Who is in the heaven that He will not cause the earth to swallow you when lo! it is convulsed?*" (67:16) "*Or have ye taken security from Him Who is in the heaven that He will not let loose on you a hurricane?*" (67:17)

In 67:15-16 Allah mentions that He may send punishment from the earth below. Then He says, "*He may send punishment from the skies above*" (67:17). Al-Sufuri explains that the threat of punishment from below (67:16) is mentioned first because the earth is mentioned in the verse immediately preceding it (67:15). This is done despite the convention to mention the highest (ie. skies) first.

In addition, Allah says in *Surah al-Anam*, "*He is the Omnipotent over His slaves*" (6:61). *Say, "He is able to send punishment upon you from above you or from beneath your feet*" (6:65).

Al-Sufuri comments that, in this instance (6:65), Allah mentions punishment from above first to reflect His being over His servants in the preceding verse 6:61. In *Surah al-Anam*, Allah mentions the punishment from above and then the punishment from below. In *Surah al-Mulk*, He mentions punishment from below then punishment from above. Hence, Allah can send punishment from above and below or below and above because He has no spatial direction; He encompasses all and is encompassed by none. Allah is Omnipresent, Omniscient, and Omnipotent and is far and beyond the physical constraints that the "Salafis" ascribe to Him.[31]

Nawawi, in his commentary on Muslim, agreed with Qadi Iyad that the words "in the heaven," in the verse "*Have you security from Him Who is in the heaven*," are interpreted figuratively. Fakhr al-Din Razi said in his *Tafsir* (3:69), "It is the anthropomorphists who used the verse, '*Have you security from Him Who is in the heaven*' to claim that Allah Himself is in the sky." The Quranic commentator Abu Hayyan al-Andalusi said

---

30 Bayhaqi, *al-Asma wa al-sifat* p. 298 and 470. For al-Khattabi see the reference to Ibn Hajar in the discussion of Allah's "laughter" further down.

31 Al-Sufuri, *Nuzhat al-majalis* p. 7.

the same thing in his *Bahr al-muhit* (8:302) and *Nahr al-madd* (2:1131-1132) with particular reference to Ibn Taymiyya.[32]

Based on the verse, *"He is Allah in the heavens and in the earth. He knoweth both your secret and your utterance, and He knoweth what you earn"* (6:3), it is established that everything that is in heaven and on earth belongs to Him. He said, *"Say, to whom belongs what is in the heavens and in the earth? Say, to Allah."* The word "what" (*ma*) here indicates rational beings as well as others, as in His saying, *"And the heaven and Him (ma) who built it, and the earth and Him (ma) who spread it .."* (91:5-6). If Allah was literally in the heavens, He would possess Himself, which is absurd.

Moreover, taking His saying, "in the heavens" in verse 6:3 to signify "inside one particular heaven" is not permissible as it contradicts the outward sense of the verse. Also, taking it to mean "inside the heavens put together" would be tantamount to saying that what of Him is contained in a given heaven is other than what is contained in the other heavens. This would require complexity and a combination of parts on Allah's behalf, which is absurd. It is therefore impossible to venture from the outward meaning of this verse, and obligatory to understand it figuratively. This figurative interpretation has several aspects.

1 It means the disposal and direction (*tadbir*) of the heavens, as when it is said, "So-and-so is in such-and-such a matter;" that is, he is engaged in disposing and directing it.

2 The words, "He is Allah" are a complete statement. He then continues with another statement, "In the heavens and in the earth, He knoweth both your secret and your utterance." That is, He knows the secret of the angels and their utterance, and He likewise knows the state of whoever is in the earth.

3 There is a precedence (*taqdim*) and a post-position (*takhir*) in the verse. The meaning implied thereby is, "And He is Allah, He knows in the heavens and in the earth your secret and your utterance."

4 Imam al-Qurtubi (d. 671) said the following in his com-

---

32 Abu Hayyan al-Andalusi, *Tafsir al-bahr al-muhit* (8:302) and *al-Nahr al-madd* (2:1131-1132).

mentary on verse 67:16, *"Have ye taken security from Him Who is in the heaven . . ."*

This may mean, "Do you feel secure that He Who is the Creator of whomever is in the heavens will not make the earth swallow you, as He did Korah?" The more exacting hold that "in the heavens" signifies, "Do you feel secure from Him who is over the heavens," just as Allah says, *"Journey in the earth"* (9:2) meaning over it; not over it by way of physical contact or spatialization, but by way of omnipotent power and control. Another position is that it means, "Do you feel secure from Him Who holds sway over *(ala)* the heavens," i.e. just as it is said, "So-and-so is over Iraq and the Hijaz," meaning that he is the governor and commander of them. The hadiths on this subject are numerous, rigorously authenticated *(sahih)*, and widely known, and indicate the exaltedness of Allah, being undeniable by anyone save an atheist or obstinate ignoramus. Their meaning is to dignify Allah and exalt Him above what is base and low, to characterize Him by exaltedness and grandeur, not by being in places, particular directions, or within limits, for these are the qualities of physical bodies. The hands are only raised skyward when one supplicates because the sky is from whence divine revelation descends and rains fall, the place of purity and the wellspring of the purified ones of the angels, and that the works of servants are raised to it and over it is the Throne and His paradise, just as Allah has made the Kabah the direction of supplication and prayer. He created all places and has no need of them. He was without space or time in His beginningless eternality before creating space and time, and is now as He ever has been.[33]

5. Ibn Hajar says in the commentary in the book of tawhid,[34] which is the last book of *Sahih al-Bukhari*:

> Bayhaqi mentioned Abu Bakr al-Dabi's saying that the Arabs use "in" *(fi)* in place of "over," as in Allah's saying, "Roam over *(fi)* the earth" and "I shall crucify you over *(fi)* the trunks of the palm-trees." Likewise, Dabi says, "In the heaven" means "Over the

---

33 Al-Qurtubi, *al-Jami li ahkam al-quran* (18:216), as cited in *The Reliance of the Traveller*, p. 860-861.
34 Ibn Hajar, on the chapter devoted to *uluw* (#23).

Throne above the heaven, as stated in the sound reports . . . And by including the hadith of Ibn Abbas containing the words, "Lord of the mighty Throne" into this chapter, Bukhari warned those that might predicate spatial elevation to Allah (*uluw fawqi*) that both the direction in which the heaven is believed to be and that in which the Throne is believed to be are created, lorded over, and brought into existence by Allah Who existed before all that and before everything else. Thus these places were created, and His existence, being eternal without beginning, precludes reference to Him as being bounded by them. And Allah knows best.[35]

3.3. INTERPRETING THE HADITH "WHERE IS ALLAH? IN THE HEAVEN" (*HADITH AYNA ALLAH*)

When the Prophet (ﷺ) asked the slave-girl, "Where is Allah?" (*ayn Allah*), she said, "In the heaven" (*fi al-sama*). She belonged to a people who worshiped stones and denied the Maker. When she confirmed the existence of Allah, however, she became a believer. If the Prophet (ﷺ) had condemned her for her answer, he would have demonstrated that she was disbelieving in the Maker. Instead he said of her, "She is a believer." He understood from her response the magnification of the Creator.

Nawawi said in his commentary on Muslim:

> This is from among the *ahadith* that deal with Allah's attributes and there are two schools of reading for it . . . The first consists in believing in it without entering into its meaning, while holding that there is nothing like unto Allah, with His elevation above the characteristics of things created. The second consists in interpreting it with what befits Him.
>
> Whoever holds the latter position says that the meaning of the tradition is that the Prophet (ﷺ) intended to test her: was she a believer in Oneness (*muwahhida*) who confirms that the Creator,

---

35 Ibn Hajar, *Fath al-bari,* "*Tawhid,*" ch. 23 last paragraph.

Disposer, and Doer is Allah alone? That He it is Who, when the petitioner invokes Him, he turns towards the heaven, and when the worshiper prays, he turns towards the Kabah? And this is not because He is circumscribed in the heaven, just as this is not because He is circumscribed in the direction of the Kabah; rather this is because the heaven is the orientation of those who invoke, just as the Kabah is the orientation of those who pray—or, on the other hand, was she of the idol-worshippers who worship the idols that are in front of them? When she replied: "In heaven," it was understood that she was a believer in Oneness and not an idol-worshiper.[36]

Qadi Iyad said:

There is no disagreement among the Muslims, all without exception; their jurists, scholars of hadith, theologians, keen-sighted ones, and imitators, that the external meanings cited pertaining to Allah being *"in the heaven"* as in His saying, *"Have you taken security from Him Who is in the Heaven that He will not cause the earth to swallow you?"* (67:16) and the like —are not as they appear (*laysat ala zahiriha*), but rather are interpreted by all of the scholars (*mutaawwila inda jamiihim*). He among the *muhaddithin, fuqaha* and *mutakallimin* who spoke to establish that there is aboveness in direction without specifying dimension or modality : he did so only by interpreting "in the heaven" (*fi al-sama*) to mean *"above the heaven"* (*ala al-sama*). And of the great multitude of the keen-sighted ones and theologians and those who establish Allah's freedom from any likeness to creation who spoke to negate the concept of limit and the inconceivability of direction with relation to Allah; they did so only by interpreting with various figurative interpretations, according to the necessity of each case.

Qadi Iyad continues, "Some of them practiced mutual tolerance in the matter of establishing a direction for Allah (i.e. they did the latter to some extent), but only with apprehension at such tolerance, for is there any difference between asking "how" and estab-

36 *Kitab* 5 *Bab* 7 Hadith 33.

lishing directions for Allah? However, whatever gen-
eralization the Law has made such as about Allah
being the Omnipotent over (*fawqa*) His slaves and
His establishing Himself over (*ala*) the Throne, it is
always with strong adherence (*tamassuk*) to the verse
which sums up the total transcendence (*al-tanzih al-
kulli*) of Allah above creation, "There is nothing like
unto Him," without which nothing of what is con-
ceived in the mind is sound. Such adherence is perfect
protection for him to whom Allah the Exalted grants
success.'"

And this, says Nawawi, is the end of Qadi Iyad's discourse.
Ali al-Qari said in relation to the hadith "Where is Allah?"

> Al-Qadi Iyad said, "By asking this, the Prophet's
> intent was not to ask about Allah's place (*makan*), for
> verily He is above and beyond space, as He is above
> and beyond time. Rather the intent of his question to
> her was to find out whether she was a believer in one-
> ness (*muwahhida*) or someone who associated part-
> ners to Allah (*mushrika*), because the disbelievers
> (*kuffar*) of the Arabs used to worship idols, and each
> tribe used to have a specific idol in its midst which it
> worshiped and aggrandized, and it may be that the
> simple-minded and ignorant ones among them did
> not know any other object of worship than that idol.
> The Prophet (ﷺ) therefore meant to determine what
> she worshiped. When she said, "in the heaven,"—and
> another narration says that she made a sign towards
> the heaven—it was understood that she was a believ-
> er in Oneness. He meant by this line of questioning
> the disavowal of the gods of the earth (*nafi al-aliha
> al-ardiyya*) which are the idols, not the establishment
> of the heaven as a location for Allah, and Allah is
> greatly exalted from the sayings of the wrong-
> doers!"37

3.4. The "Book Written Above the Throne" (*FAWQ AL-ARSH*)

Concerning the saying of the Prophet (ﷺ) cited in the Book

---

37 Ali al-Qari, *al-Mirqat sharh al-mishkat* 3:492.

of *Tawhid* of *Sahih al-Bukhari*:[38]

> When Allah created creation, He wrote with Him
> above His Throne, Verily My mercy precedeth My
> wrath;[39] when Allah created creation, He wrote a
> Book that is with Him, saying, My mercy overcometh
> or precedeth My wrath;[40] Allah wrote a Book before
> He created creation, saying: Verily My mercy pre-
> cedeth My wrath; and it is written with Him above
> the Throne.[41]

"With Him" refers to a rank, not a location, because location
does not apply to Him and the Exalted cannot be the literal
object of a preposition denoting location.

The claim that has been made by some, that "there is nothing created over the Throne," as if the Throne, which is created, was somehow the geographical limit between the creation
and the Creator is refuted by these hadiths. Not only is it
unfounded in the Book and the *sunna*, but it also suggests an
understanding of Allah's aboveness in relation to the Throne as
spatial rather than figurative and related to rank.

The passage related to the Throne in the text of the *aqida
tahawiyya*[42] has been transmitted in two different versions.
The correct version, used by al-Ghunaymi's commentary on the
aqida, reads:

> He is independent of the Throne and of what is
> beneath it; He encompasses all things and that which
> is above it (*muhitun bi kulli shayin wa bi ma fawqihi*)
> and what He has created is incapable of encompass-
> ing Him.[43]

Other versions, such as Ibn Abi al-Izz's (d. 792) commentary, read: He encompasses all things and is above it (*muhitun*

38 Chapter 22, and again, in two versions, in chapter 55.
39 Chapter 22.
40 Chapter 55 #1.
41 Chapter 55 #2.Also in Muslim (*tawba*) and Ibn Hibban. See *Riyad al-salihin*,
Chapter on hope (*al-raja*).
42 #50-51 in the translation cited above.
43 Abd al-Ghani ibn Talib al-Ghunaymi al-Maydani (d. 1881 CE), *Sharh al-aqida
al-Tahawiyya al-musammat "Bayan al-sunna wa al-jamaa*, Muhammad Muti al-Hafiz
and Muhammad Riyad al-Malih, eds. (Damascus: Maktabat al-nuri, 1970) p. 93.

bi kulli shayin wa fawqahu) and what He has created is incapable of encompassing Him.[44]

Ibn Abi al-Izz's arguments for the veracity of the latter wording are:

> The word "*wa*" has been inadvertently dropped from the text by some copyists, giving *muhitun bi kulli shayin fawqihi*—similar to the first version, which is incorrect in his view. Yet, by the same token, it could have been inserted unintentionally by some copyists.

There is nothing of creation above the Throne in his view. In this he follows Ibn Hazm, who took as his evidence *istawa* in the sense of "an act pertaining to the Throne, and that is the termination of His creation at the Throne, for there is nothing beyond it!"[45] As said earlier, this is baseless, for in the authentic hadith, Abu Hurayra narrates that the Prophet (ﷺ) said, "When Allah created creation, He wrote a book, which is with Him above the Throne, saying, My mercy overcomes My wrath." The Book which is above the Throne is the Preserved Tablet, which contains a record and decree of all things past and future. This was mentioned by Ibn Hajar in his commentary on chapter 55 of Bukhari's *Tawhid*. Neither Ibn Hazm nor Ibn Abi al-Izz make mention of this hadith in their discussions.

The word *wa* could have been deliberately expunged by some "deniers of aboveness (*fawqiyya*)"—which he takes in the literal sense. Again, who is to say that the word was not, on the contrary, interpolated by some fanatic literalists?

It should be realized that the scholars referred to by Ibn Abi al-Izz as the "deniers of aboveness" did not need to change Tahawi's text in order to present their view of *fawqiyya* as referring to rank. The Maturidi commentary of *Sharh al-aqida at-Tahawiyya* by Akmal al-Din Babarti has used the wording preferred by Ibn Abi al-Izz, and explained the *fawqiyya* as being

44 Ibn Abi al-Izz, *Sharh al-aqida al-Tahawiyya* (Beirut: Muassasat al-risala, 1416/1995) 2:372-373.

45 "*Mina qawlihi taala ala al-arshi istawa annahu filun faalahu fi al-arshi wa huwa intihau khalqihi ilayhi fa laysa bada al-arshi shayun.*" Ibn Hazm, *al-Fasl fi al-milal wa al-ahwa wa al-nihal* 2:125.

highness of rank.[46] The same is true of Basim Jabi's edition of the *aqida*.

This indicates that the wording that Ibn Abi al-Izz preferred has been used by non-"Salafis" as well as "Salafis," but interpreted differently. Thus, even if Tahawi's wording was adopted by Ibn Abi al-Izz, there is no problem with it, provided it is taken in the correct manner. As Ghazali stated in his *Ihya*,[47] "Allah is above the Throne, above the heavens, above everything, with a highness that does not make Him any closer to the Throne or the heavens, just as it does not make Him any further from the earth."

Concerning this, Ibn Hajar says in *Fath al-bari*:

> When we say, "Allah is above the Throne" (*Allah ala al-arsh*), it does not mean that He is touching it or that He is located on it or bounded by a certain side of the Throne. Rather, it is a report which is transmitted as is, and so we repeat it while at the same time negating any modality, for there is nothing like Him whatsoever, and from Him is all success.

As for "above His throne" (in the hadith) it refers to the Book. Some have taken it in the sense of "upwards from His Throne," as in Allah's saying: *"a gnat, or anything above it"* (2:26), but this is far-fetched. Ibn Abu Jamra (d. 695) said:[48]

> It may be said from the fact that the Book is mentioned as being "above the Throne" that the divine wisdom has decreed for the Throne to carry whatever Allah wishes of the record of His judgment, power, and the absolute unseen known of Him alone, so as to signify the exclusivity of His encompassing knowledge regarding these matters, making the Throne one of the greatest signs of the exclusivity of His knowledge of the Unseen. This could explain the verse *al-rahmanu ala al-arshi istawa* as referring to whatever

---

46 Akmal al-Din Babarti, commentary on *Sharh al-aqida at-Tahawiyya*, Edited by A. Yakan and A. Abu Ghuddah.

47 Ghazali, the section entitled *al-Qawaid wa al-aqaid.*

48 This is Abd Allah ibn Sad al-Azdi, known as Ibn Abu Jamra in his *Jam al-nihaya fi bad al-khayr wa ghayah*, his commentary on Bukhari.

Allah wills of His power, which is the Book He has placed above His Throne."[49]

Ibn Abu Jamra's explanation is in accordance with the sound understanding of Allah's elevation (*uluw*) as of rank, which was already mentioned. This is reminiscent of Sufyan al-Thawri's interpretation of *istiwa* in verse 20:4 as a divine command, also mentioned above. The sound understanding is confirmed by the explanation in Bukhari of the hadith of Zaynab, the Prophet's wife, when she said, "I have been married from above seven heavens," and "Allah gave me in marriage in the heaven," to refer to Allah's decree and order in the Quran, which descended from the Preserved Tablet, not to Allah Himself.

3.5. IBN HAJAR'S COMMENTARY ON THE MEANING OF THE THRONE

Ibn Hajar writes in his commentary on the twenty-second chapter of the Book of *Tawhid* in *Sahih al-Bukhari*:

> Bukhari named the Chapter on the Throne, "Chapter entitled, His Throne was on the water, and He is the Lord of the mighty Throne." In this way he mentioned two parts of two verses, and it is good to state this second part after the first one, to respond to those who misunderstood the hadith, "There was Allah, and there was nothing before Him; and His throne was on the water," mistakenly thinking that it meant that the Throne was always alongside Allah (i.e. existing without beginning). This is an incorrect position, as is the belief of some thinkers that the Throne is the Creator and the Maker! Perhaps those who held this, such as Abu Ishaq al-Harawi, used for evidence the hadith of ibn Abbas . . . narrated through Sufyan al-Thawri: "Allah was on His throne before He created anything; the first thing He created was the pen," and this "first" is interpreted as the creation of heavens and earth and their contents.

---

49 Ibn Hajar, *Fath al-bari*, "*Tawhid*," ch. 22 (#7422). (1989 ed. 13:508.)

Abd al-Razzaq mentioned in his commentary on Allah's saying, "And His throne was on the water" that this (the Throne) was the beginning of His creation before He created the heaven, and that His Throne was made from a red emerald. Thus Bukhari's mention of "The Lord of the mighty Throne" alludes to the fact that the Throne is a servant and that it is lorded over.

He ends his chapter with the hadith, "And there I saw Musa holding the leg of the Throne." By confirming that the Throne has legs, the author proves that it is an object put together, having constituent parts. Any such object must have been created. Al-Bayhaqi in his *al-Asma wa al-sifat* said:

> All the sayings of the Quranic commentators concur that the Throne is a seat or bed, and that it is an object created by Allah, Who ordered that the angels should carry, glorify, and circumambulate it in the same manner as Allah has created on earth a house and ordered the children of Adam to circumambulate it and face it during daily prayers. It is proven by the above-mentioned Quranic verses (i.e. those which Bayhaqi cites) and hadith literature that their understanding is correct.[50]

3.6. INTERPRETING ALLAH'S "DESCENT" AND THE "ASCENT" OF GOOD WORDS TO HIM

The meaning of descent (*nuzul, tanzil*) in Quran and hadith varies according to context and may mean revelation, bestowal, provision, or mercy. For example, the meaning in the verses *"Allah hath now brought down the fairest of statements"* (39:23), and *"Lo! We sent it down on the Night of the Decree"* (97:1), is revelation. According to the masters of Quranic commentary, Revelation came down to the Prophet (ﷺ) from the Preserved Tablet through Gabriel's intermediary, or Gabriel heard it directly from Allah in the same way that Moses (ﷺ) heard Allah's speech—from the right, the left, above, below, and no particular direction. Gabriel then expressed Allah's words in

---

50 Ibn Hajar, *Fath al-bari* (Beirut 1989 ed.) 13:498-499.

a language that the Prophet (ﷺ) could use to explain to his Community. This is the meaning of descent or revelation (*nuzul*). This is proven by Allah's saying, *"Lo! We have appointed it a Recitation (Quran) in Arabic that haply ye may understand"* (43:3).

The meaning of "descent" is not the downward movement of the words from Allah, at a height, to a low place. Allah said, *"And He hath sent down (anzala) for you of cattle eight kinds"* (39:6), "And We sent down iron" (57:25), and, of course, all these did not come from high to low. Ibn al-Jawzi refers to this in regard to the hadith of Allah's descent to the nearest heaven.[51]

The hadith in Bukhari and Muslim, "Our Lord descends every night to the lowest heaven when one-third of the latter part of the night is left, and says, Who supplicates Me so that I may answer him? Who asks forgiveness from Me so that I may forgive him?" is placed by al-Khattabi among the *mutashabihat*:

> This belongs to the knowledge in whose outward expression we have been ordered to believe and not seek to disclose its inward sense. It is one of the many ambiguities (*mutashabih*) which Allah has mentioned in His book.[52]

Of the hadith concerning Allah's descent in Bukhari and Muslim, Qurtubi said that it is elucidated by the hadith related by Nisai on the authority of both Abu Said al-Khudri and Abu Hurayra. The Prophet (ﷺ) said:

> Allah waits until the first part of the night is over, then He orders a herald (*munadiyan*) to say, "Is there anyone supplicating so that he may be answered? Is there anyone begging for forgiveness so that he may be forgiven? Is there anyone petitioning so that he may be granted his request?"[53]

Nisai's narration is confirmed by the hadith found in

---

51 Ibn al-Jawzi, in a section of his *Daf*.

52 Al-Khattabi, *Maalim al-sunan ala sunan Abi Dawud* (Hims ed.) 5:101.

53 Nisai, *Sunan* 6:124 (#10316) and *Amal al-yawm wa al-layla* (ed. Faruq Hammada) p. 340 #482.

Ahmad, Tabarani, and al-Bazzar on the authority of Uthman ibn Abi al-As al-Thaqafi:

> The gates of heaven are opened in the middle of the night and a herald calls out, "Is there anyone supplicating so that he may be answered? Is there anyone asking so that he may be granted? Is there anyone afflicted so that he may be delivered?" At that time there is no Muslim who invokes for anything except Allah answers him, except an adulteress who runs after her pleasure and her intimate companion.[54]

It is clear that, in the tradition of Bukhari and Muslim, the call is attributed to Allah to emphasize Allah's grandeur as the Originator of the call although the herald carries it out. When one says, "The sultan calls out for this," it is actually a herald who calls out the sultan's order, as made clear in the other two versions. It is with respect to the latter that Imam Malik reportedly said, "It is our Blessed and Exalted Lord's order which descends; as for Him, He is eternally the same, He does not move or go to and fro."[55] However, it is established that Malik forbade discourse of any kind about the hadiths of Allah's attributes,[56] that he preferred not to interpret the hadiths of descent in any way, and that he said about them, "Let them pass without entering into modality."[57]

Nevertheless, not all the Salaf let them pass; Bayhaqi relates from the *tabii* Hammad ibn Zayd that he interpreted Allah's descent to the nearest heaven as His drawing near to His servants. That is also the position of Ibn al-Jawzi in his *Daf shubah al-tashbih*. He writes "Since you understand that the One who descends towards you is near to you, content yourself with the knowledge that He is near you, and do not think in terms of bodily nearness."[58] It should also be pointed out that Ibn al-Jawzi read the verb "descend" in the hadith of Bukhari

---

54 Ahmad, Musnad 4:22, 217; al-Bazzar, *Kashf al-astar* 4:44; Tabarani, *al-Mujam al-kabir* 9:51. Haythami declared it sound in *Majma al-zawaid* 10:209.

55 A weak report related by Ibn Abd al-Barr in *al-tamhid* (7:143) and al-Dhahabi in *Syar alam al-nubala* (8:105).

56 Ibn Abi Zayd al-Qayrawani, *al-Jami* p. 124.

57 As mentioned by Tirmidhi in his *Sunan* (4:692), Ibn al-Jawzi in his *Daf shubah al-tashbih* (p. 195-196), Dhahabi in *Siyar alam al-nubala* (8:105), and others.

58 Bayhaqi, *al-Asma wa al-sifat* p. 456. Ibn al-Jawzi, *Daf shubah al-tashbih* p. 196.

and Muslim *as yunzilu* ("He orders down") instead of *yanzilu* ("He comes down"). This was also Ibn Furak's reading, according to Ibn Hajar who confirms its soundness in view of Nisai's narration. This further confirms Qurtubi's reading and Hammad's interpretation.[59]

Al-Sufuri relates that:

> Imam al-Haramayn al-Juwayni was asked, "Does Allah lie in a specific direction?" He replied, "No." He was asked, "From where did you obtain this knowledge?" He said, "From the saying of the Prophet (ﷺ), "Do not say I am superior to Yunus ibn Matta."[60] This prohibition is related to the fact that Yunus said from inside the fish at the bottom of the sea, *"There is no God save Thee. Be Thou glorified. Lo! I have been a wrong-doer"* (21:87). And Allah conversed with Muhammad, blessings and peace be upon him, above seven heavens and heard Muhammad's speech just as audibly as He heard that of Yunus. If the Lord of Truth were in a specific direction He would have heard one speech better than the other."[61]

In accordance with the above, His saying, *"Unto Him good words ascend"* (35:10) means "good words please Him." Abu Hayyan explains the "ascent" of the words as Allah's acceptance of them. This is also the explanation given by Bayhaqi.[62] Clearly, words are not in themselves endowed with locomotion.

Al-Qadi Iyad says in *al-Shifa*:

> Jafar ibn Muhammad (al-Sadiq) said, "Allah's drawing-near in the verse: *"He drew near and hung suspended and was two bows' lengths away or nearer"* (53:9) has no definition or limit. The slave's drawing near is limited." He also said, "Howness cannot be applied to drawing near. Don't you see how Gabriel was veiled from His drawing near? Muhammad drew near to the gnosis and belief in his own heart. He was

---

59 Ibn al-Jawzi, *Daf shubah al-tashbih* p. 192; Ibn Hajar, *Fath al-bari* (Beirut 1989 ed.) 3:38.

60 Bukhari, *Anbiya* ch. 24.

61 Al-Sufuri, *Nuzhat al-majalis* (Beirut: dar al-iman, n.d.) p. 8.

62 Abu Hayyan al-Andalusi, *Tafsir al-bahr al-muhit* (7:303) and Bayhaqi in Ibn Hajar's *Fath al-bari* (13:416).

suspended near by his heart's tranquility with what drew him near. Doubt and hesitation were removed from his heart."[63]

Know that what is said about drawing near and nearness to or from Allah has nothing to do with nearness of space or proximity in space. As we mentioned from Jafar as-Sadiq, "Howness cannot be applied to drawing near." The Prophet's drawing near to his Lord and his nearness to Him is made clear by his position, the honor of his rank, the splendor of the lights of his gnosis, and his witnessing the secrets of Allah's unseen world and His power. From Allah to him came kindness, intimacy, expansion and generosity.

Interpretation has to be employed here as with the words, "Our Lord descends to the nearest heaven" since one of the aspects of descent (*nuzul*) is the granting of favors, kind behavior, acceptance and kindliness. Al-Wasiti said, "Whoever speculates that the Prophet (ﷺ) himself drew near sees this in terms of distance. All that draws near to the Real hangs in the distance, i.e. far from the perception of its reality since the Real has neither nearness nor distance."[64]

Further proof of the figurative import of Allah's "descent" from high is the hadith narrated by Tirmidhi and Ahmad, on the authority of Abu Hurayra, whereby the Prophet (ﷺ) said, "By Him in Whose hand is the soul of Muhammad, if you were to extend a rope down all the way to the seventh earth, verily you would alight upon Allah!"[65] Ibn Hajar interpreted this to mean His knowledge.[66] Thus Allah's knowledge encompasses everything, according to the absolute principle that He is transcendent above place and is now as He ever was, before place was created. The same principle applies to the hadith of Allah's "descent," as Ibn Hajar demonstrates in his commentary on that hadith.[67]

---

63 Al-Qadi Iyad, *al-Shifa*, in the section entitled "His Proximity and Nearness."
64 Qadi Iyad, *al-Shifa* (Bewley trans.) Pt. 1, Ch. 3, 7.
65 Tirmidhi, *Tafsir* (Surah 57 #3298): *Aridat al-ahwadhi* 9:187; Ahmad 2:370.
66 As quoted in Ajluni's *Kashf al-khafa*, s.v. *law annakum dallaytum bi hablin. ..*
67 See the following pages.

3.7. IBN HAJAR'S COMMENTARY ON THE HADITH OF DESCENT

Ibn Hajar says the following in his commentary on the hadith of Bukhari and Muslim concerning Allah's "descent" to the lowest heaven:

> Those who assert direction for Allah have used this hadith as proof that He is in the direction of aboveness. The vast majority of the scholars (*al-jumhur*) reject this, because such a saying leads to establishing boundaries for Him and Allah is exalted above that.

The meaning of "descent" is interpreted differently: Some say that the external meaning is meant literally: these are the *mushabbiha* and Allah is exalted above what they say.

• Some reject the validity of the hadiths cited in that chapter altogether. These are the Khawarij and the Mutazila and they display arrogance. What is strange is that they interpret figuratively what is related to this in the Quran, but they reject what is in the hadith either out of ignorance or out of obstinacy.

• Some have taken them as they have come, believing in them without specificity, declaring Allah to be transcendent above modality (*kayfiyya*) and likeness to creation (*tashbih*): these are the vast majority of the Salaf. That position is reported by Bayhaqi and others from the four Imams, Sufyan ibn Uyayna, Sufyan al-Thawri, Hammad ibn Salama, Hammad ibn Zayd, al-Awzai, al-Layth, and others.

• Some interpreted them in a way that befits the linguistic usage of the Arabs.

• Some have over-interpreted them to the point that they almost tampered with their text.

• Some have made a difference between a kind of interpretation that is likely and current in the linguistic usage of the Arabs, and another kind which is far-fetched and archaic, interpreting in the former case and committing the meaning to Allah in the latter. This is reported from Malik, and among the Khalaf it is asserted decisively by Ibn Daqiq al-Id (d. 702).[68]

Bayhaqi said, "The safest method is to believe in them without modality, and to keep silence concerning what is meant except if the explanation is conveyed from the Prophet (ﷺ) himself, in which case it is followed." The proof for this is the agreement of the scholars that the specific interpretation is not obligatory, and that therefore the commitment of meaning to Allah is safest . . .

Ibn al-Arabi al-Maliki said:

> It is reported that the innovators have rejected these hadiths, the Salaf let them pass as they came, and others interpreted them, and my position is the last one. The saying, "He descends" refers to His acts not His essence, indeed it is an expression for His angels who descend with His command and His prohibition. And just as descent can concern bodies, it can also concern ideas or spiritual notions (*maani*). If one takes the hadith to refer to a physical occurrence, then descent would be the attribute of the angel sent to carry out an order. If one takes it to refer to a spiritual occurrence, that is, first He did not act, then He acted; this would be called a descent from one rank to another, and this is a sound Arabic meaning.

In sum, it is interpreted in two ways; the first is, His command or His angel descends; the second is, it is a metaphor for His regard for supplicants, His answering them, and so forth.

Abu Bakr ibn Furak has said that some of the masters have read it *yunzilu* (He sends down) instead of *yanzilu* (He descends), that is, He sends down an angel. This is strengthened by Nisai's narration through al-Aghurr from Abu Hurayra and Abu Said al-Khudri, "Allah waits until the first part of the night is over, then He orders a herald to say: Is there anyone supplicating so that he may be answered? . . ." There is also the hadith of Uthman ibn Abi al-As, "The gates of heaven are

---

68 Ibn Hajar reports Ibn Daqiq al-Id's words in full elsewhere: "We say concerning the various attributes that they are real and true according to the meaning Allah wills for them. As for those who interpret them, we look at their interpretation: if it is close to the rules of language in use among the Arabs we do not reject it, and if it is far from them we relinquish it and return to believing while declaring transcendence." Ibn Daqiq al-Id in Ibn Hajar, *Fath al-bari* (Dar al-fikr ed.) 13:383.

opened in the middle of the night and a herald calls out, Is there anyone supplicating so that he may be answered? . . ." Al-Qurtubi said, "This clears all ambiguity, and there is no interference by the narration of Rufaat al-Jahni whereby "Allah descends to the nearest heaven and says, No-one other than I asks about My servants," for there is nothing in this which precludes the above-mentioned interpretation.

Al-Baydawi said:

> Since it is established with decisive proofs that the Exalted is transcendent above having a body or being circumscribed by boundaries, it is forbidden to attribute to Him descent in the sense of displacement from one place to another place lower than it. What is meant is the light of His mercy; that is, He moves from what is pursuant to the attribute of Majesty entailing wrath and punishment, to what is pursuant to the attribute of Generosity entailing kindness and mercy."[69]

Let us turn to the two footnotes appended by Bin Baz to Ibn Hajar's words here, because they are indicative of his approach to this landmark of Muslim scholarship. It is a remarkable fact that his commentary of *Fath al-bari* is actually an evisceration of the doctrine of mainstream Islam and an attempt to replace it with anthropomorphism. This is particularly clear in light of the fact that any discussion of hadiths regarding the attributes is replete with slander. Such is the quality of most of this "commentary." For example, when Ibn Hajar mentions that "the vast majority of the scholars" reject the notion of Allah having a direction, Bin Baz inserts this footnote:

What he means by "the vast majority of the scholars" is the vast majority of the scholars of *kalam*. These are the Companions and those who followed them in excellence—they assert a direction for Allah, and that is the direction of elevation, believing that the Exalted is above the Throne, without giving an example and without entering into modality. The proofs from the Quran and the *sunna* for this are innumerable, so take heed and beware. And Allah knows best.[70]

This statement being noted, the reader is encouraged to

69 Ibn Hajar, *Fath al-bari* (1989 ed.) 3:37-38.
70 *Ibid.* p. 37n.

decide for himself whether any one of the above statements is true. Also noted is Bin Baz's indiscriminate expulsion of all *kalam* scholars from the fold of mainstream Islam, by separating them into two distinct groups. *Kalam* scholars include Asharis, and it is clear, from the discussion above, that their enemies are none other than the enemies of Islam. In regard to the heresy of those who attribute a direction to Allah, the reader is referred below, where the position of Sunnis on this issue is stated.

Bin Baz's reaction to the quotation of Ibn al-Arabi's position is particularly virulent: [71]

> This is an obvious mistake which goes against the plain import of the texts that have come to us concerning the descent, and likewise what is cited of Baydawi later is null and void. The correct position is that of the pious Salaf who believed in the descent and let pass the texts as they came to them, asserting Allah's descent in the sense that befits Him, without asking how nor giving an example, just as the rest of His attributes. That is the safest, straightest, most knowledgeable, and wisest way. Therefore hold on to it, cling to it stubbornly, and beware what contravenes it so that you may reach safety. And Allah knows best.[72]

It has already been mentioned that the Salaf did apply interpretation in many places, therefore it cannot be "an obvious mistake" to interpret the hadiths of the attributes. Also mentioned were al-Khattabi's, al-Izz ibn Abd al-Salam's, al-Nawawi's, and al-Subki's explanation that interpretation is an obligation in the face of innovations that thrive on ambiguity, such as *tajsim*, with which the Salaf did not have to deal in the way that the Khalaf did after them. There is no better illustration of the soundness of the Salaf's rulings than Bin Baz's blatant declaration that mainstream Islam attributes a direction to Allah. Here now is the actual position of mainstream Islam concerning those who attribute a direction to Allah.

---

71 Ibn al-Arabi: "It is reported that the innovators have rejected these hadiths, the Salaf let them pass as they came, and others interpreted them, and my position is the last one."

72 *Ibid.* p. 38n.

3.8. MAINSTREAM ISLAM'S REFUTATIONS OF THOSE WHO ATTRIBUTE A DIRECTION TO ALLAH

Imam Bukhari (d. 256) believed that Allah exists without a place. Ibn Hajar repeats the belief that Allah is without place many times.[73]

Ibn Jarir al-Tabari (d. 311) said in his commentary on the verse *"Then turned He (thumma istawa) to the heaven"* (2:29):

> The meaning of *istiwa* in this verse is height and elevation . . . but if anyone claims that this means displacement for Allah, tell him, He is high and elevated over the heaven with the height of sovereignty and power, not the height of displacement and movement to and fro.[74]

Imam al-Ashari (d. 324) said in the authentic version of his Ibana:[75]

> Allah is established on the Throne in the sense that He said and the meaning that He wills, with an establishment that transcends touch, settlement, location, immanence, and displacement. The Throne does not carry him, rather the Throne and its carriers are carried by the subtleness of His power, subdued under His grip, and He is above the Throne and above everything down to the extremities of the lower earth, with an aboveness that does not make him any closer to the Throne or to the heavens. Rather, He is as exalted high over the Throne as He is exalted high over the lower earth, and together with this He is near every creature, and He is nearer to His servant than his jugular vein, and He is witness over everything.[76]

Shahrastani (d. 548) relates that Imam Ashari also said:

> The vision of Allah does not entail direction,

---

73 Ibn Hajar, *Fath al-bari* 13:357; Cf. 3:23, 6:102, 13:309, 328, 351, 354, 355, 357, 366, 369-370, 414.

74 Ibn Jarir al-Tabari, *Tafsir* 1:192.

75 Imam al-Ashari, *Ibana*, published by Dar al-ansar and edited by Fawqiyya Husayn Mahmud.

76 Al-Ashari, *al-Ibana an usul al-diyana*, ed. Fawqiyya Husayn Mahmud (Cairo: dar al-Ansar, 1977), p. 21.

place, or form, or face to face encounter either by impingement of rays or by impression, all of which are impossible.[77]

Mulla Ali al-Qari states:

It is obligatory that you believe that your God . . . is not contained in any place or direction.[78]

He states elsewhere:

Allah is not located in a place, whether above or below, or any other than these, and time is inapplicable to Him, unlike what the *mushabbiha* and *mujassima* and *hululiyya* or incarnationists believe.[79]

He also cites *al-hafiz* Zayn al-Din al-Iraqi's statement that all four Imams agree that anyone who believes Allah lies in a specific direction has committed disbelief.[80]

Al-Izz ibn Abd al-Salam does not declare those who attribute a direction to Allah disbelievers, but only innovators:

The correct position is that the one who holds belief in Allah's direction is not declared a disbeliever, because the scholars of Islam did not bring such as these out of Islam, rather, they adjudicated inheritance from Muslims for them, burial in Muslim grounds, sanctity of their blood and property, and the obligation to pray over their remains. The same is true of all the upholders of innovations.[81]

Imam Ghazali said: The Hashwiyya asserted direction for Allah while guarding themselves from divesting Allah of His attributes (*tatil*), falling thereby into likening Allah to creation (*tashbih*).

Allah has granted success to Sunnis in establishing the truth. They have recognized the proper goal in establishing

---

77 Shahrastani, *al-Milal wa al-nihal* as translated by A.K. Kazi and J.G. Flynn, Muslim Sects and Divisions (London: Kegan Paul International, 1984) p. 85.

78 Mulla Ali al-Qari, in *Sharh ayn al-ilm.*

79 Mulla Ali al-Qari, in *Sharh al-fiqh al-akbar.*

80 Al-Qari, *Sharh ayn al-ilm wa zayn al-hilm 1:34; Sharh al-fiqh al-akbar* (Beirut: Dar al-kutub al-ilmiyya, 1404/1984) p. 57; al-Mirqat, cited by Kawthari, Maqalat p. 321, 362.

81 Al-Izz ibn Abd al-Salam, *Fatawa* p. 151, 153.

their method, and understood that direction is denied and disallowed for Allah because it pertains to bodies and complements them; while vision of Him is firmly established because it directly follows knowledge and attends it as its perfecting component.[82]

Ibn al-Jawzi says in his *Daf shubah al-tashbih*:

> Some claim the verses *"Good words ascend to Him"* (35:10) and *"He is the Omnipotent over His servants"* (6:18, 6:61) as proof that He is above in sensory fashion, forgetting that sensory aboveness is only applicable to bodies or atoms, and that aboveness can also be expressed for loftiness of rank.
>
> Furthermore, just as He said, "above His servants," He also said, *"and He is with you"* (57:4). Therefore whoever interprets the latter as meaning "with you in knowledge," permits his counterpart to interpret *istiwa* (in 20:4) as "subduing" (*al-qahr*) . . .

Abu Yala says, "What is meant by "aboveness" is Allah's *istiwa* in person on the Throne, which is a limit for him in the direction that is bounded by the Throne. As for the other directions, such as above, behind, in front, and left, they are not bounded." I say, these words are the very root of anthropomorphism, because what bounds is either greater or smaller than what is bounded, and these dimensions only apply to bodies.[83]

Ibn Hajar states:

> The fact that the two directions of "above" and "below" are inapplicable and impossible for Allah does not preclude His being described with the attribute of elevation (*uluw*), for such description is only from the standpoint of the meaning of elevation, not that of sensory perception.[84]

Al-Kirmani said, "The outward meaning of the saying, "He Who is in the heaven" (*man fi al-sama*) is not meant. Allah is transcendent above immanence and place. However, because the direction of aboveness is nobler than any other direction, Allah linked it to Him to indicate the loftiness of the Essence

---

82 Al-Ghazali, *al-Iqtisad fi al-itiqad* (Beirut: Dar al-kutub al-ilmiyya, 1409/1988) p. 48.
83 Ibn al-Jawzi, *Daf shubah al-tashbih* p. 131, 135, 260.
84 Ibn Hajar, *Fath al-bari* 6:136 (Jihad).

and the Attributes." He addresses the other expressions of aboveness in the same manner.[85]

Ibn al-Humam al-Hanafi (d. 681) said in *al-Musayara*, a commentary on Ghazali's tenets of belief:

> The seventh foundation of Islamic belief is that Allah, the Exalted, is not characterized by a direction, because directions above, below, right, etc. are created with creatures . . . and if, by "direction" other than that is meant, which does not suggest the immanence of boundaries or corporeality, let it be made plain (i.e. that it is a loftiness of rank, not space), so that it can be examined whether it belongs truly to transcendence, if it is misphrased or other than that, then it must be shown to be corrupt.[86]

Imam al-Yafii (d. 768), in the end of his *Kitab marham al-ilal al-mudila*, devotes an entire chapter to the refutation of the anthropomorphists. It begins with the words:[87]

> The true Imam and teacher of the scholars of *kalam*, Imam al-Haramayn said, "The madhhab of the People of Truth (*Ahl al-Sunna*) is absolutely unanimous on the question that Allah is exalted above boundaries and above being characterized by directions. The Karramiyya and some of the Hashwiyya have said that He is bounded and that He is characterized by the direction of aboveness . . . and each of these two positions is tantamount to declaring that Allah has a dimension or that He has parts, and constitutes pure disbelief." . . . I quoted this from his book *al-Irshad*.[88]

Abu Bakr ibn al-Arabi al-Maliki (d. 543) labels believers in Allah's direction "followers of Pharaoh":

> Your conclusion shows that you are indeed the fol-

---

85 *Ibid.* 13:412.

86 Ibn al-Humam, *al-Musayara* p. 16-17.

87 The title of the chapter is: *Bayan al-istidlal ala nafi al-jiha wa al-jismiyya wa batalan madhhab man qala bihima min al-karramiyya wa al-hashwiyya wa mutaakhkhiri al-hanbaliyya* (The exposition of the proofs upon which are based the negation of direction and corporeality and the invalidity of the school of those who assert them among the *karramiyya* and the *hashwiyya* and the late Hanbalis).

88 Al-Yafii, *Marham al-ilal al-mudila*, ed. E. Denison Ross (Calcutta: Asiatic Society of Bengal, 1910) p. 244, 246.

lowers of Pharaoh, who believed that the Creator lies in a certain direction, and so he desired to climb up to Him on a ladder. He congratulates you for being among his followers, and he is your imam![89]

Even Ibn Hazm al-Zahiri (d. 456), the arch-enemy of Ashari and the Ashari school, says:

> By no means whatsoever is Allah in a place or in a time. This is the position of the vast majority of the scholars (*al-jumhur*) and ours as well, and other than this position is not permissible, for anything other than it is false.[90]

3.9. IBN AL-ARABI AL-MALIKI'S REFUTATION OF THE ANTHROPOMORPHISTS IN THE COMMENTARY ON THE HADITH OF DESCENT

Bin Baz attacks Ibn al-Arabi's position favoring interpretation despite the fact that this Maliki scholar is one of the most respected authorities among scholars of both jurisprudence and hadith. Also, he is scrupulous in his adherence to the strictest principles in most matters. Like al-Khattabi, Ibn Battal, Nawawi, Ibn Hajar, and so many others, Ibn al-Arabi represents the most sound of the Sunni positions. This is demonstrated by his commentary in *Aridat al-ahwadhi* on the hadith of descent in Tirmidhi, which is cited in full:

> People are divided into three opinions regarding this hadith and the like: Some of them reject it, because it is a single narration and its external sense is not suitable for Allah. These are the Innovators. Some of them accepted it and took it as it came without interpreting it or discussing it, while believing that there is nothing that resembles Allah. Some of them interpreted it and explained it (and this is my position) because its meaning is easy in pure Arabic. Some ignorant people, however, trespassed bounds in interpreting it. They say that in this Hadith there is

---

89 Abu Bakr Ibn al-Arabi, *Aridat al-ahwadhi* 2:235.
90 Ibn Hazm, *al-Fasl fi al-milal wa al-ahwa wa al-nihal* 2:125.

proof that Allah is in the Heaven on the Throne above the Seven Heavens. We say that this is a sign of tremendous ignorance.[91]

What the hadith said is "He descends to Heaven" without specifying from where He descends or how He descends. Yet they said, and their proof is again based on the external sense, "The Merciful is firmly established on the Throne" (al-rahmanu ala al-arshi istawa).

We ask, "What is the Throne in Arabic, and what is istawa?"

They reply, "As Allah said, 'That they may mount (li yastawu) upon their backs' (43:13)."

We say, "Allah is Mighty and Higher than to have His istiwa on His Throne compared to our sitting on the backs of animals!"

They say, "And as He said, 'And the ship came to rest (istawat) upon al-Judi' (11:44)."

We say, "Allah is Mighty and Higher than a ship that sailed and then docked and stopped!"

They said, "And as He said, 'When you and those who are with you settle on the ship' (23:28)."

We say, "Allah forbid that His istiwa (being seated) be similar to that of Noah and his people! Everything in the latter case is created, as it consists in istiwa (sitting on) an elevated place and a settling in a place involving physical contact. The entire Community (umma) is in agreement, even before hearing the hadith of descent and the arguments of those who rejected it, that istiwa (being seated) in regard to Allah does not involve any of those things. Therefore do not give examples from His creation for Him!"

They say, "Allah said, 'Then He made istiwa on

---

91 There is in this implicit criticism of Ibn Abi Zayd al-Qayrawani. He belonged to Ibn al-Arabi's own school and was criticized for stating in his Risala (or Epistle on Islamic belief and law according to the Maliki school) that "Allah is on His glorious Throne in person" (innahu fawqa arshihi al-majid bi dhatihi). This was something that Imam Malik never said, since it has no precedent in the Quran and hadith, and is therefore rejected. Ibn Abi Zayd did not include "in person" in his other statement of creed in al-Jami fi al-sunan although he said, "He is above His heavens, on His Throne, outside His earth" (innahu fawqa samawatihi ala arshihi duna ardihi).

Like Ibn Arabi, al-Izz ibn Abd al-Salam and Ibn Hajar al-Haytami consider the saying, "on His Throne in person" unacceptable and characterize it as a reprehensible innovation which is not permissible to follow. Ibn Abi Zayd al-Qayrawani, al-Jami li al-sunan wa al-adab wa al-maghazi wa al-tarikh p. 108; al-Izz Ibn Abd al-Salam, Fatawa p. 153; al-Haytami, Fatawa hadithiyya p. 110-113.

the Throne' (20:4) means 'Then He was sitting (*istawa*) in Heaven' (2:29)."

We say, "This is a contradiction. First you say that He is on the Throne above Heaven, then you say He is in Heaven according to His saying, '*Have you taken security from Him Who is in the Heaven'* (67:16) - and you say that it means 'above the Heaven.' Therefore you must say that 'The Merciful is firmly established on the Throne' means 'to the Throne'!"

They say, "*Allah said, 'He rules all affairs from the Heaven to the Earth'* (32:5)."

We say, "This is true, but it does not provide any proof for your innovation!"

They say, "All the firm believers in the Oneness of Allah raise their hands to the Heavens when supplicating him, and if Musa had not said to Pharaoh, 'My Lord is in the Heaven,' Pharaoh would not have said, 'O Haman, build me a tower.'"

We say, "You are telling lies about Musa, he never said that. But your conclusion shows that you are indeed the followers of Pharaoh, who believed that the Creator lies in a certain direction, and so he desired to climb up to Him on a ladder. He congratulates you for being among his followers, and he is your imam!"

They say, "What about Umayya ibn Abi al-Salt who said, 'Glory to Him Whom creatures are unable to know in the way He deserves to be known, Who is on His Throne, One and One Alone, Sovereign and Possessor over the Throne of Heaven, unto Whose Majesty faces are humbled and prostrate?' and he (Umayya) had read the Torah, the Bible, and the Psalms."

We say, "It is like you and your ignorance to cite as proof, first Pharaoh, then the discourse of a pre-Islamic Arab supported by the Torah and the Bible, which have been distorted and changed! And of all of Allah's creation the Jews are the most knowledgeable in disbelief and likening Allah to creation."[92]

What we must believe is that Allah existed and nothing existed with Him; that He created all creation, including the Throne, without becoming indicatable through them, nor did a direction arise for

92 Ibn Hajar said in *al-Isaba fi tamyiz al-sahaba,* "There is no disagreement among the authorities in history that Umayya ibn Abi Salt died an unbeliever." (Ibn Hajar, al-Isaba (Calcutta, 1853) 1:133 (#549).)

Him because of them, nor did He acquire a location in them; that He does not become immanent, that He does not cease to be transcendent, that he does not change, and that He does not move from one state to another.

Istiwa in the Arabic language has fifteen meanings both literal and figurative. Some of these meanings are suitable for Allah and the meaning of the verse (20:4) is derived from them. The other meanings are not accepted under any circumstances. For example, if it is taken to mean being in a place (*tamakkun*), settling (*istiqrar*), connecting (*ittisal*), or being bounded (*muhadhat*): then none of these are suitable for the Creator—Exalted is He—and no one should try to find His likeness in His creation.

One may refrain from explaining the verse, as Malik and others have said:

"The *istiwa* is known"—he means: its lexical sense—"and the modality is unknown"[93] That is: the modality of whatever is suitable for Allah among the senses of *istiwa*: therefore who can specify such modality? "And asking about it is innovation" because, as we have just made clear, probing this matter is looking for dubious matters and that is asking for *fitna*.

Hence, from what the Imam of Muslims Malik has said we can conclude that the *istiwa* is known; that what is suitable for Allah is left unspecified; and that He is declared transcendent above what is impossible for Him. As for specifying what is not suitable for Him, it is not permissible for you, since you have completed the declaration of oneness and belief by negating likeness for Allah and by negating whatever it is absurd to believe concerning Him. There is no need for you for anything beyond that, and we have already explained this in detail.

As for His saying, "He descends", "He comes," "He arrives," and similar phrases whose meanings are not allowed to apply to His essence, they refer to His

---

93 *Wa al-kayfu majhul.* The more authenticated version of Imam Malik's saying has: "and the modality is not conceivable by reason" (*wa al-kayfu ghayru maqul*). See for the latter: Ibn Abi Zayd al-Qayrawani al-Maliki's *Jami fi al-sunan wa al-adab wa al-maghazi wa al-tarikh* p. 123. Ibn Hajar mentions a third wording similar to it and authentically reported by Bayhaqi through Malik's companion Abd Allah ibn Wahb: "It is not said how about him, and howness is excluded concerning Him" (*wa la yuqalu kayfu wa al-kayfu anhu marfuun*) in *Fath al-bari* (Beirut 1989 ed.) 13:501.

actions . . . Al-Awzai explained this when he said, about this hadith ("Allah descends"), "Allah does what He wishes."[94] Or it suffices to know, or simply to believe that Allah is not to be defined by any of the characteristics of created things and that there is nothing in His creation that resembles Him and there is no interpretation that can explain Him.

They said, 'We must say "He descends"' without asking how. We say, 'We seek refuge in Allah from saying that! We only say whatever Allah's Messenger has taught us to say and what we have understood from the Arabic language in which the Quran was revealed. And the Prophet (ﷺ) said':

Allah says, O My servant, I was ailing and you did not visit me, I was hungry and you did not feed me, I was thirsty and you did not give me drink. . .[95]

None of this is suitable of Allah whatsoever, but He has honored all these actions by expressing them through Him. In the same way, the saying "Our Lord descends" expresses His servant and angel that descends, in His name, with His order concerning whatever He bestows of His Mercy and gives of his generosity and showers His creation of His bounty.

The poet says:
I have descended
therefore do not suspect me of jealousy! -
in the station of the generous lover.

A descent can be either figurative or physical. The descending that Allah spoke about, if understood as physical, would mean His angel, Messenger, and slave. However, if you can understand it to mean that He was not doing any of this and that He then turned to do it in the last third of the night, thereby answering prayers, forgiving, bestowing, and that He has named this "descending from one degree to another and from one attribute to another," then that - ironically enough - is addressed to those who have more knowledge than you and more intelligence, who are firmer in belief in Allah's Unity and are less confused than you - nay, who are not confused at all!

They say in ignorance that if He meant the descending of his Mercy he would not make that only

---

94 Cf. al-Fudayl ibn Iyad in Bukhari's *Khalq afal al-ibad* (Beirut: Muassasat al-risala, 1411/1990) p. 14, and Yahya ibn Main in *al-Lalikai sharh usul itiqad ahl al-sunna*.

95 Muslim relates it.

in the last third of the night, because His Mercy
descends day and night. We say, "Yes, he singled out
the night, and the day of Arafat, and the hour of
Juma, because the descent of His mercy in them is
more abundant, and its bestowal is even greater
then." Allah warned us of this when He said, "And
those who beg forgiveness in the early hours of the
morning" (3:17).[96]

3.10. "HE IS WITH YOU WHEREVER YOU ARE" (*WA HUWA MAAKUM AYNAMA KUNTUM*)

The Salaf applied *tawil*, or interpretation, to this verse in a
variety of ways. The most known is that of Imam Sufyan al-
Thawri, being "He is with you in His knowledge."[97] However, it
has also been said to mean, with His acceptance, with His help,
with His tolerance, with His will, with His punishment, etc.

When Imam Sufyan al-Thawri's teacher, Abu al-Qasim al-
Junayd (d. 298)[98] was accused of heresy by the anthropomorphists of Baghdad, Abu al-Hasan al-Nuri (d. 295) was asked by
the chief judge, in the presence of the Sultan al-Mutawakkil,
"Where is your Lord in relation to you?" He replied:

He is, in relation to me, wherever I am in relation to Him,
since He said: "*He is with you wheresoever you are (wa huwa
maakum aynama kuntum)*" (57:4).

That is, He is with us in whatever way we are with Him. If
we are with Him with obedience, He is with us with help and
guidance; if we are with Him with heedlessness, He is with us
with His will; if we are with Him with disobedience, He is with
us with His delay; if we are with Him with repentance, He is
with us with acceptance; if we are with Him with abandonment
of His commands, He is with us with punishment.[99]

96 Abu Bakr ibn al-Arabi, *Aridat al-ahwadhi* 2:234-237.

97 In al-Dhahabi, *Siyar alam al-nubala* 7:274.

98 The "Imam of the World of his time" according to Ibn al-Athir.

99 In Ibn Ajiba, *Iqaz al-himam fi sharh al hikam* (Beirut: al-Maktaba al-
thaqafiyya, n.d.) p. 397.

4

THE ABERRATIONS OF THE WAHHABIS AND "SALAFIS" REGARDING THE ATTRIBUTES AND THE VIEWS OF MAINSTREAM ISLAM CONCERNING THEM

The aberrations of the anthropomorphists with regard to the verses and hadiths of the attributes are easily detectable, with a little preparation. They will add "in person" (*bi al-dhat*) or "literally" (*haqiqatan*) to the mention of verse 20:5, claiming that this was the way of the Salaf and the Four Imams. Worse, they declare as innovators and misguided (and sometimes as disbelievers) those who give a figurative interpretation of the attributes, claiming that this was never the way of the Salaf and the four Imams. Yet, as shown already and again in the next section, the Prophet (ﷺ), the Companions, the Salaf and the four Imams did sometimes apply figurative interpretation, yet the expressions "in person" or "literally" in relation to the attributes never found acceptance among them. Rather, this breach of the Salafs' *bila kayf* was practiced by Wahhabis and "Salafis," who worked to alter the method of the Salaf. Following are some examples of their aberrations past and present.

4.1. IBN ABD AL-WAHHAB'S *FATWA* ON THE HAND OF ALLAH AND SPECIFYING LIMBS AND PLACES FOR ALLAH

Muhammad ibn Abd al-Wahhab declares in one of his *fatawa*:

> He who believes that the meaning of Allah's hand in verses such as "Allah's hand is over their hand" is His power; or that Allah's establishment (*istiwa*) is his overpowering (*istila*), or that Allah is in every place, is an ignorant, misguided innovator who has contravened the "Salafi" doctrine (*al-aqida al-salafiyya*) followed by the Prophet (ﷺ), his Companions, and their pious followers such as the Four Imams and the scholars who succeeded them, but he is not declared an unbeliever until he insists on following his belief after being corrected about it.[1]

It is strange that ibn Abd al-Wahhab shuns the name "Islam," given by Allah to His religion, and the name "Sunni (*Ahl al-Sunna*)" used by Muslims to refer to those of sound belief. He names it instead "the 'Salafi' doctrine," an invented name in Islam that suggests that there is more than one doctrine among Sunnis. What is worse, he makes the Prophet (ﷺ) the adherent of a doctrine—his own doctrine - when in fact it is the Salaf who are, by the very definition of the term "Salaf," the adherents and followers of the Prophet (ﷺ)!

Another incoherence is Abd al-Wahhab's equating the beliefs of Sunnis and the Jahmis, who believed that Allah is in every place. By mentioning Sunnis and the Jahmis together, ibn Abd al-Wahhab allows himself to condemn both of them as one and the same group. This is a common device in Wahhabi and "Salafi" arguments today.

---

1 Ibn Abd al-Wahhab, *Rasail wa fatawa li al-shaykh Muhammad ibn Abd al-Wahhab wa abnaih*, p. 14 (Question 14).

One of the obvious proofs that ibn Abd al-Wahhab's practice departs from the school of Imam Ahmad is that the latter, although he faced the Jahmi heresy at its peak, never declared the Jahmis disbelievers, nor the rest of the Mutazila. Ibn Abd al-Wahhab may be said to be following Ibn Taymiyya's ideas in this matter.

Finally, as seen above, there are many interpretations of the Hand among the Imams and their schools, including Power, Mercy, or Generosity. The interpretation of the Establishment as the overpowering is in the same line. On the other hand if Ibn Abd al-Wahhab is implying, by his words, a spatial establishment over the Throne, then as quoted before, this convicts him of disbelief by consensus.

4.1.1. THEY SPECIFY LIMBS AND PLACES FOR ALLAH

The views of Muhammad ibn Nasir ibn Muammar al-Najdi al-Tamimi (d. 1810 CE), one of the students of Ibn Abd al-Wahhab and of his brother Sulayman, are collected in *Al-hadiyya alsaniyya wa al-tuhfa al-wahhabiyya al-najdiyya* and in *Majmuat al-rasil wa al-masil al-najdiyya*. Al-Tamimi declares in the latter:

> Allah is on the Throne, and the Chair (*kursi*) is where He places His feet . . . He is on His Throne, but He has no limits.[2]

This sheds new light on Darimi's claim that to say "Allah has no limits" was the invention of Jahm ibn Safwan.[3] At the same time, the literal understanding of Ibn Abbas' saying, "the Chair is where He places His two feet"[4] conforms with Darimi's ideas and those of the anthropomorphists of Ibn al-Jawzi's time. Al-Qurtubi said in his *Tadhkira*, "The *mujassim* one who attributes a body to Allah is an idol-worshiper." Ghazali states in *Iljam*, "Whoever worships a body is a disbeliever according to the consensus of the Community." The correct understanding of Ibn Abbas' statement is, as Ibn al-Jawzi said, to represent the smallness of the Chair in relation to the

---

2 *Majmuat al-rasail wa al-masail al-najdiyya*, ed. Muhammad Rashid Rida (Cairo: Matbaat al-manar, 1345/1926) Pt. 1 _3, p. 560.

3 Ibn Said al-Darimi, *Kitab al-naqd* p. 23. See above.

4 Al-Hakim (sahih) 2:282, confirmed by Dhahabi, and by Haythami in *Majma al-zawaid* 6:323.

Throne.[5] This is confirmed by Ibn Abbas' own explanation of the Throne as meaning Allah's knowledge,[6] which Ibn Kathir cites with his chain of transmission through Ibn Abi Hatim.[7] This is also the meaning given by Nasafi.[8]

Another Wahhabi edict (fatwa) states in the same book, "The denial that Allah is on the Throne is disbelief."[9] This is also found in a fatwa given by Ibn Khuzayma that goes on to state that such a person must be killed unless he repents.[10] According to Ibn Khuzayma, therefore, Imam al-Baydawi must be killed, along with every Muslim who is not an anthropomorphist. Another descendent of Ibn Abd al-Wahhab declares:

The meaning of istawa in verse 20:5 is: He settled Himself (istaqarra) and ascended (irtafaa) and rose above (ala), and all three of them are one meaning which none but a Jahmi atheist will deny in order to divest Allah from His names and attributes.[11]

According to the grandson of ibn Abd al-Wahhab, Imam Abu Hanifa and his school are Jahmi atheists for saying, "We assert that Allah is established on the throne without His need (haja) nor settlement (istiqrar) upon it"![12] This condemnation was indeed the position of some of the literalists, such as the early narrator Yazid ibn Harun, who is reported by Bukhari as saying:

Whoever claims that the Merciful is established on the Throne in any other way than what occurs in the mind of the uneducated is a Jahmi, and Muhammad al-Shaybani (Abu Hanifa's student) is a Jahmi.[13]

This is clearly a gross and unwarranted attack on an actu-

---

5 Cf. Ibn al-Jawzi, Daf shubah al-tashbih p. 258.

6 As cited by al-Khazin in his tafsir of 2:255.

7 Tafsir Ibn Kathir (Beirut: Dar al-fikr ed.) 1:381.

8 Al-Khazin and al-Nasafi in Majma al-tafasir 1:398-399.

9 Majmuat al-rasail al-najdiyya, Pt. 11, p. 198.

10 Cited by Ahmad ibn Hajar Al Butami in his book al-Aqaid al-salafiyya p. 139.

11 Abd al-Rahman ibn Hasan ibn Muhammad ibn Abd al-Wahhab in Majmuat al-tawhid al-najdiyya cited in Ibn Khalifa Ulyawi al-Azhari's book: Hadhihi aqidatu al-salaf wa al-khalaf fi dhat Allahi taala wa sifatihi wa afalihi wa al-jawab al-sahih li ma waqaa fihi al-khilaf min al-furu bayna al-dain li al-salafiyya wa atba al-madhahib al-arbaa al-islamiyya (This is the doctrine of the Predecessors and the Descendants concerning the divergences in the branches between those who call to al-salafiyya and the followers of the four Islamic Schools of Law) (Damascus: Matbaat Zayd ibn Thabit, 1398/1977) p. 19.

12 Abu Hanifa, Wasiyyat al-imam al-azam Abu Hanifa, ed. Fuad Ali Rida (Beirut: Maktabat al-Jamahir, 1970) p. 10.

13 Bukhari, Khalq afal al-ibad p. 15.

al enemy of the Jahmis, reminiscent of the attack of al-Dhuhli on Bukhari for saying that the pronunciation of Quran is created, and the Wahhabi Mashhur al-Salman's suggestion that Bukhari is a Jahmi, which is cited further down. How could Muhammad al-Shaybani be a Jahmi when he wrote the following lines?

> The scholars of the divine law have agreed from East to West that belief is obligatory in Allah's attributes as mentioned in the Quran and the hadiths conveyed from the Prophet (ﷺ) by the trustworthy narrators, without likening Allah to creation and without explaining them. Whoever explains them and says what Jahm says has departed from the practice of the Prophet (ﷺ) and the Companions and parted with the Congregation of Muslims, because He has described His Lord as nothing.[14]

The truth is that some of the anthropomorphists took the words of the Salaf (originally directed against Jahm) and turned them against mainstream Muslims, including some of the Salaf like Bukhari, Ibn Hibban, and al-Shaybani. Ibn Taymiyya mastered the practice of attacking anti-anthropomorphists and calling them Jahmis, like al-Razi and the Asharis, although no scholars before him ever suggested that the Asharis were anything other than Sunnis, unlike the Jahmis. This blurring of boundaries and misnaming within Islam has served until now to deflect attention from the deviation of the *mujassima* themselves. One might say that Imam Abu Hanifa had foreseen this state of affairs when he said, "Two heresies have come to us from the East: Jahm who divests Allah of His attributes, and Muqatil who likens Allah to creation."[15]

Although many of the true Salaf cited the meanings of *irtafaa* and *ala* for *istawa* in 20:5, as already mentioned, none of them cited *istaqarra* because, unlike the other two, it cannot be interpreted figuratively and suggests anthropomorphism. In the mind of Wahhabis, however, *istaqarra* is the paramount meaning for the verse, and all other meanings come second. Ibn Battal and Ibn al-Arabi's statement that *istaqarra* typifies

---

14 Muhammad al-Shaybani as cited in Ibn Hajar's *Fath al-bari* (Beirut 1989 ed.) 13:501.
15 In al-Dhahabi, *Siyar alam al-nubala* 7:202.

the anthropomorphists has already been cited. Thus Abd al-Rahman ibn Hasan's bizarre assertion that "all three of them are one meaning"—although "to settle" has nothing to do with "rising" or "ascending" - betrays his intention to gain acceptance for the meaning "to settle" by trying to associate it with long established meanings. In fact it is contradicted by scholars of the same school; for instance, Albani declares in his *Mukhtasar al-uluw* that the attribution of *istaqarra* to Allah is groundless and impermissible![16] This is important in view of Ibn Taymiyya and Ibn Qayyim's refusal to declare this impermissibility. Ibn Taymiyya defines *istawa* as "*saida* (he climbed), *ala* (he towered high), *irtafaa* (he rose), *istaqarra* (he settled),"[17] while they both, as already mentioned, believe with al-Khallal that Allah and the Prophet (ﷺ) sit on the Throne together.[18] Thus on the one hand Abd Allah ibn Ahmad ibn Hanbal, Uthman al-Darimi, Ibn Taymiyya, Ibn Qayyim, Ibn Hasan Al al-Shaykh Ibn Abd al-Wahhab, and, as shown further down, Ibn Uthaymin, all accept *istaqarra* as a meaning for *istawa* in 20:5, while Albani rejects it. Finally, Abd al-Rahman ibn Hasan's familiar accusation of Jahmism, again, provides the usual smokescreen.

4.2. UTHAYMIN COMPARES ALLAH TO THE SUN

Muhammad Salih al-Uthaymin, a "Salafi" scholar, writes: "Allah's establishment on the throne means that He is sitting in person on His throne."[19]

As shown in the sections above, neither the word "sitting" nor the words "in person" have ever been said by any of the true Salaf, though they have been used by the Karramis. These words are a clear-cut example of likening Allah to creation, addition to original text, and innovation on the part of the "Salafis." Moreover, this is the kind of addition, moreover, that

16 Albani, *Mukhtasar al-uluw* p. 17.

17 Ibn Taymiyya, *al-Tasis al-radd ala asas al-taqdis* 1:568. See also Abu Hayyan, *Tafsir al-nahr al-madd* 1:254 (Ayat al-kursi).

18 Ibn Taymiyya, *Majmu al-fatawa* 4:374; Ibn Qayyim, *Badai al-fawaid* 4:39-40. (Cairo: al-matbaa al-muniriyya, 1900?) 4:39-40; al-Khallal, *Kitab al-sunna* p. 209-268, commentary on the verse: "*It may be that your Lord will raise you to an exalted station*" (17:79).

19 Uthaymin, *Aqidat al-muslim*, 2nd ed., Saudi Arabia, p. 11, translated as "The Muslim's Belief."

leaves no doubt in the mind of the reader as to its corporeal imagery. It matters little that al-Uthaymin says just two lines later, "Nobody except He knows exactly *how* He is sitting,"[20] for the anthropomorphism remains in the words "sitting" and "in person." This aberration is perpetuated by such glosses for the word *kursi* in the verse of the Throne (2:255) as "seat," found in one of the most widespread translations of the Quran today.[21]

Already mentioned is Ibn Taymiyya's comparison of Allah to the moon, and his comparison of Allah's knowledge to the moon's rays. Al-Uthaymin, aiming higher, replaces the moon with the sun in his commentary on Ibn Taymiyya's lines, and declares that although Allah is in the heavens "in person" (*bi dhatihi*), He does draw near to the servant during prayer, "just as the sun is in the heaven, while its rays reach creatures on earth." He continues his explicit similes with indifference to his blatant commitment of *tamthil*:

> The proof that Allah is in front of the person who prays is the Prophet's saying "If one of you stands in prayer, let him not spit in front of him for Allah is in front of him;" and so this facing (*muqabala*) is established for Allah literally (*thabitatun lillahi haqiqatan*), in the way that befits Him. Nor does it contradict His elevation (*uluwwahu*), for what reconciles the two matters is that with respect to the creature both can be put together, just as the sun at its rising is facing him who faces the East, at the same time being in the heaven. And if this is true for created things, then it is more rightfully true for the Creator.[22]

Since when do created things serve as an analogy for the Creator? Allah spoke the truth when He said, *"They measured not Allah with His true measure"*! (6:91) According to the terms of Uthaymin's astral simile, Allah's words, *"Prostrate thyself, and draw near"* (96:19) would indicate physical proximity.

20 Italics by the author.

21 *The Holy Quran: English Translation of the Meanings and Commentary*, Revised and Edited by The Presidency of Islamic Research, Ifta, Call and Guidance (Madinah: King Fahd Holy Quran Printing Complex, 1410H) Surah 2:255; footnote #298.

22 Uthaymin, *Sharh al-aqida al-wasitiyya* (Cairo: Maktabat al-ilm) p. 44.

However, no rational person can say that such meaning is intended here, for when the person in prayer prostrates, he does not draw near to any body. The proximity in question is to His mercy, and the words "in front of him" in the above hadith mean that Allah is looking over the worshiper and taking account of his works. This is not to say that He is there literally, as this would be ascribing to Him a place, which is an aberration.

Uthaymin also declares his belief in Allah's displacement to and fro, adding the formula, "in the way that befits Him," which is his common disclaimer:

> Coming and arrival are among Allah's active attributes. These two are established as belonging to Him in the way that befits Him. Their proof is that He says: *"And thy Lord shall come with angels, rank on rank"* (89:22) and *"Wait they for naught else than that Allah should come unto them in the shadows of the clouds with the angels?"* (2:210). To explain these verses as a reference to the coming or arrival of Allah's order (*amr*) is unsound, because it contravenes the external meaning of the verse and the consensus of the early generations, and there is no proof-text for it.[23]

4.3 IMAM AHMAD'S INTERPRETATION OF ALLAH'S "COMING" AS "HIS ORDER"

As mentioned above, it is established that Imam Ahmad explained Allah's "coming" in verse 2:210 as the coming of His order (*amr*).[24] Similarly, Imam Ahmad explained verse 89:22 to mean Allah's order, according to Ibn Hazm,[25] and Bayhaqi, who relates that Ahmad took as its elucidation verse 16:32, "Wait they aught save that thy Lord's command (*amr*) should come to pass?"[26] According to Uthaymin, therefore, Imam Ahmad contradicts the consensus of the early generations and his expla-

23 Uthaymin, *Sharh al-wasitiyya*, p. 23.

24 As related by Bayhaqi in his *Manaqib Ahmad* with a sound chain cited by Ibn Kathir in his *al-Bidaya wa al-nihaya*. This is also Ibn al-Jawzi's explanation of the verse in his *Daf shubah al-tashbih*.

25 Ibm Hazm, in *al-Fasl fi al-milal*.

26 Bayhaqi, *al-Asma wa al-sifat*, ed. Kawthari, p. 292; Ibn Kathir, *al-Bidaya wa al-nihaya* 10:327; Ibn al-Jawzi, *Daf shubah al-tashbih* p. 13, 110, 141; Ibn Hazm, *al-Fasl fi al-milal wa al-ahwa wa al-nihal* 2:173. See also Buti, *al-Salafiyya* p. 134.

nations should be rejected as unsound. Instead, Uthaymin's understanding should be adopted. Such is the "Salafi" school.

Dr. Ahmad al-Saqqa of the University of al-Azhar remarked on the absurdity of such positions with the following words:

> The commentator (al-Uthaymin) is saying that "the coming" is not explained as "the coming of the order," rather it is explained as a coming which befits the majesty of Allah without anthropomorphic imagery nor suggestion of modality, *min ghayri tash-bihin wa la takyif.* That is, he is establishing that there is a body that moves by coming and by returning, however, he does not declare it openly as a bodily entity. And this is the "Salafi" *madhhab.*[27]

Al-Uthaymin, like Ibn Said al-Darimi before him, calls the kursi, "The place of the two feet, and the *arsh* is that upon which Allah made *istiwa.*[28] The reader understands plainly that the meaning of his words is that Allah sits on the *arsh* and then places his feet on the *kursi*. This is anthropomorphism, but matters are made worse by the comments that he makes a few pages later:

> It is established that Allah the Exalted has feet, and Sunnis have explained the leg (*rijl*) and the foot (*qadam*) as being literal according to what befits Allah; whereas *Ahl al-tawil* have explained *al-rijl* as being the group which Allah will place in the fire, and *al-qadam* as being those sent forth (*muqaddamin*) to the fire . . . and I reject and return their explanation to them on the grounds that it contravenes the external meaning of the words.[29]

Observe how Al-Uthaymin, like Darimi before him, makes a mockery of the name of *Ahl al-Sunna* by assigning it to those who hold his anthropomorphist views, and relegating those who apply *tawil* outside the fold of the *sunna*.

---

27 Ahmad Hijazi al-Saqqa, *Daf al-shubuhat an al-shaykh Muhammad al-Ghazali* (Cairo: Maktabat al-kulliyyat al-azhariyya, 1410/1990) p. 58.

28 Uthaymin, *Sharh al-wasitiyya*, p. 15.

29 Uthaymin, *Sharh al-wasitiyya*, p. 42.

4.4. THE SALAF'S INTERPRETATION OF
QADAM, RIJL, AND SAQ

The following mainstream Islamic scholars are, according to Uthaymin, actually outside the mainstream for denying Allah bodily appendages and the position of sitting on a seat.

- Ibn Abbas, who calls Allah's *kursi* "His knowledge," according to the authorities of Quranic commentary already mentioned.
- Al-Hasan al-Basri, who calls Allah's *qadam* "those whom Allah has sent forth (*qaddamahum Allah*) from the most evil of creatures, and has established as inhabitants of the fire," which is also the understanding of Ibn al-Jawzi.[30]
- The lexicographer *al-hafiz* al-Nadr ibn Shumayl (b. 122), who said, "*Qadam* means those whom Allah in His foreknowledge knows to be the inhabitants of the fire."
- Al-hafiz al-Bayhaqi, who relates Ibn Shumayl's saying in his *al-asma wa al-sifat*.[31]
- Ibn Hibban (d. 354), who says in his *Sahih*, "The Arabs use *qadam* to mean 'repository' (*mawdi*). Exalted is Allah far above placing His 'foot' in the fire or any other such meaning!"[32]
- Al-Khattabi, who adheres to the explanation of al-Hasan al-Basri, taking for its elucidation the verse 10:2 "They have a sure foundation (*qadam*) with their Lord" with reference to one's good works.[33]

All of these scholars are part of mainstream Islam. What they say is correct and their way is the path of truth.

Ibn Abbas said, when he was asked about Allah's saying *"On the day the leg shall be uncovered"* (68:42), "If you find something from the Quran to be obscure, seek its meaning from poetry; verily poetry is the register (*diwan*) of the Arabs. Have you not heard the poet's saying:

Your people have opened the way
   of sword-blows upon the necks
And war or battle rose on every leg
   (i.e. it was impossible to flee)"

---

30 Ibn al-Jawzi, *Daf shubah al-tashbih* p. 15.
31 Al-Bayhaqi, *al-Asma wa al-sifat*, p. 352.
32 Ibn Hibban, *Sahih* 1:502.
33 Al-Khattabi, *Maalim al-sunan ala sunan Abi Dawud* 5:95. Cf. Buti, *al-Salafiyya* p. 140. See the excerpt from al-Buti's work above.

Then he said, "This is a day of affliction and violence." Thus the meaning of verse 68:42 is, "On the day when affliction befalls them in earnest."[34]

Ibn al-Jawzi relates from Ibn Abbas, Mujahid, Ibrahim al-Nakhi, Qatada, and "the vast majority of the scholars," the same meaning. He cites Ibn Qutayba's explanation that the leg or shank is a metaphor for the action in which one hitches up one's lower garments, baring his legs.[35]

4.5. UTHAYMIN'S REDUCTIVE MENTION OF PROPHETS

Al-Uthaymin says in his book: "We believe that Allah possesses two real eyes . . . We believe that all messengers are created human beings who have none of the divine qualities of Allah."

Compare this unprecedented manner of speech with words used by such scholars as al-Tahawi in his *aqida*, cited above:

34. Anyone who describes Allah as being in any way the same as a human being has become an unbeliever.

38. He is beyond having limits placed on Him, or being restricted, or having parts or limbs.

Even Ibn Hazm, the arch-enemy of Asharis, declares:

> Saying: He has two eyes is null and void and part of the belief of anthropomorphists . . . Allah said, *ayn* (eye) and *ayun* (eyes) . . . and it is not permissible for anyone to describe Him as possessing "two eyes", because no text has reached us to that effect.[36]

As for the demeaning reference to the Messengers, peace be upon the Prophet and upon all of the prophets, as "created human beings who have none of the divine qualities of Allah," it is replied that Allah Himself calls the Prophet (ﷺ) *raufun rahim*. These are two of His own attributes meaning "kindest, merciful."

Disrespectful reference to prophets encapsulates the demeaning manner in which Wahhabi propagandists aim to

---

34 It was mentioned by Ibn Hajar in *Fath al-bari* (13:428) and Ibn Jarir al-Tabari in his *Tafsir* (29:38) from Mujahid, Said ibn Jubayr, and Qatada.

35 Ibn al-Jawzi, *Daf shubah al-tashbih* p. 118-119.

36 Ibn Hazm, *al-Fasl fi al-milal* 2:166.

misrepresent the Prophet Muhammad (ﷺ) and is sufficient in itself to convict them of deviation from the doctrine of mainstream Islam. The sound position on the topic, and the appropriate language, are found in al-Qadi Iyad's *al-Shifa* in a section entitled, "On Allah honoring the Prophet (ﷺ) with some of His own Beautiful Names and describing him with some of His own sublime qualities":

> Know that Allah has bestowed a mark of honor on many of the Prophets by investing them with some of His names, for instance, He calls Isaac and Ishmael (ﷺ) "knowing" (*alim*) and "forbearing" (*halim*), Abraham (ﷺ) "forbearing", Noah (ﷺ) "thankful" (*shakur*), Jesus (ﷺ) and John (ﷺ) "devoted" (*barr*), Moses (ﷺ) "noble" (*karim*) and "strong" (*qawi*), Joseph (ﷺ) "a knowing guardian" (*hafiz, alim*), Job (ﷺ) "patient" (*sabur*), and Ishmael (ﷺ) "truthful to the promise" (*sadiq al-wad*) . . . Yet He has preferred our Prophet Muhammad (ﷺ).[37]

4.6. HARRAS ASSERTS APPENDAGES AND DIRECTION FOR ALLAH

Another "Salafi," Muhammad Khalil Harras, asks in his edition of Ibn Taymiyya's *al-Aqida al-wasitiyya*:

> How can Allah's "hand" be interpreted to mean power when the text proves mentioning of palm, fingers, right and left, closing, opening, etc. which can happen only in the case of a real hand?[38]

This case of *tashbih*, or likening Allah to His creation, demonstrates that the struggle of mainstream Islamic scholars against the anthropomorphists is far from over. Ibn al-Jawzi said in his day:

> They refuse to construe "hand" (*yad*) as meaning "favor" and "power" . . . Instead they said, "We construe them in their customary external senses, and the external sense is what is describable in terms of well-known human characteristics, and a text is only construed literally if the literal sense is feasible."

37 Al-Qadi Iyad, *al-Shifa* as translated by Aisha A. Bewley, *Muhammad Messenger of Allah: al-Shifa of Qadi Iyad* (Granada: Madinah Press, 1992) p. 126.
38 Harras, *Sharh al-wasitiyya* (Salafi Press, 1989) p. 44.

> Then they become vexed when imputed with *tashbih*
> (likening Allah to His creation) and they express
> scorn at such an attribution to themselves, clamoring,
> "We are *Ahl al-Sunna!*" Yet their discourse is clearly
> couched in terms of *tashbih*. And some of the masses
> follow them.[39]

Indeed, which of the mainstream Muslims ever said such
an enormity as "sitting in person" or "hands with palm, fingers,
right and left, closing, opening" in reference to Allah? Have
Uthaymin and Harras not heard about the treatment recommended by the school of Imam Ahmad for those who suggest
the resemblance of Allah's hand to "a real hand"? Here is
Shahrastani's text again:

> Ibn Karram used to say, "Allah is firmly seated on
> the throne and he is in person (*dhatan*) on the upper
> side of it . . . Imam Ahmad and his school abhorred
> likening Allah to His creation (*tashbih*) to such an
> extent that they used to say, "Whoever moves his
> hand while reciting the verse "I created with My
> Hand", or gestures with his fingers when narrating
> the hadith "The heart of the believer is between two
> fingers of the Merciful," cut their hands or fingers
> off!"[40]

It is seen from all of the above that it is al-Ashari who is the
closer to Imam Ahmad's position prohibiting any form of *tashbih*, since his writings clearly report the condemnation of views
like theirs. For example, Harras insists that the vision of Allah
in the Hereafter must entail direction, "for it is necessary for a
thing being seen to be in the direction of the seer."[41] This is the
position of the Mutazila who used this false axiom to deny the
sight of Allah by believers, and who think that to assert sight
is to assert direction. Al-Ghazali replied to them in his *al-
Iqtisad fi al-itiqad*:[42]

> The consensus agrees that the senses are not lim-
> ited by direction . . . Of the strongest proofs of seeking
> His vision (without direction) is Moses' prayer, "*Let*

---

39 Ibn al-Jawzi, *Daf shubah al-tashbih* p. 100-101.
40 Shahrastani, *al-Milal wa al-nihal* (Cairo, 1317) p. 145, 137-138.
41 Harras, *Sharh al-wasitiyya* p. 73.
42 "The retrenchment in sound belief."

me see You" (7:143), and it is impossible for a prophet whose rank was that Allah spoke to him directly not to know, concerning His attributes, what the Mutazila have discovered! . . . Ignorance consists in denying the possibility of vision because, in their view, His essence cannot be seen since He does not lie in any direction - and this must be declared as disbelief or misguidance. Did Moses not know that He did not lie in any direction? And knowing this, did He not know that the vision of what does not have a direction is absurd?

The Hashwiyya—vulgar anthropomorphists—are unable to conceive that anything exists except that it lies in a direction, so they have asserted direction for Allah until it obliged them unavoidably to assert corporeality, dimension, and a share in the characteristics of creation.

The Mutazila—separatists—denied direction for Allah (like the Sunnis) but then could not conceive that Allah can be seen without direction. In this they contravened the decisive evidence of the Law, and think that to assert vision is to assert direction.

The Mutazila became enmeshed in a false concept of transcendence (*tanzih*) while guarding from likening Allah to creation (*tashbih*), falling thereby into excess; the Hashwiyya asserted direction for Allah while guarding themselves from divesting Allah of His attributes (*tatil*), falling thereby into likening Allah to creation (*tashbih*).

Allah has granted success to followers of mainstream Islam in establishing the truth. They have recognized the proper goal in establishing their method, and understood that direction is denied and disallowed for Allah because it pertains to bodies and complements them; while vision of Him is firmly established because it directly follows knowledge and attends it as its perfecting component.

The assertion of Ibn Taymiyya, in his anti-Ashari work of *kalam*, that "the clever ones among the later Asharis have agreed with the Mutazila in denying the vision,"[43] is a fabricated charge reminiscent of Ibn Hazm's utter misrepresentations of Ashari and Baqillani.[44] The position of late Asharis on

---

43 Ibn Taymiyya, *Dar taarud al-aqli wa al-naql*, ed. Julaynid (Cairo: Muassasat al-ahram, 1409/1988) p. 172.

44 Such as classifying them among the Murjia: Ibn Hazm, *al-Fasl fi al-milal* 4:203-226.

the vision is the same as that of these early Asharis. This is stated explicitly by Ibn Hajar in his commentary on the line, "Worship Allah as if you saw Him" from the hadith of Gabriel.[45]

Another notorious trait of Ibn Taymiyya's work is its repeated attribution of the book *al-Radd ala al-jahmiyya* to Imam Ahmad, which is incorrect. Ibn Taymiyya credits him with examples from that book. For example, Imam Ahmad is made to say:

> Just as a man who holds a bottle of water in his hand encompasses it with his sight, also does Allah encompass the world with His sight while established on His Throne; similarly, a man who builds a house and exits it knows what is in it, and Allah who created the world knows what is in it despite His elevation.[46]

It is no doubt with Imam Ahmad's false precedent that Ibn Taymiyya felt bold enough to compare Allah to the moon, and with Ibn Taymiyya's real precedent that Ibn Uthaymin felt bold enough to compare Allah to the sun.

Imam Ahmad's text continued:

> The denial of corporeality necessitates the denial of direction that is one of its obligatory characteristics. The assertion of our knowledge of Allah necessitates the assertion of the vision of Him, since the latter is one of the characteristics that follow and complement knowledge and properly belong to it . . . And that, as every reasonable person knows, is the retrenchment in sound belief.[47]

Another answer to al-Harras is Imam Ashari's denial of direction:

> The vision of Allah does not entail direction, place, or form, or face to face encounter either by

---

45 Ibn Hajar, in *Fath al-bari.*
46 Ibn Taymiyya, *Dar taarud al-aqli wa al-naql* p. 164.
47 Al-Ghazali, *al-Iqtisad fi al-itiqad* p. 46-48.

impingement of rays or by impression, all of which are impossible.[48]

It has been mentioned previously that Bin Baz goes so far as to assign mainstream Islam with the attribution of direction to Allah, and to credit its disallowance to *Ahl al-Kalam*. He mentions the two groups as though they were separate entities, excluding Ibn Hajar from the first and including him in the second. Let us now turn to more of these assaults on the great scholars of the Community by the so-called "Salafis."

4.7. DWARVES CHALLENGING GIANTS: BAZ AND SALMAN "CORRECTING" THE *AQIDA* OF IBN HAJAR AND NAWAWI

One of the worst innovations Muslims are presently having to face is the "Salafi" inquisition of highly respected scholars whose soundness of doctrine has never been questioned in the Community. Their scrutiny does not affect areas in which disagreement is allowed as a matter of course, such as *fiqh*, but does affect the area of belief in which no disagreement is allowed among the scholars of mainstream Islam. Therefore today, one will see "Salafi" authors such as Harras, Bin Baz, Salman, and Albani disagreeing in the area of *aqida* with scholars like Nawawi and Ibn Hajar al-Asqalani.[49] One of these revisionists wrote an entire book to cast aspersions on the doctrine of Imam Nawawi, calling it "The refutations and criticism of Imam Nawawi for committing figurative interpretations in *Sharh sahih Muslim*." He begins with the words:

> He [Imam Nawawi] has committed in his book some lapses and a host of mistakes related to Allah's names and attributes, among other important matters, which pass by his commentators, not to mention his readers, without any reference back to the school of the pious Salaf in those all-encompassing matters, which ought to be made as clear as the sun . . .[50]

48 In Shahrastani, as translated by A.K. Kazi and J.G. Flynn, *Muslim Sects and Divisions* (London: Kegan Paul International, 1984) p. 85.

49 These scholars have been refuted in their most major works, including *Sharh sahih Muslim* and *Sharh sahih al-Bukhari!*

50 Salman, *Al-rudud* p.8.

The author then proceeds in three hundred pages to reject Imam Nawawi's explanations of the hadiths that pertain to the attributes, calling them wrong, rejected, unsound, and deviant. At the same time, he specifies that Nawawi's views are founded on Qadi Iyad's earlier commentary of Muslim, and that the "refutations and criticism" apply to him also.

Another example of this "Salafi" practice is Bin Baz's aspersion of the greatest hadith master of the Khalaf, Ibn Hajar al-Asqalani, found in his scant comments in a recent re-edition of *Fath al-bari*. It is Bin Baz's own doctrine that is questionable, not Ibn Hajar's. Bin Baz's slander of Ibn Hajar and the Maliki hadith master, Ibn al-Arabi's, condemnation of anthropomorphism have already been mentioned. Following are more of Bin Baz's derogatory remarks against Ibn Hajar.

4.8. ALLAH'S LAUGHTER

Bin Baz suggests that Ibn Hajar "abandons the way of the Companions, the Followers, and their excellent followers" by interpreting Allah's "laughter" as His good pleasure (*rida*), in his commentary on the hadith, "Allah laughs at two who enter paradise . . ."[51] The critic does not address the fact that Ibn Hajar is merely reiterating the view of the *hafiz* al-Khattabi (d.386),[52] who himself quotes Bukhari's (d. 256) view that Allah's laughter means His mercy. Apparently Bin Baz does not believe that al-Khattabi and Bukhari follow what he calls "the way of the Companions, the Followers, and their excellent followers?"

Bin Baz again explicitly charges Qadi Iyad (d. 544) with abandonment of the way of mainstream Islam for his statement, among others, that Allah's Hand does not pertain to a bodily appendage.[53] He goes further and openly blames Ibn Hajar for saying, "the attribution of hoarding (*wai*) to Allah [in the hadith, "Do not hoard so Allah will not hoard from you"] is a metaphor for withholding." Bin Baz writes:

> This is a mistake unbecoming of the commenta-
> tor, and the correct position is to affirm the literal

---

51 Ibn Hajar, *Fath al-bari* (Beirut 1989 ed.) 6:50n. in *Jihad* Ch. 28 #2826.
52 This is the hadith master Abu Sulayman Hamd ibn Muhammad ibn Ibrahim al-Khattabi al-Busti to whom Ibn Hajar often refers in his commentary on Bukhari.
53 Ibn Hajar, *Fath al-bari* (Beirut 1989 ed.) 3:357n.

description of Allah by that attribute, in the sense that befits Him, as with all attributes . . . that is the saying of *Ahl al-Sunna wa al-Jamaa*, so keep to it![54]

On the Prophet's saying, in Bukhari and Muslim, "Allah smiled/laughed last night at the good deed of both of you," Ibn Hajar comments, "The attribution of laughter and wonder to Allah is figurative (*majaziyya*) and their meaning is Allah's good pleasure at their deed." Bin Baz says here:

> Would that the author had cleansed his work from declarations other than the Prophet's own declarations. It would have sufficed for him to say, laughter and wonder that befit His majesty. What is said about the Attributes is the same as what is said about the Essence; affirming them without giving an example, and asserting transcendence without divestiture. "There is nothing like Him whatsoever, and He is Hearer, Seer," and that is the school of the Companions and the Successors, and their successors until the Day of Judgment.

Ibn Hajar quotes Al-Khattabi:

> The literal attribution of wonder to Allah is absurd and its meaning is good pleasure (*rida*) . . . and it could mean that Allah causes His angels to wonder at the good deed of the couple . . . Abu Abd Allah (al-Bukhari) said, "The meaning of Allah's laughter here is mercy (*rahma*)."

Ibn Hajar comments, "I did not see this in the manuscripts of Bukhari which have reached us." Bayhaqi confirms al-Khattabi.[55]

Al-Khattabi continues, "The interpretation of laughter as good pleasure is more likely than its interpretation as mercy, because the laughter of the recording angels (*al-kiram*) indicates good pleasure." Ibn Hajar comments, "Good pleasure on

---

54 Ibn Hajar, *Fath al-bari* (Beirut 1989 ed.) 3:383n.
55 Bayhaqi, *al-Asma wa al-sifat* p. 298, 470 through Farabari.

Allah's part necessitates mercy from Him, since the two necessarily go together."[56]

Nawawi says something similar:

> Al-Qadi Iyad said, What is meant by Allah's wonder is His good pleasure, and it could mean that it was the angels who wondered, but the Prophet (ﷺ) attributed it to Allah as a mark of honor.[57]

Salman also attacks Nawawi, and Qadi Iyad before him, for interpreting Allah's "laughter" as His good pleasure. Salman is not satisfied to declare that such an interpretation is null and void. Instead he goes so far as to identify it as the negation and divestiture (*nafi wa tatil*) of an attribute of Allah, as practiced by the *Muattila* or Divesters, a name given chiefly to the Jahmis:

> The explanation of the laughter by its inseparable attribute, such as good pleasure, love, or the will to bestow goodness: all these are negations and divestitures of this attribute (laughter) imposed by the divesters' bad thoughts about their Lord, since they imagine that these meanings apply to Him just as they apply to creatures.[58]

It is ironic that the "Salafis," in their ignorance, are calling "Jahmi" one of the chief enemies of the Jahmis, Imam Bukhari, who himself undoubtedly interpreted Allah's laughter as His mercy.[59] Also, Ibn al-Jawzi (d. 597) considered it obligatory to interpret Allah's laughter to mean the disclosure of His generosity and of His goodness (*ibda karam Allah wa ibanat fadlih*). He supports his position using the meaning of Allah's "running" in the hadith in Bukhari and Muslim, "Whoever comes to me walking, I come to him running." Before him, Ibn Battal (d. 449) interpreted this as Allah's promptness in granting His reward. Like Ibn Hajar, Ibn al-Jawzi quotes al-Khattabi's view that the laughter means Allah's good pleasure.[60] Thus, on the one hand, there are those such as Bin Baz,

---

56 Ibn Hajar, *Fath al-bari* (Beirut, 1989 ed.) 7:151, 8:816.
57 Nawawi, *Sharh sahih Muslim* (ed. al-Mays, Beirut, n.d.) 13/14:256.
58 Salman, *al-Rudud* p. 133.
59 As related by Bayhaqi and Ibn Hajar.
60 Bayhaqi, *al-Asma wa al-sifat* p. 298, 470; Ibn Hajar, *Fath al-bari* 7:82 (6:50 in Beirut 1989 ed.) For Ibn Battal's interpretation: *Fath al-bari* 13:513. Cf. Buti, *al-Salafiyya* p. 135, and Ibn al-Jawzi, *Daf shubah al-tashbih* (Saqqaf ed.) p. 180, 183.

Harras, and Salman, who pretend to represent the view of the true Salaf, and on the other the prestigious names of the great hadith masters (*huffaz*), such as:

- ° Bukhari
- ° Khattabi
- ° Ibn Battal
- ° Qadi Iyad
- ° Ibn al-Jawzi
- ° Nawawi
- ° Ibn Hajar

4.9. ALLAH'S "SCHEMING"

Salman also blames Nawawi for interpreting Allah's "scheming" in the verse, *"They schemed, and Allah schemed"* (3:54) as an example of repeating the same term but using two different meanings; literal and metaphorical.[61] Both Bin Baz and Salman use literalism as an excuse to assert blameworthy traits to the Creator, even as they overtly reject sound scholarship that points away from this view. Furthermore, the books of Albani, which have already been touched upon, are many times as full with enormities couched in terms of disputation.

In light of their attempt to pass revisionism for scholarship, it must be asked, who are these writers who question the doctrines of Ibn Hajar and Nawawi? Like dwarves battling giants they attack and refute those of the highest repute; building for themselves a name through faultfinding, which the public misinterprets as wisdom. Unfortunately, this is proof of the spreading of the poison of division and ignorance in the Muslim world today.

These views are presented to Muslims so that they will not be fooled by the false scholarship that is being spread in the name of Islam. This false scholarship is but the end of a 200-year-old campaign to contradict and dismantle everything that scholars of mainstream Islam have been raised with since the dawn of Islam. One of the most flagrant proofs of the "Salafis'" guilt in this regard is the contradiction of their own scholars when they oppose the hard line of *tajsim* advocated by the

---

61 Salman, *al-Rudud* p. 149.

group. Albani's contradiction of those who accept the meaning of "settling" (*istaqarra*) in reference to the verse of *istiwa* (20:5), and Ibn Uthaymin's contradiction of Albani on the same point (see Appendix 2). Ironically enough, Ibn Abd al-Wahhab's grandson, Sulayman ibn Abd Allah, refuted the doctrine of his own grandfather:

Allah the Exalted is not the locus of any created phenomena, and He is not immanent in any created thing, nor is He circumscribed by any created thing whatsoever. Therefore, whoever believes or says: Allah is in person (*bi dhatihi*) in every place, or in one place: he is a disbeliever (*kafir*). It is obligatory to declare that Allah is distinct from His creation, established over His throne without modality, or likeness, or examplarity. Allah was and there was no place, then He created place and He is exalted as He ever was before He created place, and He is not perceived by the senses, nor measured by human measure, and there is not even the beginning of an analogy for His Essence, His attributes, and His acts . . . He resembles nothing and nothing resembles Him. Therefore whoever draws a resemblance between Him and a created object has committed disbelief.[62]

---

62 Sulayman ibn Abd Allah b. Muhammad b. Abd al-Wahhab, *al-Tawdih an tawhid al-khallaq fi jawab ahl al-Iraq* (1319/1901) p. 34. New ed.: al-Riyad : Dar tibah, 1984.

5
CONCLUSION: SALAF AND PSEUDO-SALAF

5.1. NEITHER IBN TAYMIYYA NOR IBN QAYYIM REPRESENT THE TEACHING OF THE SALAF

In conclusion, it is now clear that by attributing to Allah Almighty motion and descent, bodily confinement in a space above the created Throne, spatial elevation, and so forth, Ibn Taymiyya, Ibn Qayyim al-Jawziyya, Ibn Abd al-Wahhab, and their followers follow neither the pious Salaf nor the pious Khalaf. Instead they follow the rudest examples of anthropomorphism among the strange sayings of some scholars, among them the like of Abu Muhammad Hisham ibn al-Hakam of Kufa, about whom al-Ashari says:

> His Lord is in a specific place distinct from other places, and that place is the Throne, and He touches the Throne, and the Throne contains and circumscribes Him . . . and He has length, breadth and height and a body with six sides.[1]

By resuscitating grave errors that had been rejected and

---

1 Al-Ashari, *Maqalat al-islamiyyin wa ikhtilaf al-musallin*, ed. Muhammad Muhyi al-din Abd al-Hamid (Cairo: Maktabat al-nahda al-misriyya, 1969-70) p. 260.

condemned more than once before, these self-pronounced "Salafi" authors declared their enmity to the doctrinal unity of mainstream Islam. The major scholars of their time, who were not blinded by private loyalty or discipleship, and who were not stifled by Wahhabi tyranny, were quick to see the threat the "Salafis" posed to sound belief. In every century, strong, familiar *fatawa* have been issued against them, and the struggle of the Saved Sect has been waged indefatigably.

Let it be restated for clarity that:

• **Neither Ibn Taymiyya nor Ibn Qayyim al-Jawziyya belong to the true Salaf or to their school of thought.**

• **The school of thought of the Salaf is entirely represented and contained in the scholars of the schools of law, their methods, and their Imams.**

• **Those who belong to that collective school of thought are the Saved Group who follow mainstream Islam.**

• **Those who contradict the belief of that group and oppose them in their writings, such as these two scholars and their Wahhabi and "Salafi" subscribers in later times, are outside mainstream Islam and even farther from the school of the Salaf.**

5.2. IBN TAYMIYYA'S GREAT ARROGANCE

It is found that pseudo-Salafi authors routinely consider their own *ijtihad* superior to that of the recognized *madhahib* altogether. As Ibn Hajar al-Asqalani reported of Ibn Taymiyya, they are prone to correct everyone great and small, including the Companions:

> Al-Tufi said: A time came when his companions took to over-praising him and this drove him to be satisfied with himself until he became proud before his fellow human beings, and became convinced that he was a scholar capable of independent reasoning. Henceforth he began to answer each and every scholar great and small, past and recent, until he went all the way back to Umar and faulted him in some mat-

ter. He also spoke against Ali and said, He made mistakes in seventeen matters. Some considered him a dissimulator of disbelief (*munafiq*) because of what he said about Ali; namely, that he had been forsaken everywhere he went, had repeatedly tried to acquire the *khilafa* and never attained it, fought out of lust for power rather than religion, and said that "he loved authority while Uthman loved money." He would say that Abu Bakr had declared Islam in his old age, fully aware of what he said, while Ali had declared Islam as a boy, and the boy's Islam is not considered sound upon his mere word. In sum he said ugly things such as these, and it was said against him that he was a dissimulator, in view of the Prophet's saying to Ali: "Only a dissimulator would show you hatred."[2]

The "Salafis" claim to follow the school of Imam Ahmad ibn Hanbal, although he never provided the example that they follow. Rather, they object to following any of the recognized *madhahib* in countless matters, whether that of Imam Malik, Abu Hanifa, al-Shafii, or Ahmad ibn Hanbal. Nowhere is their deviation from these Imams greater than in the area of *aqida*.

5.3. "SALAFIS" CLAIM IBN TAYMIYYA AS A REFORMER BUT HE INAUGURATED CONFUSION

Ibn Taymiyya viewed himself as a reformer of Islam, much as Martin Luther believed himself to be the reformer of Christianity. However, Islam does not recognize reform, only renewal. All the same, Ibn Taymiyya is sported by his admirers as the reformer who would bring Islam back to the way of the Salaf, as suggested by the Prophet (ﷺ) in the hadith, "Mine is the best century, then the one following it, then the one following it." Ibn Taymiyya and his followers seem to dismiss the fact that while he did not live in the times described by the Prophet (ﷺ) as the best, the recognized Imams (whose verdicts they oppose and distort in so many instances) did, and are rightfully respected as the true Salaf.

There never was nor is there now any disagreement among

---

2 Ibn Hajar, *al-Durar p.* 154-155.

mainstream scholars about issues of belief. The mainstream scholars have, since the third century, agreed on the formulations of Abul-Hasan al-Ashari and Maturidi in *aqida*, and have never deviated from them. Only Ibn Taymiyya, who came much later than the Salaf, likened Allah to creation—in terms that the Salaf shunned—and incorporated into his school a strange literalist understanding of Quran and hadith in their name, and so disregarded verses warning against just that. It is unfortunate that today a small but vocal minority of Muslims have taken this scholar, to the exclusion of all mainstream scholars, as their model and as their Imam. They have no understanding of his wrong beliefs, and simply parrot his *fatawa*, and those of his follower Muhammad ibn Abd al-Wahhab, blindly.

5.4. THE WORST EVIL IS AN EVIL SCHOLAR

The Prophet (ﷺ) said, "The worst evil consists in learned men who are evil, and the best good consists in learned men that are good," and "Beware the lapse of the learned man." He also said that the one with the worst position in Allah's sight on the day of resurrection is a learned man who did not profit from his learning.

Umar ibn al-Khattab said that three things demolished Islam:

* The slip of the learned man,
* The disputation of a hypocrite about the Book, and
* The rule of leaders who lead people astray.[3]

Umar's descendant and the Renewer of the eleventh century, Imam Ahmad Sirhindi, said, "The good scholar is the best of mankind. The bad scholar is the worst of mankind. Men's happiness and disaster depend upon scholars."

From these warnings it can be concluded that a person of intellect, wisdom, and powerful memory, if set towards good, has the ability to revive and renew the religion. According to the Prophet, "At the head of every hundred years, Allah will

---

3 Al-Darimi transmitted them in the introduction of his *Sunan* and al-Tibrizi mentioned them in the *Mishkat*, Book of Knowledge.

send this Community one who will revive its religion."[4] However, if, as in the case of Ibn Taymiyya, this man is corrupted in his own beliefs, he can cause irreparable damage that is greater than that of the external enemies of Islam.

The greatest indication of the damage done by Ibn Taymiyya is the fact that no single scholar in the history of Islam has helped polarize the Muslim Community to the extent that he has. Only about Ibn Taymiyya has it been said at the same time that, on one hand he was a Shaykh al-Islam[5] or reformer of the religion and,[6] on the other hand, he was "a slave which Allah has forsaken, misguided, blinded, deafened, and debased,"[7] and to call him Shaykh al-Islam was to commit disbelief![8] Shaykh al-Islam al-Taqi al-Subki said of him, "His learning exceeded his intelligence." Ibn Taymiyya's teachings remained ignored and abased for nearly five hundred years. Then, Muhammad ibn Abd al-Wahhab came forth with even less learning and less intelligence, and hammered home the wedge that Ibn Taymiyya first inserted into the heart of Islamic unity.

5.5. "SALAFIS" PERPETUATE REBELLION AGAINST THE ISLAMIC STATE

Was Ibn Abd al-Wahhab a reviver? Yes, but a reviver of corrupt ideas and dubious beliefs whose followers took up the sword against the Commander of the Faithful and proclaimed him the head of the rebels (*bughat*) of his time, like the Khawarij. Yet, as Ibn Abidin al-Hanafi pointed out in the excerpt already cited, "The name of Khawarij is applied to those who part ways with Muslims and declare them disbelievers, as took place in our time with the followers of Muhammad ibn Abd al-Wahhab . . ."

Ibn Abd al-Wahhab's sons and followers pillaged the lands of the Two Holy Sanctuaries, killing the descendants of the

---

4 Abu Dawud, *Malahim* (Book 36) 1.

5 "Abu al-Hajjaj al-Mizzi (654-742) did not give this title to anyone else among his contemporaries besides Ibn Taymiya." Shams al-Din al-Sakhawi, *al-Jawahir wa al-durar fi tarjamat shaykh al-islam Ibn Hajar* (al-Asqalani) (Cairo: Lajnat ihya al-turath al-islami, 1986) p. 16.

6 E.g. by al-Nadwi and others who seem unaware that the renewers of the eighth century are al-Bulqini and Zayn al-Din al-Iraqi by near-consensus, and some have said: *Hafiz* Taqi al-Din al-Subki.

7 Ibn Hajar al-Haytami, *Fatawa hadithiyya* (Cairo: al-halabi, 1390/1970) p. 114.

8 According to Ala al-din al-Bukhari.

Prophet (☙), and destroying the Prophet's home and the homes of his relatives and Companions. They formed a sect called al-Wahhabiyya to insure that Ibn Abd al-Wahhab's design would be carried out until the caliphate was destroyed little more than a century after his death. In the golden age of European colonialism, no British, French, German, or Italian armies killed as many Muslims as the Wahhabis killed in al-Hijaz in the 19th century. Yet the Prophet (☙) defined the Muslim as he from whose harm other Muslims are safe.

The intellectual descendants of al-Wahhabiyya are the modern day "Salafis." Like the Wahhabis, the "Salafis" accuse Muslims at large of disbelief, they wish harm to the Prophet (☙) and those who love him but, unlike them, do not have the means to carry arms against the innocent. The Prophet (☙) asked after the battle of Uhud, "How will a people who harm their Prophet (☙) prosper?" This is the way of the "Salafis," the Wahhabis, and the way of Ibn Taymiyya, not the way of mainstream Islam and the Salaf, and not the way of the Prophet (☙) and the Companions.

5.6. WARNING OF MUSLIMS SCHOLARS AGAINST THE "SALAFIS"

The Mufti of Makka, Ahmad Zayni Dahlan, wrote several books exposing Ibn Abd al-Wahhab's heresy. Many others did the same, including Ibn Abd al-Wahhab's own father, his brother Sulayman ibn Abd al-Wahhab, and hundreds of Sunni scholars in his own time, and afterwards, when the Wahhabi name was updated to "Salafi."[9] Yet, today there are financed printing presses, "scholars," and associations publishing the teachings of Ibn Taymiyya, Ibn Qayyim, Ibn Abd al-Wahhab and their like. They deliberately ignore the refutations of the Wahhabi and "Salafi" views already in place according to the consensus of mainstream Islamic scholars. This suggests that these are the last days of the Nation of the Prophet (☙), as he said, "The most vulgar, the basest people will come to preside over Muslims," and:

---

[9] These works form a treasury of late Sunni heresiology, of which we have listed about eighty titles in the introduction to our translation of al-Sidqi al-Zahawi's *al-Fajr al-sadiq* under the title *The Doctrine of Ahl al-Sunna versus the "Salafi" Movement.* Published by Al-Sunnah Foundation of America, 1996.

One of the foreshadows of Doomsday is that knowledge will vanish, the ignoramuses of religion will increase in number, and there will be more of those who have alcoholic drinks and who commit fornication.[10]

---

[10] Bukhari.

APPENDIX 1:
A BRIEF HISTORY OF THE WAHHABI
MOVEMENT[1]

The Wahhabiyya is a sect whose origin can be traced back to Muhammad Ibn Abd al-Wahhab (d.1207/1792). Although he began proselytizing as early as 1143 A.H., the subversive current that Ibn Abd-al-Wahhab initiated took some fifty years to spread. His doctrine first appeared in Najd, the same district that produced the false prophet, Musaylima in the early days of Islam. Muhammad Ibn Saud, governor of this district, aided Ibn Abd al-Wahhab's effort and forced people to follow him. One Arab tribe after another allowed itself to be deceived until sedition became commonplace in the region, Ibn Abd al-Wahhab's notoriety grew and his power soon passed beyond anyone's control. The nomadic Arabs of the surrounding desert feared him. He used to say to the people, "I call upon you only to confess *tawhid* (monotheism) and to avoid *shirk* (i.e., not to associate partners with Allah in worship)." The people of the countryside followed him; where he walked, they walked, until his dominance increased.

Muhammad Ibn Abd-al-Wahhab was born in 1111/1699 and died in 1207/1792. At the outset of his career, he used to go back and forth to Makka and Madina in search of knowledge. In Madina, he studied with Shaykh Muhammad Ibn Sulayman al-Kurdi and Shaykh Muhammad Hayah al-Sindi. These two shaykhs, as well as others whom he studied with early on, detected the heresy of Ibn Abd al-Wahhab's creed. They used to say, "Allah will allow him to be led astray; but even unhappier will be the lot of those misled by him." Even his father, Abd al-Wahhab, a pious scholar of the religion, detected his son's heresy and began to warn others about him. His own brother (Sulayman) soon followed suit, going so far as to write a book

---

1 Excerpted from Jamal Effendi al-Sidqi al-Zahawi's *al-Fajr al-sadiq*, translated by the author as *The Doctrine of Ahl as-Sunna Versus the "Salafi" Movement* (ASFA, 1996). The book is available in its entirety at the website http://www.sunnah.org/publi-cation/fajr.htm.

entitled *al-Sawaiq* to refute the innovative and subversive creed manufactured by Ibn Abd al-Wahhab.[2]

Famous writers of the day made a point of noting the similarity between Ibn Abd al-Wahhab's beginnings and those of the false prophets who were prominent in Islam's initial epoch —like Musaylima the Prevaricator, Sajah al-Aswad al-Anasi, Tulayha al-Asadi and others of their kind. What was different in Ibn Abd al-Wahhab's case was that he did not make an outright claim to prophecy. Undoubtedly, he was unable to gain enough support to openly proclaim it. Nevertheless, he would call those who came from abroad to join his movement "Muhajirun," and those who came from his own region "Ansar," in patent imitation of those who took flight from Makka with the Prophet Muhammad. Ibn Abd al-Wahhab habitually ordered anyone who had made hajj prior to their joining him to remake it, since they made their first hajj as disbelievers and Allah had not accepted it. He was also given to telling people who wished to enter in his innovative religion, "You must bear witness against yourself that you were a disbeliever and you must bear witness against your parents that they were disbelievers and died as such."

His practice was to declare a group of famous scholars of the past disbelievers. If a potential recruit to his movement agreed and testified to the truth of that declaration, he was accepted; if not, an order was given and he was summarily put to death. Ibn Abd al-Wahhab made no secret of his view that the Muslim community had existed for the last six hundred years in a state of unbelief (*kufr*) and he said the same of anyone who did not follow him. Even if a person was the most pious and God-fearing Muslim, Ibn Abd al-Wahhab would denounce him as an idolater (*mushrik*), making the shedding of their blood and confiscation of their wealth permitted (*halal*).[3]

On the other hand, Ibn Abd al-Wahhab affirmed the faith of

2 Sulayman Ibn Abd al-Wahhab al-Najdi, *al-Sawaiq al-ilahiyya fi al-radd ala al-Wahhabiyya* (Divine lightnings in answering the Wahhabis), ed. Ibrahim Muhammad al-Batawi (Cairo: Dar al-insan, 1987). Offset reprint by Waqf Ikhlas, Istanbul: Hakikat kitabevi, 1994. Prefaces by Shaykh Muhammad ibn Sulayman al-Kurdi al-Shafii and Shaykh Muhammad Hayyan al-Sindi (Muhammad Ibn Abd al-Wahhab's shaykh) to the effect that Ibn Abd al-Wahhab is *"dall mudill"* ("misguided and misguiding").

3 According to the noted Western historian, M. Cooke, ". . .he (M. Ibn abd al-Wahhab) considered most of the professed Muslims of his day to be polytheists who should be fought until they accepted Islam." See "On the Origins of Wahhabism," Royal Asiatic Society Journal. Series 3, vol 2, 2 (1992) p. 191-202.

anyone who followed him even though they were persons of notoriously corrupt and profligate styles of life. He always played on the dignity that he felt Allah had entitled him to. Ibn Abd al-Wahhab's personal aggrandizement directly correspond-ed to his claim that less reverence was due to the Prophet (ﷺ). He frequently depreciated the Prophet's status as the Messenger of Allah by describing him with language fit to describe an errand boy rather than a divinely commissioned apostle. He would say things such as, "I looked up the account of Hudaybiyya and found it to contain this or that lie." Ibn Abd al-Wahhab was in the habit of using such contemptuous speech that one of his followers felt free to say, in his presence, "This stick in my hand is better than Muhammad because it benefits me by enabling me to walk. But Muhammad is dead and bene-fits me not at all." This statement, of course, expresses nothing less than disbelief (*kufr*) and counts legally as such in the Four Schools of Islamic Law.

Returning always to the same theme, Ibn Abd al-Wahhab used to say that invoking blessings on the Prophet (ﷺ) was rep-rehensible and disliked (*makruh*) in the Sharia. He prohibited the recitation of blessings of the Prophet (ﷺ) (*salawat*) on the eve of Friday. He forbade its public utterance from the *minbar*, and he harshly punished anyone who pronounced such prayers. He even went so far as to kill a blind *muadhdhin* (a profes-sional caller to prayer) who did not comply when Ibn Abd al-Wahhab commanded him to stop praying for the Prophet (ﷺ) at the conclusion of his call to prayer. Ibn Abd al-Wahhab deceived his followers by saying that all that was done to keep monothe-ism pure.

Ibn Abd al-Wahhab also burned many books containing prayers for the Prophet (ﷺ); among them *Dalail al-khayrat* and others, similar in content and theme. In this fashion, he destroyed countless books on Islamic law, commentaries on the Quran, and volumes of hadith whose common fault lay only in their contradiction of his own vacuous creed. At the same time, however, Ibn Abd al-Wahhab never stopped encouraging his fol-lowers to interpret Quran and hadith for themselves, and to act on their interpretations in light of their own understanding —

darkened though it was by Ibn Abd al-Wahhab's heretical indoctrination and errant belief.

Ibn Abd al-Wahhab clung fiercely to his practice of denouncing people as disbelievers. To do this he used Quranic verses originally revealed about idolaters, and extended their application to monotheists. It has been narrated by Abdullah Ibn Umar and recorded by Imam Bukhari that the Khawarij[4] transferred Quranic verses intended to refer to disbelievers and applied them to believers.There is another narration that has been transmitted, on the authority of Ibn Umar, that relates that the Prophet (☵), said, "What I most fear in my community is a man who interprets verses of the Quran out of context." These two hadiths both apply to Ibn Abd al-Wahhab and his followers.

Ibn Abd al-Wahhab statements and actions reveal that his intention was to found a new religion.[5] Consequently, the only thing he accepted from the religion of our Prophet (☵) was the Quran. However, even this was only for show, as it helped to hide from people what his aims really were. Ibn Abd al-Wahhab and his followers used to interpret the Quran according to their own whims and ignored the commentaries provided by the Prophet (☵) his Companions, the pious ancestors of our faith (*al-salaf al-salihun*) and the Imams of Quranic commentary. He did not argue based on the strength of the Prophet's narrations and the sayings of the Companions, the Successors to the Companions, and the Imams (i.e. those who derived rulings in the Sharia by means of *ijtihad*). He did not adjudicate legal cases based on the principles of the law (*usul*); that is, he did not adhere to Consensus (*ijma*), nor to sound analogy (*qiyas*). Although he claimed to belong to the legal school (*madhhab*) of Imam Ahmad Ibn Hanbal, this claim was made in falsehood and dissimulation. The scholars and jurists of the Hanbali school rejected his multifarious errors. They, including his own brother,[6] wrote numerous articles refuting him.

The learned Sayyid al-Haddad al-Alawi said:

---

4 See Glossary.

5 The first Western traveller to Arabia, C. Neibuhr, actually believed Ibn Abd al-Wahhab to have begun anew religion, it was so unlike traditional Sunni Islam. See C. Neibuhr, *Travels through Arabia and Other Countries in the East*. 9 Edinburgh, 1792). Vol. II, p.131.

6 His book touching on Ibn Abd al-Wahhab's errors was mentioned earlier.

> In our opinion, the one element in the statements
> and actions of Ibn Abd al-Wahhab that makes his
> departure from the foundations of Islam unquestion-
> able is the fact that he, without support of any gener-
> ally accepted interpretation of Quran or *sunna* (*bi la
> tawil*), takes matters in our religion necessarily well-
> known to be objects of prohibition (*haram*) agreed
> upon by consensus (*ijma*) and makes them permissi-
> ble (*halal*) [e.g. asking Muslims to repeat their *sha-
> hada*, or killing them]·[7]

Furthermore, Ibn Abd al-Wahhab disparages the prophets,
the messengers, the saints, and the pious. The willful dispar-
agement of anyone falling under these categories is unbelief
(*kufr*) according to the consensus reached by the major Imams
of the Sunni schools of Islamic law.

Ibn Abd al-Wahhab wrote an essay entitled, "The
Clarification of Unclarity Concerning the Creator of heaven
and earth" for Ibn Saud. In this work, he declared that all present-day Muslims, and Muslims from the past 600 years, are
disbelievers. He applied the Quranic verses, intended to refer
to disbelievers in the tribe of the Quraysh, to most God-fearing
and pious individuals in the Muslim community. Ibn Saud naturally used this work as a device in subjecting the Arabs to his
dominance and fortifying his political sovereignty. Ibn Abd al-
Wahhab called people to his religion by instilling in their hearts
the idea that everyone under the sun was an idolater. What's
more, according to Ibn Abd al-Wahhab, anyone who slayed an
idolater would go directly to paradise when he died.

Among the narrations transmitted from the Prophet (ﷺ),
on him be peace, is the statement, "At the end of time, a man
will rise up in the same region as once rose Musaylima. He
would change the religion of Islam." Another saying reads,
"From Najd a satan will appear on the scene causing the Arab
peninsula to erupt in earthquake from discord and strife."

Among Ibn Abd al-Wahhab's abominations were his burn-
ing the books of Islamic science, and his slaughter of Islamic

7 Al-Habib Alawi ibn Ahmad ibn Hasan ibn Qutb al-Irshad al-Habib Abd Allah ibn
Alawi al-Haddad, *Misbah al-anam wa jala' al-zalam fi radd shubah al-bidi al-najdi al-
lati adalla biha al-awamm* (The Beacon of humanity and the dispelling of darkness in
refuting the Najdii Innovator that misguided the innocent). Excerpts from the original
Arabic text of this book are available at the website http://www.sunnah.org/publica-
tion/beacon/cover.htm.

scholars and people of every class. He not only made the shedding of their blood and confiscation of their property and wealth licit, but also allowed the desecration and exhumation of the graves of the Friends of Allah (*awliya*). In Ahsa, for example, he ordered that some of the saints' graves be used by people to relieve themselves.

He forbade people to read Imam Jazuli's *Dalail al-khayrat*, to perform supererogatory acts of devotion, to utter the names of Allah in His remembrance, and to recite the *mawlid* celebrating the Prophet's birth. What's more, he killed anyone who dared to do any of these things. He forbade any kind of act of worship after the canonical prayers. He would publicly declare a Muslim a disbeliever for requesting a prophet or individual of saintly life to join his prayers as an intercessor, though it is encouraged by Allah and mentioned in Quran and hadith many times. He also said anyone who addressed a person as lord or master (*sayyid*) was a disbeliever.

Undoubtedly, one of the worst abominations perpetrated by the Wahhabis under the leadership of Ibn Abd al-Wahhab was the massacre of the people of Taif. They killed everyone in sight, slaughtering child and adult, ruler and ruled, lowly and high-born. They began with a suckling child nursing at his mother's breast and moved on to a group studying Quran, slaying all of them, down to the last man. When they had wiped out the people they found in the houses, they went into the streets, the shops and the mosques, killing whoever happened to be there. They even killed people in prayer until they had annihilated every Muslim in Taif and until only some twenty or more people remained.

Survivors were contained in Bayt al-Fitni, armed and guarded against the Wahhabi approach. There was another group at Bayt al-Far numbering two-hundred and seventy who fought the Wahhabis that day. They were followed by a second and third group until the Wahhabis presented a guarantee of clemency. They made this proposal as a trick. When the defenders entered, the Wahhabis seized their weapons and slew them each and every man. Others, they brought out with a guarantee of clemency to the valley of Waj, where they abandoned men and women in the cold and snow, barefoot, naked, and exposed in shame. Then, they plundered their possessions, wealth of any kind, household furnishings and cash.

The Wahhabis cast books into the streets to be blown to and fro, including copies of the Quran, volumes of Bukhari, Muslim, and other canonical collections of hadith, and books of *fiqh*, all mounting to the thousands. Books remained in the streets for several days, trampled on by the Wahhabis. Not one among them made the slightest attempt to remove even one page of Quran from under foot and preserve it from the ignominy and disrespect of this display. Then, they razed the houses and made what was once a town a barren waste land. That was in the year 1217 A.H.

Ibn Abd al-Wahhab believed that prophethood was only a matter of political leadership that the cleverest people attain when circumstances offer them an ignorant and uninformed crowd. However, since Allah the Exalted had shut tight the door of prophecy after the Seal of the Prophets (ﷺ) there was no way to realize this goal except to claim that he was a renewer of the faith (*mujaddid*) and an independent thinker in the formulation of legal rulings (*mujtahid*). Such an attitude—or rather the worst and most profound state of moral misguidance and religious disbelief— brought Ibn Abd al-Wahhab to the point of declaring every group of Muslims disbelievers and idolaters. He set out to apply verses of Quran, specifically revealed to single out the idolaters of the Arabs, to include all Muslims who visit the grave of their Prophet (ﷺ) and seek his intercession with their Lord.

Ibn Abd al-Wahhab cast aside anything that contradicted his own invalid claims and vain desires to work mischief with the explicit statements of the Master of all messengers, the Imams, and the *mujtahid*s of Islam (that is, those who have the capacity to exercise independent reasoning in the process of legal discovery). Hence, when he saw a consensus of legal opinion in matters of faith that clashed with his own thinking, he rejected it as a matter of principle, asserting, "I do not entertain any opinion of people coming after the Quran which contains all that pertains to Islam, the fresh and the dry." The Quran says:

> With Him are the keys of the unseen, the treasures that none knoweth but He. He knoweth whatever there is on the earth and in the sea. Not a leaf doth fall but with His knowledge. There is not a grain in the darkness (or depths) of the earth, nor anything fresh or dry (green or withered), but is (inscribed) in a record clear (to those who can read) (6:59).

Thus, he failed to heed what the Quran itself declared, "He who follows the path of those other than the Muslims" inasmuch as he accepted from Quran only what it reveals about idolaters among the Arabs. He interpreted these verses in his own obscure fashion, having the gall to stand before Allah and use the unwarranted and unjustified exegesis of His Holy Text to facilitate the accomplishment of his own personal and political ambitions!

In the narration where the angel Gabriel assumes human form to question him about the creed of Islam, the Prophet (ﷺ) declared, "Islam is to testify that there is no god but Allah and Muhammad is the Messenger of Allah."[8] Again, in the narration of Umar he says, "Islam is built upon five articles of faith (the first being): "Testimony that there is no god but Allah, Muhammad is His servant and Messenger." There is also his declaration to the delegation of Abd al-Qays, where he says,[9] "I am commanding you to believe in Allah alone. Do you know what belief in Allah alone is? It is to testify: There is no god but Allah and Muhammad is the Messenger of Allah." Also cited is his exhortation, "I order you to fight people until they say, "There is no god but Allah and that Muhammad is the Messenger of Allah." Finally, the Prophet (ﷺ) says, "It is sufficient that folk say, There is no god but Allah."

It is amazing how Ibn Abd al-Wahhab misrepresents the use of the Prophet's name in petitions to Allah or *tawassul* that are within the pretenses of monotheism (*tawhid*) and divine transcendence (*tanzih*). He claims that use of a Prophet's name in this manner constitutes association of a partner with Allah.

8 Bukhari and Muslim.
9 Also cited in Bukhari and Muslim.

At the same time, however, he asserts that Allah's mounting His throne is like sitting on it and affirms that Allah has hands, face, and spatial dimension! Ibn Abd al-Wahhab says it is possible to point to Allah in the sky and claims that He literally descends to the lower heavens. What happens to Divine transcendence when the lowliest of animate creatures shares properties with their Creator? To what is He, the Exalted, transcendent, when He is characterized in so deprecating a fashion and His divinity is couched in terms so redolent of ridicule and contempt?

One of Ibn Abd al-Wahhab's more enormous stupidities is that when reason contradicts his claims, he casts it aside and gives it no role in his judgment. He endeavors to make people like dumb beasts when it comes to matters of faith. He prohibits the involvement of reason in religious affairs, despite the fact that there is no contradiction between reason and faith. On the contrary, whenever human minds reach their full measure of completeness and perfection, religion's merits and prerogatives with regard to reason become totally manifest. Is there in this age, an age of the mind's progress, anything more abominable than denying reason its proper scope, especially when the cardinal pivot of religion is based on the ability to reason? The obligation to carry out the duties of Islam disappears when mental capacity is absent. Allah has addressed his servants in many places in the Quran as "O you who possess minds," alerting them to the fact that knowledge of the realities of religion is an obligation only of those possessing minds.

Now a summation of the vain and empty prattle of the renegade Wahhabi sect that it aspires to issue as doctrine. Their invalid creed consists of a number of articles:

1 Affirming the face, hand, and spatial direction of the Creator and making Him a body that descends and ascends.
2 Applying principles derived from narration (naql) prior to those derived from reason (aql).
3 Denial and rejection of consensus as a principle (asl) of Sharia legislation.
4 Prohibiting copying and emulating the judgments of the

Imams who have the status of those capable of exercising independent reasoning in matters of Sharia.

5 Declaring Muslims who contradict them disbelievers.

6 Prohibition of using the name of the Messenger in petitions to Allah (*tawassul*) or the name of someone else among the friends of Allah (*awliya*) and pious (*salihin*).

7 Making the visiting of the tombs of prophets and of pious people illicit.

8 Declaring a Muslim a disbeliever who makes a vow to someone other than Allah or sacrifices at the grave or final resting place of *awliya* or the pious.

APPENDIX 2:
NASIR AL-DIN AL-ALBANI'S ATTACKS ON
THE SCHOLARS
AND HIS INNOVATIONS IN DOCTRINE

A modern day scholar, Shaykh Hasan Ali al-Saqqaf, has documented Nasir al-Din al-Albani's derogatory style in his book called *Qamus shataim al-albani wa alfazihi al-munkara al-lati yatluquha ala ulama al-umma*" (Dictionary of Albani's insults and the heinous words he uses against the scholars of the Community).[1] Here are some of his examples of Albani's criticism and manner of mentioning the hadith masters:

He [Albani] compares Hanafi *fiqh* to the Gospel in respect to distance from Quran and *sunna*.[2]

He says of Imam Abu Hanifa, "The imams have declared him weak for his poor memorization"[3] although Ibn Hajar al-Asqalani reports no such position in his *Tahdhib al-tahdhib*.

He describes Suyuti as a "loudmouth" (*jaja*)[4] who "contradicts himself" (4:386) and he says of Suyuti, "Has he no shame?"[5]

He refers to Dhahabi as one with little sagacity and scholarly skill[6] and cautions against "the extent of Dhahabi's self-contradiction" as an example why one should not imitate men.[7]

He blames al-Hakim, al-Mundhiri, and al-Dhahabi's "poor scholarliness and proneness to imitation" because they all declared a hadith sound and he—Albani—disagrees with them.[8]

---

1 Shaykh Hasan Ali al-Saqqaf, *Qamus shataim al-albani wa alfazihi al-munkara al-lati yatluquha ala ulama al-umma* (Dictionary of Albani's insults and the heinous words he uses against the scholars of the Community). Amman: Dar al-imam Nawawi, 1993.

2 In Albani's commentary of Mundhiri's *Mukhtasar sahih Muslim,* 3rd ed. (al-Maktab al-islami 1977) p. 548. The comparison was removed from later editions.

3 In Albani's commentary of Ibn Abi Asim's *Kitab al-sunna* 1:76. This falsehood is categorically refuted in another volume.

4 Albani, *Daifa* 3:189.

5 Albani, *Daifa* 3:479.

6 Albani, *Ghayat al-maram* p. 35.

7 Albani, *Daifa* 4:422.

8 Albani, *Daifa* 3:416.

Of Ibn al-Jawzi he also says, "He contradicts himself."[9]

Of al-Hakim, "Grossly mistaken"[10] and "self-contradictory."[11]

Of Ibn Hajar al-Asqalani, "Self-contradictory."[12]

Of al-Subki, "He shows fanaticism."[13]

Of al-Munawi, he refers to "his fanaticism"[14] and says "I find no excuse for his self-contradictions."[15]

Here are some of Albani's' targets among contemporary shaykhs of hadith and other scholars:

Ahmad al-Ghumari, "One of the innovators."[16]

Abd Allah al-Ghumari the author of *al-Qawl al-muqni fi al-radd ala al-albani al-mubtadi* (The persuasive discourse in refutation of Albani the innovator). Albani calls him "deluded" and imputes him with "wickedness" and "perfidy."[17]

Shaykh al-Islam, Imam al-Kawthari. The hatred of Albani and his followers for him is well-known.

Shuayb al-Arnaut: Albani classifies him among the People of Idle Desires (*ahl al-ahwa*)[18] and declares "he blinds himself."[19]

Abd al-Fattah Abu Ghudda. Albani curses him, "May Allah maim your hand and cut off your tongue."[20]

Muhammad Awwama: see below.

Muhammad Said Ramadan al-Buti. Albani imputes him and Awwama with "blind-following" and "animal stupidity."[21]

Mahmud Said the author of "Warning to the Muslim concerning Albani's attack on *Sahih Muslim*." Albani says of him, "A new jealous, loathsome rebel."[22]

Ismail al-Ansari. Albani speaks of his "perfidy," says that his heart "drips with the blood of jealousy and envy," calls him

9 Albani, *Sahiha* 1:193.
10 Albani, *Daifa* 3:458.
11 Albani, *Tawassul* p. 106.
12 Albani, *Daifa* 3:267.
13 Albani, *Daifa* 2:285.
14 Albani, *Daifa* 2:345.
15 Albani, *Daifa* 4:34.
16 Albani, *Daifa* 4:6.
17 Albani, *Sifat al-salat* (Riyad: dar al-maarif, 1991) p. 21.
18 Albani, *Adab al-zifaf* p. 21.
19 Albani, *Sifat al-salat* p. 16.
20 Albani, *Kashf al-niqab* p. 52.
21 Albani, *al-Ayat al-bayyinat*, 4th ed. (al-maktab al-islami 1405) introduction.
22 Albani, *Adab al-zifaf* p. 49.

"crafty" and "rebellious" and asks, "Is he one of the shaykhs of *kashf* who claim they see what is in the hearts of people and know their secrets, and practice disbelief?"[23]

Nasib al-Rifai, whom Albani calls together with al-Sabuni "Two of the most ignorant of those who spoke on this matter, especially al-Rifai who is the most audacious in his extensive ignorance"[24] "they lied, by Allah."[25]

Muhammad Ali al-Sabuni, the commentator on the Quran. Albani calls him "a thief, a liar, an ignorant and one who misguides others."[26]

Habib al-Rahman al-Azami, the Indian *muhaddith*. Albani calls him "one of the enemies of the Sunna and of the people of hadith and of the callers to *tawhid*."[27]

It is no wonder that Albani shows everybody who does not agree with him such enmity, considering the extent of his own innovations in religion:

1. He prohibits women from wearing gold rings despite the *ijma* of scholars permitting it. This was exposed by Saqqaf, in his treatise *Ihtijaj al-khaib bi ibarat man iddaa al-ijma fa huwa kadhib* (Albani's recourse to the phrase: "Whoever claims consensus he is a liar!").

2. He claims that 2.5 % *zakat* is not due on money obtained from commerce; i.e. the main activity whereby money circulates among Muslims.

3. He prohibits fasting on Saturdays. This was exposed by Saqqaf in his treatise *al-Qawl al-thabtu fi siyami yawm al-sabt* (The firm discourse concerning fasting on Saturdays).

4. He prohibits *itikaf* in any but the Three Mosques. This was exposed by Saqqaf in his treatise *al-Lajif al-dhuaf li al-muta-laib bi ahkam al-itikaf* (The Lethal strike against the one who toys with the rulings of *itikaf*).

5. He claims that it is lawful to eat in Ramadan before *maghrib* as it is defined by the law, and after true dawn.

6. He compares Hanafi fiqh to the Gospel as mentioned above.

7. He calls people to imitate him rather than the Imams of the Salaf, such as the founders of the four schools of law. His fol-

---

23 Albani, *Daifa*.
24 Albani, *Daifa* 1988 ed. 4:51.
25 Albani, *Daifa* 3:361.
26 Albani, Page H of the beginning of his *Sahiha* vol. 4.
27 Albani, *Adab al-zifaf*, new ed. al-maktaba al-islamiyya p. 8.

lowers invalidate the ahadith that contradict his views.

8. He prohibits the make-up performance of prayers missed intentionally. Saqqaf exposed this in his treatise, *Sahih sifat salat al-nabi sallallahu alayhi wa sallam* (The sound description of the Prophet's prayer).

9 He claims that it is permissible for menstruating women and those in a state of major defilement (*junub*) to recite, touch, and carry the Quran. This was exposed by Saqqaf in his treatise, *Ilam al-khaid bi tahrim al-quran ala al-junub wa al-haid* (The appraisal of the investigator into the interdiction of the Quran to those in a state of major defilement and menstruating women).

10 Albani claims that among the religious innovations in Madina is the presence of the Prophet's grave in the mosque.[28]

11 He claims that whoever travels to visit the Prophet (ﷺ) or to ask him for his intercession is a misguided innovator.[29]

12 He claims that whoever carries *dhikr* beads in his hand to remember Allah is misguided and innovating. This was exposed in the *muhaddith* Mahmud Said's *Wusul al-Tahani bi ithbat sunniyyat al-sibha wa al-radd ala al-albani* (The alighting of mutual benefit and the confirmation that the *sibha* is a *sunna*, and the refutation of Albani).

13 He claims that Allah is in a place above the Throne called *al-makan al-adami*, or "the place of non-existence." This was exposed by Saqqaf in his book *Talqih al-fuhum al-aliya* (The inculcation of lofty discernment).

14 He claims in *Tamam al-minna* that masturbation does not annul the fast.

Some of the points mentioned above will be refuted in more detail in the other volumes of this series. It is enough for now to show the legacy of Ibn Taymiyya and of the anthropomorphists, and to note that the wealth of proofs provided by mainstream Islamic scholars against the innovators in previous times are still current today.

---

28 Albani, *Manasik al-hajj wa al-umra* (4th ed. Al-maktaba al-isla-miyya) p. 60-61.
29 *Ibid.*

APPENDIX 3:
RECOMMENDED BOOKS OF SOUND DOCTRINE

In view of the profusion of "Salafi" views among young Muslims today, this section concludes with two lists of books on doctrine. The first is of recommended books of sound doctrine, which are recommended to all who desire to protect their religion. The second list is of rejected books of unsound doctrine, which Muslims are warned against with the strongest of warnings.

Bayhaqi's *al-Asma wa al-sifat*, ed. al-Kawthari.

Bayhaqi's *al-Itiqad wa al-hidaya ila sabil al-rashad*.

Imam al-Haramayn al-Juwayni's *al-Aqida al-nizamiyya fi al-arkan al-islamiyya*.

Imam al-Haramayn's *Kitab al-irshad ila qawati al-adilla fi usul al-itiqad*.

Tahawi's *Aqida* in Ghunaymi's or Saqqaf's commentary.

Ibn Hajar al-Asqalani's *Kitab al-tawhid in Fath al-bari*.

His *Kitab al-iman* in *Fath al-bari*.

Nawawi's commentary of *Sharh sahih Muslim*.

Abd al-Qahir al-Baghdadi's Usul al-din and the conclusion of his *Farq bayn al-firaq*.

Ghazali's *Qawaid al-aqaid* in *Ihya ulum al-din*, his *Iqtisad fi al-itiqad*, and his *Iljam al-awamm*.

The commentary on the above by al-hafiz al-Zabidi, in the second volume of his *Ithaf al-sadat al-muttaqin*.

Another commentary and edition of Ghazali's text by Hasan al-Saqqaf entitled *Aqidat ahl al-sunna wa al-jamaa*.

Ali al-Qari's commentary on Imam Abu Hanifa's *al-Fiqh al-akbar*.

Kawthari's *Maqalat* (articles).

Ibn al-Jawzi's *Daf shubah al-tashbih* ed. Hasan Saqqaf.

Tabdid al-zalam, which is Kawthari's commentary of Subki's refutation of Ibn al-Qayyim entitled *al-Sayf al-saqil*.

al-Bajuri's Quranic commentary and that of Abu Hayyan.

Qadi Iyad's *al-Shifa* and his commentary on *Sahih Muslim*.

APPENDIX 4:
REJECTED BOOKS OF UNSOUND DOCTRINE

The following books on *aqida* (belief and doctrine) are rejected for their deviant stance on many matters, such as Allah's essence and attributes, interpretation of Quran, anthropomorphism, and *tawassul* (seeking a means in Islam).

al-Sunna by Abdullah the son of Ahmad ibn Hanbal, shown by al-Kawthari to be replete with pure anthropomorphism.

al-Sunna by al-Lalikai and his *Itiqad ahl al-sunna*.

al-Sunna by Abu Bakr al-Khallal, Imam Ahmad's student;

The books of al-Barbahari.

al-Radd ala bishr al-marisi also called *Kitab al-naqd* by Uthman ibn Said al-Darimi (this is not the author of the *Sunan*).

al-Ibana of Ibn Batta.

Ibtal al-tawil by Abu Yala whom Ibn al-Jawzi called *mujassim*.

Kitab al-tawhid of Ibn Khuzayma, a book renamed by Imam Fakhr al-Din Razi: *Kitab al-shirk* and which Ibn Khuzayma later disavowed.

al-Sifat and *Ruyat* Allah falsely attributed to al-Daraqutni.

al-Iman by Ibn Mindah.

Dhamm al-kalam of al-Harawi, which Ibn Hajar considered a model of how not to write.

The books of Ibn Taymiyya, particularly: *al-Tasis*, *al-Ziyara*, and others.

Those of his student Ibn Qayyim on the same topics.

al-Uluw of al-Dhahabi, written in his youth, and which many of his later writings disavow.

The books of Ibn Abd al-Wahhab whose *fitna* is mentioned in the hadiths on Najd and those on the Khawarij.

Modern day books based upon the above works, where the dates of birth of the earlier writers are cited to fool innocent Muslims into taking them as authorities among the Salaf, when in fact they further heretical views. This is true of the books of al-Albani, Ibn Uthaymin, Ibn Baz, Mashhur Al Salman, Harras, and their propagandists in English such as Dawud Burbank, Bilal Phillips, and others.

GLOSSARY

ahkam: legal rulings.

ahl al-bida wa al-ahwa: the People of Unwarranted Innovations and Idle Desires.

ahl al-sunna wa al-jamaa: the Sunnis; the People of the Way of the Prophet and the Congregation of Muslims.[1]

aqida pl. *aqaid*: doctrine.

azaim: strict applications of the law. These are the modes of conduct signifying scrupulous determination to please one's Lord according to the model of the Prophet (ﷺ).

bida: blameworthy innovation.

faqih, pl. *fuqaha*: scholar of *fiqh* or jurisprudence; generally, "person of knowledge."

faqir, pl. *fuqara'*: Sufi, lit. "poor one."

fatwa, pl. *fatawa*: legal opinion.

fiqh: jurisprudence.

fitna: dissension, confusion.

hadith: saying(s) of the Prophet, and the sciences thereof.

hafiz: hadith master, the highest rank of scholarship in hadith.

haqiqi: literal.

hashwiyya: uneducated anthropomorphists.

hijri: adjective from *hijra* applying to dates in the Muslim calendar.

hukm, pl. *ahkam*: legal ruling.

ibadat: worship, acts of worship.

ihsan: perfection of belief and practice.

ijtihad: personal effort of qualified legal reasoning.

isnad: chain of transmission in a hadith or report.

istinbat: derivation (of legal rulings).

jahmi: a follower of Jahm ibn Safwan (d. 128), who said: "Allah is the wind and everything else."[2]

jihad: struggle against disbelief by hand, tongue, and heart.

kalam: theology.

khalaf: "Followers," general name for all Muslims who lived after the first three centuries.

khawarij: "Outsiders," a sect who considered all Muslims who did not follow them, disbelievers. The Prophet said about them as related by Bukhari: "They will transfer the Quranic verses meant to refer to disbelievers and make them refer to believers." Ibn Abidin applied the name of khawarij to the Wahhabi movement.[3]

madhhab, pl. *madhahib*: a legal method or school of law in Islam. The major schools of law include the Hanafi, Maliki, Shafii, and Hanbali and Jafari.

majazi: figurative.

manhaj, minhaj: Way, or doctrinal and juridical method.

muamalat (pl.): plural name embracing all affairs between human beings as opposed to acts of worship *(ibadat)*.

muattila: those who commit *tatil*, i.e. divesting Allah of His attributes.

muhaddith: hadith scholar.

muhkamat: texts conveying firm and unequivocal meaning.

mujahid, pl. *mujahidin*: one who wages *jihad*.

mujassima (pl.): those who commit

---

1 See the section entitled "Apostasies and Heresies" in our *Doctrine of Ahl al-Sunna Versus the "Salafi" Movement* p. 60-64.

2 See Bukhari, *Khalq afal al-ibad*, first chapter; Ibn Hajar, *Fath al-bari*, *Tawhid*, first chapter; and al-Baghdadi, *al-Farq bayn al-firaq*, chapter on the Jahmiyya.

3 al-Sayyid Muhammad Amin Ibn Abidin al-Hanafi, *Radd al-muhtar ala al-durr al-mukhtar*, *Kitab al-iman*, *Bab al-bughat* [Answer to the Perplexed: A Commentary on "The Chosen Pearl," Book of Belief, Chapter on Rebels] (Cairo: Dar al-Tibaa al-Misriyya, 1272/1856) 3:309.

tajsim, attributing a body to Allah.

mujtahid: one who practices *ijtihad* or personal effort of qualified legal reasoning.

munafiq: a dissimulator of his disbelief.

mushabbiha (pl.): those who commit *tashbih*, likening Allah to creation.

mushrik, pl. *mushrikun*: one who associate partners to Allah.

mutakallim, pl. *mutakallimun*: expert in *kalam*.

mutashabihat (pl.): texts which admit of some uncertainty with regard to their interpretation.

mutazila: rationalist heresy of the third century.

sahih: sound (applied to the chain of transmission of a hadith).

salaf: the Predecessors, i.e. Muslims of the first three centuries.

salafi: what pertains to the "Salafi" movement, a modern heresy that rejects the principles of mainstream Islam

shafaa: intercession.

sharia: name embracing the principles and application of Islamic law.

suluk: rule of conduct, personal ethics.

tawil: figurative interpretation.

tafwid: committing the meaning to Allah.

tajsim: attributing a body to Allah

tajwid: Quran reading.

takyif: attributing modality to Allah's attributes.

tamthil: giving an example for Allah.

taqlid: following qualified legal reasoning.

tariqa: path, specifically the Sufi path.

tasawwuf: collective name for the schools and sciences of purification of the self.

tashbih: likening Allah to His Creation.

tatil: divesting Allah from His attributes.

tawassul: seeking a means.

tawhid: Islamic doctrine of monotheism.

tazkiyat al-nafs: purification of the self.

usul: principles.

wasila: means.

BIBLIOGRAPHY

"A Brief Introduction to the Salafi Dawah" (Ipswich, U.K.: *Jamiat Ihyaa Minhaaj al-Sunnah*, 1993)

Abbasi, Mohammad, "Protestant Islam," which is available at http://ds.dial.pipex.com/masud/Islam/MISC/pislam.htm.

Abidin, Imam Muhammad, *Hashiyat radd al-muhtar ala al-durr al-mukhtar.*

Ahmad, *Musnad.*

Ajiba, *Iqaz al-himam fi sharh al-hikam* (Beirut: al-Maktaba al-thaqafiyya, n.d.).

Ajluni, *Kashf al-khafa, s.v. law annakum dallaytum bi hablin...*

Ajurri, *Sharia.*

Al-Munawi, *Fayd al-Qadir* (6:251-252 #9141-9142).

Albani, *Adab al-zifaf.*

Albani, *al-Ayat al-bayyinat,* 4th ed. (al-Maktab al-islami 1405).

Albani, *Daifa.*

Albani, *Ghayat al-maram.*

Albani, *Kashf al-niqab.*

Albani, *Manasik al-hajj wa al-umra* (4th ed. al-Maktaba al-isla-miyya).

Albani, *Mukhtasar al-uluw.*

Albani, on Ibn Abi Asim's *Kitab al-Sunna.*

Albani, on Mundhiri's *Mukhtasar Sahih Muslim,* 3rd ed. (al-Maktab al-isla-mi 1977).

Albani, *Sahiha.*

Albani, *Sifat al-salat* (Riyad: Dar al-maarif, 1991).

Albani, *Tawassul, Its Types and Rulings.*

Andalusi, Abu Hayyan, *al-Nahr al-madd.*

Andalusi, Abu Hayyan, *Tafsir al-bahr al-muhit.*

Arabi, Abu Bakr ibn, *Aridat al-ahwadhi.*

Arabi, Abu Bakr, *al-Awasim.*

Asakir, *Bayan al-wahm wa al-takhlit fi hadith al-atit* (The exposition of error and confusion in the narration of the groaning).

Asakir, *Tabyin* (Damascus 1347/1929).

Asakir, *Tarikh Dimashq.*

Ashari, *al-Ibana an usul al-diyana,* ed. Fawqiyya Husayn Mahmud (Cairo: Dar al-Ansar, 1977).

Ashari, *al-Ibana an usul al-diyana,* Hyderabad: *Dairat al-maarif,* 1321/1903; Cairo: *Idarat al-Matbaa al-muniriyya,* 1348/1930; ed. Fawqiyya Husayn Mahmud, 2 vol. (Cairo: Dar al-ansar, 1977); ed. Abbas Sabbagh (Beirut: Dar al-Nafais, 1994); also translated as Abu al-Hasan Ali ibn Ismail al-Ashari's *al-Ibana an usul al-diyana* (The elucidation of Islam's foundation): a translation with introduction and notes by Walter C. Klein (New York: Kraus Reprint Corp., 1967; Reprint. Originally published: New Haven, Conn.: American Oriental Society, 1940).

Ashari, *Istihsan al-khawd fi ilm al-kalam,* Hyderabad: Dairat al-maarif, 1344/1925. Reprinted in Richard J. McCarthy, *The Theology of al-Ashari*

(Beirut: Imprimerie Catholique, 1953).

Ashari, *Kitab al-luma fi al-radd ala ahl al-zaygh wa-al-bida,* Ed. Abd al-Aziz Izz al-Din Sayrawan (Beirut: Dar lubnan li al-tibaa wa al-nashr, 1987).

Ashari, *Maqalat al-islamiyyin wa ikhtilaf al-musallin,* Ed. H. Ritter, 2 vol. (Istanbul: Government Press, 1929-1930); (Damascus and Beirut: al-Hikma, 1994).

Ashari, *Maqalat al-islamiyyin wa ikhtilaf al-musallin*, ed. Muhammad Muhyi al-din Abd al-Hamid (Cairo: Maktabat al-nahda al-misriyya, 1969-70).

Ashari, *Usul ahl al-sunna wa al-jamaa,* Ed. Muhammad al-Sayyid al-Julaynad (Cairo: Matbaat al-taqaddum, 1987).

Asim, Ibn Abi, *Sunna*.

Asqalani, Ibn Hajar, *Fath al-bari*.

Asqalani, Ibn Hajar, *Lisan al-mizan* (Hyderabad: Da'irat al-maarif al-nizamiyya, 1329).

Athir, *al-Kamil*.

A. A. *Maqalat al-Kawthari* (*Riyadh: Dar al-ahnaf,* 1414/1993)

Babarti, Akmal al-Din, commentary on *Sharh al-aqida al-Tahawiyya,* Edited by A. Yakan and A. Abu Ghuddah.

Badran, Abu al-Aynayn, *Usul al-fiqh al-islami* (Alexandria: Muassasat shabab al-jamia, 1402/1982).

Baghawi, *Tafsir*.

Baghdadi, Khatib, *Tarikh Baghdad*.

Baghdadi, *Usul al-din* (Istanbul: Dar al-funun fi madrasat al-ilahiyyat, 1928).

Baghdadi, Abd al-Qahir, *al-Farq bayn al-firaq* (Beirut: Dar al-kutub al-ilmiyya, n.d.)

Baghdadi, Abd al-Qahir, *al-Tabsira al-baghdadiyya, al-Asma' wa al-sifat,* and *al-Farq bayn al-firaq.*

Baqillani, *Tamhid* (1366/1947) (Cairo edition).

Barr, Ibn Abd, *al-Tamhid*.

Bayhaqi, *al-Asma wa 'l-sifat,* ed. Kawthari.

Bayhaqi, *al-Madkhal*.

Bayhaqi, *Manaqib al-Imam Ahmad*.

Bayhaqi, *Shuab al-iman*.

Bazzar, *Kashf al-astar*.

Bukhari, *Anbiya*.

Bukhari, *Khalq afal al-ibad* (Beirut: Muassasat al-risala, 1411/1990).

Bukhari, *Sahih*. English.

Bukhari, Abd al-Aziz, *Kashf al-Asrar,* ed. Muhammad al-Baghdadi (Dar al-kitab al-arabi).

Butami, Ahmad ibn Hajar, *al-Aqaid al-salafiyya*.

Buti, Muhammad S. Ramadan, *al-Salafiyya marhalatun zamaniyyatun mubarakatun la madhhabun islami.* "The Salafiyya is a blessed period of history, not an Islamic school of law" (Damascus: Dar al-fikr, 1408/1988).

Cooke, M. "On the Origins of Wahhabism," *Royal Asiatic Society Journal.* Series 3, vol 2,2 (1992) p. 191-202.

Dahlan, Ahmad Zayni, *Khulasat al-kalam fi umara al-balad al-haram*.
Darimi, Uthman ibn Said, *Kitab al-naqd ala al-jahmiyya* (Cairo, 1361/1942).
Dawud, *Kitab al-Sunna*.
Dawud, *Malahim*.
Dawud, *Sunan*.
Dhahabi, *al-Nasiha al-dhahabiyya*, Damascus in 1347.
Dhahabi, *Bayan zaghal al-ilm*. (Damascus: Qudsi, 1347 (1928-1929)).
Dhahabi, *Mizan al-itidal fi naqd al-rijal* (Cairo: al-Halabi, 1382).
Dhahabi, *Mujam al-Mashaikh* (Taif: maktabat al-siddiq, 1408/1988).
Dhahabi, *Siyar alam al-nubala*.
Fayruzabadi, *al-Qamus al-muhit*.
Furak, Abu Bakr, *Mujarrad Maqalat al-Ashari* (Beirut, 1987).
Ghazali, *al-Iqtisad fi al-itiqad* (Beirut: Dar al-kutub al-ilmiyya, 1409/1988).
Ghazali, *al-Mustasfa min ilm al-usul* (Cairo: al-Maktaba al-tijariyya, 1356/1937).
Ghazali, Hujjat al-Islam Abu Hamid, *Iljam al-awam an ilm al-kalam* (Restraining the uneducated from the science of theology). (Istanbul : s.n., 1287/1870, repr. Istanbul: Waqf Ikhlas offset, 1994).
Ghudda, on al-Subki's *Qaida*.
Haddad, Al-Habib Alawi ibn Ahmad ibn Hasan ibn Qutb al-Irshad al-Habib Abd Allah ibn Alawi, *Misbah al-anam wa jala' al-zalam fi radd shubah al-bidi al-najdi al-lati adalla biha al-awamm* (The Beacon of Humanity and the Dispelling of Darkness in Refuting the Najdi Innovator That Misguided the Innocent). Excerpts from the original Arabic text of this 0 book are available at the website http://www.sunnah.org/publication/beacon/cover.htm.
Haddad, Abd Allah ibn Alawi, *Misbah al-anam*.
Haddad, Abdullah, "The Book of Assistance," trans. Mostafa Badawi (London: Quilliam Press, 1989).
Hajar, *Al-durar al-kamina fi ayan al-mi'at al-thamina* (The hidden pearls: notable people of the eighth century] (Hyderabad: Dairat al-maarif al-uthmaniyya, 1384 H).
Hajar, *al-Durar al-kamina*.
Hajar, *al-Isaba fi tamyiz al-sahaba*. (Calcutta, 1853).
Hakim, *Mustadrak*.
Hanafi, Ali al-Qari, *al-Shifa* (Qadi Iyad).
Hanbal, Abd Allah ibn Ahmad, *Kitab al-sunna* (Cairo: al-Matbaa al-Salafiya, 1349/1930).
Hanbali, Abu al-Hasan Ali ibn Ubayd Allah al-Zaghuni, *al-Idah*.
Hanbali, al-Qadi Abu Yala ibn al-Farra, *Tabaqat al-Hanabila* (d. 458).
Hanbali, Ibn al-Jawzi, *Daf shubah al-tashbih*.
Hanifa, *Kitab al-fiqh al-akbar bi sharh al-Qari* (Cairo: Dar al-kutub al-arabiyya al-kubra, 1327/1909).
Hanifa, *Wasiyyat al-imam al-azam Abu Hanifa*, ed. Fuad Ali Rida (Beirut : Maktabat al-Jamahir, 1970).
Harras, *Sharh al-wasitiyya* (Salafi Press, 1989).
Haytami, Ibn Hajar, *Fatawa hadithiyya* (Cairo: al-halabi, 1390/1970).
Haythami, Ibn Hajar, *Majma al-zawaid*.

Hayyan, *Tafsir al-nahr al-madd min al-bahr al-muhit* (The commentary of the river extending from the ocean).

Hazm, *al-Fasl fi al-milal wa al-ahwa wa al-nihal.*

Hazm, *al-Fasl fi al-milal.*

Hibban, *Sahih.*

Hisham, *Sira.* English version.

Holy Quran: English Translation of the Meanings and Commentary, Revised and Edited by The Presidency of Islamic Research, *Ifta,* Call and Guidance (Madinah: King Fahd Holy Qur-an Printing Complex, 1410H).

Humam, *al-Musayara fi ilm al-kalam wa al-aqaid al-tawhidiyya al-munjiya fi al-akhira* (Cairo: al-matbaa al-hamawiyya, 1348/1929).

Husni, Taqi al-Din, *Dafu shubahi man shabbaha wa tamarrada wa nasiba dhalika il al-sayyid al-jalil al-imam Ahmad* (Cairo: Dar ihya al-kutub al-arabiyya, 1350/1931).

Imad, *Shadharat.*

Iyad, Al-Qadi, *al-Shifa* as translated byAisha A. Bewley, *Muhammad Messenger of Allah: al-Shifa of Qadi Iyad* (Granada: Madinah Press, 1992).

Izz, Ibn Abi, *Sharh al-aqida al-tahawiyya* (Beirut: Muassasat al-risala, 1416/1995).

Jawzi, *Daf shubah al-tashbih bi akuff al-tanzih,* ed. Hasan al-Saqqaf (Amman: Dar al-imam Nawawi, 1412/1991).

Jawzi, *Sifat al-safwa.*

Jawziyya, Ibn Qayyim, *Badai al-fawaid* (Misr: al-Matbaa al-Muniriya, 1900?).

Julaynid, Muhammad al-Sayyid and Abd al-Sabur Shahin as *Dar taarud al-aqli wa al-naql* (The prevention of contradiction between reason and transmitted texts) (Cairo: Muassasat al-ahram, 1409/1988).

Juwayni, al-Haramayn, *al-Irshad ila qawati al-adilla fi usul al-itiqad* (The guidance to the decisive proofs in the foundations of belief).

Juwayni, al-Haramayn, *Luma al-adilla fi qawaid aqaid ahl al-Sunna;* ed. Hammuda Ghuraba (Cairo: al-Maktaba al-azhariyya li al-turath, 1993). Ed. and trans. in McCarthy, *The Theology of al-Ashari.*

Kabbani, Muhammad Hicham, *Doctrine of Ahl al-Sunna wa al-Jamaa Versus the "Salafi" Movement.* As-sunnah foundation of America 1996.

Kathir, *al-Bidaya wa al-nihaya.*

Kathir, *Tafsir Ibn Kathir* (Beirut: Dar al-fikr ed.).

Kawthari, Muhammad Zahid, *Maqalat al-Kawthari* (Riyadh: dar al-ahnaf, 1414/1993; Cairo: *al-maktaba al-azhariya li al-turath,* 1415/1994).

Kazi, A.K. and J.G. Flynn trans., *Muslim Sects and Divisions* (London: Kegan Paul International, 1984).

Keller, Nuh, "Who or what is a Salafi? Is their approach valid?"

Keller, Nuh, editor and translator. *The Reliance of the Traveller: A Classic Manual of Islamic Sacred Law,* by Ahmad ibn Naqib al-Misri (Dubai: Modern Printing Press, 1991).

Khajnadee, Muhammad Al-Masoomee, *Blind Following of Madhhabs* (Birmingham: al-Hidaayah, 1993).

Khallal, *Kitab al-sunna.*

Khattabi, *Maalim al-sunan ala sunan Abi Dawud* (Hims ed.).

Khazin and al-Nasafi, *Majma al-tafasir*.

Khazin, *Tafsir*.

Khuzayma, Muhammad ibn Ishaq, *Kitab al-tawhid wa-ithbat sifat al-rabb allati wasafa biha nafsahu*.. (Cairo: Idarat al-tibaa al-muniriyya, 1354/1935).

Lalikai, *al-Sunna*.

Lalikai, *Sharh usul itiqad ahl al-Sunna*.

Makki, Ibn Hajar al-Haytami, *Fatawa hadithiyya* (Cairo: Halabi, 1390/1970).

Maliki, Ibn Abi Zayd al-Qayrawani, *Jami fi al-sunan wa al-adab wa al-maghazi wa al-tarikh*.

Maliki, Qadi Iyad, *Sahih Muslim*.

Marzuq, *al-Tawassul bi al-nabi wa bi al-salihin* (Istanbul: Hakikat kitabevi, 1993).

Maturidi, Abu Mansur Muhammad ibn Muhammad, *Majmuat rasa'il* (Hyderabad: Matbaat majlis dairat al-Maarif al-Nizamiyya, 1321/1903).

Maturidi, *Sharh al-fiqh al-akbar* in *Majmuat rasail* (Hyderabad: Matbaat majlis dairat al-Maarif al-Nizamiyya, 1321/1903).

Maydani, Abd al-Ghani ibn Talib al-Ghunaymi, *Sharh al-aqida al-Tahawiyya al-musammat "Bayan al-sunna wa al-jamaa*, Muhammad Muti al-Hafiz and Muhammad Riyad al-Malih, eds. (Damascus: Maktabat al-nuri, 1970).

Madani, Ibn Abi Umar, *Musnad*.

Muhammad Rashid Rida, editor, *Majmuat al-rasa'i wa al-masail al-najdiyya*, ed. Muhammad Rashid Rida (Cairo: Matbaat al-manar, 1345/1926).

Najdi, Sulayman Ibn Abd al-Wahhab, *al-Sawaiq al-ilahiyya fi al-radd 'ala al-Wahhabiyya* (Divine lightnings in answering the Wahhabis), ed. Ibrahim Muhammad al-Batawi (Cairo: Dar al-insan, 1987). Offset reprint by Waqf Ikhlas, Istanbul: Hakikat Kitabevi, 1994.

Nawawi, *al-Majmu sharh al-muhadhdhab* (Cairo: Matbaat al-asima, n.d.).

Nawawi, *Sharh Sahih Muslim*.

Nawawi, *Tahrir al-tanbih* (Dar al-fikr 1990 ed.)

Neibuhr, C. *Travels through Arabia and Other Countries in the East.* (Edinburgh, 1792). Vol. II.

Nisai, *Sunan*.

Nisai, *Amal al-yawm wa al-layla* (ed. Faruq Hammada).

Qalyubi, Shihab al-Din Ahmad, *Kanz al-raghibin sharh minhaj al-talibin*. (commentary).

Qari, Mulla Ali, *al-Mirqat sharh al-mishkat*.

Qari, Mulla Ali, *Sharh al-fiqh al-akbar* (Beirut: dar al-kutub al-ilmiyya, 1404/1984).

Qari, Mulla Ali, *Sharh ayn al-ilm wa zayn al-hilm*.

Qayrawani, Ibn Abi Zayd, *al-Jami fi al-sunan wa al-adab wa al-maghazi wa al-tarikh*, ed. M. Abu al-Ajfan & Uthman Battikh (Beirut: Mu'assasat al-risala; Tunis: al-maktaba al-atiqa, 1402/1982).

Qayrawani, Ibn Abi Zayd, *al-Jami li al-sunan wa al-adab wa al-maghazi wa al-tarikh.*

Qayyim, *Badai al-fawaid.* (Cairo: al-Matbaa al-muniriyya, 1900?).

Qurtubi, *al-Jami li ahkam al-quran.*

Qutayba, *Gharib al-hadith.*

Rajab, *Dhayl tabaqat al-hanabila.*

Razi, Fakhr al-Din, *al-Tafsir al-kabir.*

Razi, Fakhr al-Din, *Asas al-taqdis* (The foundation of declaring Allah transcendent).

Sakhawi, Shams al-Din, *al-Ilam bi al-tawbikh li man dhamma ahl al-tawrikh* (Damascus: Matbaat al-taraqqi, 1349; repr. Baghdad: Matbaat al-Ani, 1382).

Sakhawi, Shams al-Din, *al-Jawahir wa al-durar fi tarjamat shaykh al-islam Ibn Hajar (al-Asqalani)* (Cairo: lajnat ihya' al-turath al-islami, 1986).

Sakhawi, Shams al-Din, *Kitab tarjimat shaykh al-islam, qutb al-awliya' al-kiram wa faqih al-anam, muhyi al-sunna wa mumit al-bida Abi Zakariyya Muhyiddin al-Nawawi* (Biography of the Shaykh al-Islam, the Pole of the Noble Saints and the Jurist of Mankind, the Reviver of the Sunna and the Slayer of Innovation Abu Zakariyya Muhyiddin al-Nawawi) (Cairo: Jamiyyat al-nashr wa al-talif al-azhariyya, 1354 / 1935).

Saksaki, *al-Burhan fi marifat aqa'id ahl al-adyan* (The demonstration concerning the knowledge of the doctrines of the people of religion).

Salam, al-Izz ibn Abd, *Fatawa,* ed. Abd al-Rahman ibn Abd al-Fattah (Beirut: dar al-marifa,1406/1986).

Salman, Mashhur Ibn Hasan, *al-Rudud wa al-taaqqubat ala ma waqaa li al-imam al-nawawi fi Sharh Sahih Muslim min al-tawil fi al-sifat wa ghayriha min al-masail al-muhimmat* (Riyad: Dar al-hijra, 1413/1993).

Sanani, Muhammad ibn Ismail, *Raf al-astar li-ibtal adillat al-qailin bi-fana al-nar* (Exposing the nullity of the proofs of those who claim that the Fire will pass away), ed. Albani. Beirut: al-Maktab al-Islami, 1984.

Sanani, Muhammad ibn Ismail, *Risala sharifa fi ma yataallaqu bi kam al-baqi min umr al-dunya?* (Precious treatise concerning the remaining age of the world) ed. al-Wasabi al-Mathani. Sana': *Maktabat Dar al-Quds,* 1992.

Saqqa, Ahmad Hijazi, *Daf al-shubuhat an al-shaykh Muhammad al-Ghazali* (Cairo: Maktabat al-kulliyyat al-azhariyya, 1410/1990).

Saqqaf, Hasan Ali, *Al-tandid bi man addada al-tawhid* (Slander of him who counts several tawhids).

Saqqaf, Hasan Ali, *Qamus shataim al-albani wa alfazihi al-munkara al-lati yatluquha ala ulama' al-umma"* (Dictionary of Albani's insults and the heinous words he uses against the scholars of the Community).Amman: *Dar al-imam Nawawi,* 1993.

Shafii, *al-Fiqh al-akbar fi al-tawhid li al-imam Abi Abd Allah Muhammad ibn Idris al-Shafii,* 1st ed. (al-Azbakiyya, Cairo: al-Matbaa al-adabiyya, 1324/1906 or 1907).

Shahrastani, *al-Milal wa al-nihal.* Trans. A.K. Kazi and J.G. Flynn, *Muslim Sects and Divisions* (London: Kegan Paul International, 1984).

Shahrastani, *al-Milal wa al-nihal.* Trans. A.K. Kazi and J.G. Flynn, *Muslim*

Sects and Divisions (Cairo, 1317).

Shawkani, *Irshad al-fuhul.*

Siddiqui, M.Z., *Hadith Literature and its Early Developments* (Islamic Texts Society).

Subki, Taj al-Din, *Qaida fi al-jarhi wa al-tadil*, ed. Abd al-Fattah Abu Ghudda, 5th ed. (Aleppo and Beirut: Maktab al-matbuat al-islamiyya, 1404/1984).

Subki, Taj al-Din, *Tabaqat al-shafiiyya al-kubra*, ed. Nur al-Din Shariba (Cairo: al-Halabi, 1373/1953).

Subki, Taqi al-Din, *Al-durra al-mudiyya fi al-radd ala Ibn Taymiyya* (The luminous pearl: a refutation of Ibn Taymiyya) Ed. Imam Kawthari (1284-1355 A.H.). Damascus: Matbaat al-taraqqi, 1929.

Subki, Taqi al-Din, *Al-rasa'il al-subkiyya fi al-radd ala Ibn Taymiyya wa tilmidhihi Ibn Qayyim al-Jawziyya* (Subki's treatises in answer to Ibn Taymiyya and his pupil Ibn Qayyim al-Jawziyya) Ed. Kamal al-Hut. Beirut: Alam al-Kutub, 1983.

Subki, Taqi al-Din, *Al-sayf al-saqil fi al-radd ala Ibn Zafil* (The burnished sword in refuting Ibn Zafil, i.e. Ibn Qayyim al-Jawziyya) Ed. Imam Kawthari. Cairo: Matbaat al-saada, 1937.

Sufuri, *Nuzhat al-majalis* (Damascus and Beirut: Dar al-iman, n.d.)

Suyuti, *Jami al-saghir.*

Suyuti, *Tadrib al-rawi sharh taqrib al-nawawi* (al-Maktaba al-ilmiyya, 1379).

Suyuti, *Tahdhir al-khawass min akadhib al-qussas* (The warning of the elect against the lies of story-tellers).

Tabarani, *al-Awsat.*

Tabarani, *al-Mujam al-kabir.*

Tabari, Ibn Jarir, *Kitab ikhtilaf al-fuqaha* (The differences among jurists), ed. Frederik Kern, Egypt 1902.

Tabari, Ibn Jarir, *Tafsir al-Tabari.*

Tahawi, *Ikhtilaf al-fuqaha li al-imam Abu Jafar Ahmad ibn Muhammad al-Tahawi*, ed. Muhammad Saghir Hasan al-Masumi (Islamabad: Mahad al-abhath al-islamiyya, 1971).

Taymiyya, *al-Iman,* ed. Muhammad Nasir al-Din al-Albani (Cairo: Maktabat Anas ibn Malik, 1400/1980).

Taymiyya, *al-Tasis al-radd ala asas al-taqdis.*

Taymiyya, *al-Aqida al-wasitiyya* (Salafiyya ed. 1346 / 1927).

Taymiyya, *Bayan muwafaqat sahih al-manqul wa sarih al-maqul* (The exposition of the conformity of sound transmitted proof-texts with what is evidently reasonable).

Taymiyya, *Dar taarud al-aqli wa al-naql*, ed. Julaynid (Cairo: Muassasat al-ahram, 1409/1988).

Taymiyya, *Fatawa al-kubra.*

Taymiyya, *Majmu al-fatawa.*

Taymiyya, *Majmuat al-fatawa.*

Taymiyya, *Minhaj ahl al-sunna al-nabawiyya fi naqd kalam al-shia wa al-qadariyya* (The open road of the prophetic sunna in the criticism of the sayings of Shias and predestinarians) (Bulaq: al-Matbaa al-kubra al-amiriyya, 1321/1904).

Taymiyya, *Muwafaqat al-maqul...* on the margins of *Minhaj al-sunna* (Bulaq: al-matbaa al-kubra al-amiriyya, 1321/1904) .

Tibrizi, *Mishkat*.

Tirmidhi, *Sunan*.

Uthaymin, *Sharh al-aqida al-wasitiyya* (Cairo: Maktabat al-ilm).

Uthaymin, *Aqidat al-muslim*, 2nd ed., Saudi Arabia. (The Muslim's Belief).

Wahhab, Ibn Abd, *Rasail wa fatawa li al-shaykh Muhammad ibn Abd al-Wahhab wa abnaih*.

Wahhab, Sulayman ibn Abd Allah b. Muhammad b. Abd, *al-Tawdih an tawhid al-khallaq fi jawab ahl al-Iraq* (1319/1901) p. 34. New ed. al-Riyad: Dar tibah, 1984.

Wahhab, Sulayman ibn Abd Allah b. Muhammad b. Abd, *al-Tawdih an tawhid al-khallaq fi jawab ahl al-Iraq* (1319/1901) New ed.: *al-Riyad : Dar tibah*, 1984.

Wahhab, Abd al-Rahman ibn Hasan ibn Muhammad ibn Abd, *Majmuat al-tawhid al-najdiyya* cited in Ibn Khalifa Ulyawi al-Azhari, *Hadhihi aqidatu al-salaf wa al-khalaf fi dhat Allahi taala wa sifatihi wa afalihi wa al-jawab al-sahih li ma waqaa fihi al-khilaf min al-furu bayna al-dain li al-salafiyya wa atba al-madhahib al-arbaa al-islamiyya* (This is the doctrine of the Predecessors and the Descendants concerning the divergences in the branches between those who call to *al-salafiyya* and the followers of the Four Islamic Schools of Law) (Damascus: Matbaat Zayd ibn Thabit, 1398/1977).

Yafii, *Kitab marham al-ilal al-mudila*.

Yafii, *Marham al-ilal al-mudila*, ed. E. Denison Ross (Calcutta: Asiatic Society of Bengal, 1910).

Yala, *Musnad*.

Zabidi, *Taj al-arus*.

Zahawi, *al-Fajr al-sadiq*.

Zahawi, Jamal Effendi al-Sidqi, *al-Fajr al-sadiq*, translated by the author as *The Doctrine of Ahl as-Sunna Versus the "Salafi" Movement* (ASFA, 1996).

INDEX TO QURANIC VERSES

We did not send you except as a
Mercy to the worlds, 20

We feed you for the sake of Allah's
face, 118

We have built the heaven with (Our)
hands, 102

When you and those who are with
you settle on the ship, 154

Wheresoever you turn there is
Allah's face, 109, 118

With Him are the keys of the
unseen, 195

INDEX TO HADITH

GENERAL INDEX

ENCYCLOPEDIA OF ISLAMIC DOCTRINE SERIES